PEACE PROSPERITY AND THE COMING HOLOCAUST

Dave Hunt

HARVEST HOUSE PUBLISHERS
Eugene, Oregon 97402

OTHER BOOKS BY DAVE HUNT:

The Cult Explosion
Death of a Guru
God of the Untouchables
Mission: Possible
The Devil and Mr. Smith
Confessions of a Heretic
The Power of the Spirit (Edited)

Except where otherwise indicated, all Scripture quotations in this book are taken from the New American Standard Bible, Copyright © The Lockman Foundation 1960, 1962, 1963, 1968, 1971, 1972, 1973, 1975, 1977. Used by permission.

PEACE, PROSPERITY, AND THE COMING HOLOCAUST

Copyright © 1983 by Dave Hunt
Published by Harvest House Publishers
Eugene, Oregon 97402

Library of Congress Catalog Card Number 82-084069
ISBN 0-89081-331-0

Printed in the United States of America.

Dedicated to **Mission: Possible** *and those they faithfully serve at great risk: prisoners of conscience, their families, and all the others who are suffering the loss of basic freedoms in the Soviet Union and under other oppressive regimes.*

CONTENTS

INTRODUCTION

As the title of this book indicates, this is not your ordinary gloom-and-doom book about Armageddon. In fact, this is not your ordinary book. If you have already read everything that is available on the subject of prophecy, the Antichrist, and end-of-the-world scenarios, then you still have not read most of what this book is about. Its premises and conclusions may startle you.

We will carefully consider the future of planet Earth from every angle: scientific, occult, political, military, Biblical. We will come to some startling conclusions about the Antichrist, and from a different perspective than you are likely to have heard or read about. You may find these conclusions hard to believe in spite of the evidence that will be given. What the Bible says about the Antichrist is indeed hard to believe: 1) that he will unite the entire world under a one-world government with himself as the absolute dictatorial head; and 2) that he will deceive the entire human race into embracing a new one-world religion, of which he will also be the head. In fact, it is declared that everyone on earth will *worship* him, except for those few people who know his real identity and are able to see through his lies.

The normal response to such predictions is scornful skepticism. Russia, China, Islamic nations all part of a new one-world government, in submission to the dictatorial control of some "Antichrist"? Preposterous! Soviet-led International Communism, for example, has its own plans for controlling the world, which have been proceeding with extraordinary success. What could cause the Kremlin to surrender its growing empire to anyone else? This seems inconceivable!

And *worship* this new world dictator? That is even more preposterous! For 65 years the Soviet Union has been involved in a determined campaign to stamp out all religion. Surely if worshiping the Antichrist is required, this would be resisted by Soviet leaders to the last nuclear bomb in their arsenal! And isn't Russia, according to Bible prophecy, supposed to attack Israel and thereby set off World War Three and a global nuclear holocaust? That hardly sounds as though she is under the control of a world ruler.

Moreover, the increasing secularization of Western society and worship of science in the space age hardly fit the idea that a new religion will shortly become the faith of the whole world. Nevertheless, the Bible prophecies are clear. And when we take them seriously, a door swings open to fascinating new insights, provided only that we take into consideration certain factors that most "experts on the future"—both Christian and non-Christian—have overlooked.

It is these factors that we will carefully explore in the following pages. We begin with the proposal of "A Contrary Scenario," which is very different from the theories on this subject that are currently in vogue.

—Dave Hunt

1

A Contrary Scenario

Peddling gloom and doom has become a huge and prosperous business. Investment advisors have made fortunes frightening millions of people with their solemn warnings about the "death of the dollar" and the "collapse of the world financial system." Self-proclaimed "experts" at peering into the future, from psychic seers to social scientists and Christian fundamentalists, warn of spreading famine compounded by the population explosion and the alarming loss of farming land by erosion and pollution. We are told that cataclysmic upheavals of the land and oceans will soon change major coastlines, wiping out large cities at the cost of billions of dollars and millions of lives. Even the CIA has gotten into the act, predicting that capriciously changing weather patterns will so disrupt production of major crops that the end of this decade could well see hordes of starving people marching across continents in search of food.

Ecologists add their dire predictions to the thickening gloom: that our oceans and lakes are dying and even earth's atmosphere is being polluted beyond remedy. Scientific studies warn that earth is running out of potable water and that complete ecological collapse could come with surprising suddenness. According to some experts, the only thing that may save us from completing the gradual destruction of planet earth is a nuclear holocaust. This horrifying prospect is persuasively presented as all but inevitable by the dual argument that: 1) no hope remains to stop the daily and insane continued production and deployment of more and more nuclear weapons (said to be a million times more destructive than the Hiroshima bomb), in spite of the fact that we already have enough to destroy the earth ten times over; and 2) humanity has never failed to use any major weapon it has developed.

Apocalypse Now?

The only question among the gloom-and-doomers seems to

be whether a nuclear or economic holocaust will hit us first. As to the latter, there is almost unanimous agreement that the world is headed for a repeat performance of the Great Depression of the 1930's, except that this one will be far worse! The *Daily News Digest,* a sophisticated investment advisory letter that condenses the important news from many sources, sent out a promotional mailing in October 1982 warning that "the coming economic, cultural and political upheaval could be unequaled in modern history....Remember: erupting deficits, artificially low interest rates, skyrocketing taxes, a falling money supply and a stock market boom were the final warning signs just prior to the crash of 1929...and are now signalling an even more devastating collapse directly ahead!" At about the same time, the highly regarded weekly investment advisory service *International Moneyline* issued the following dire predictions:

> Reaganomics will fail...it's just about over. The casino is still open, but the hour is late...we're on the brink of disaster.
>
> After the financial panic, the economy will fall faster and farther than anyone now expects....the world is headed for an economic abyss and there's literally nothing that anyone can do to stop it....
>
> There never has been a more certain scenario.

A very similar gloom-and-doom scenario is endorsed by leading international bankers and government agencies. The annual report of the World Bank, released in August 1982, "painted a gloomy economic picture...the continuing worldwide recession...high and volatile interest rates...and growing debt repayment burdens."[1] The nine largest U.S. banks have a debt exposure to developing countries and Eastern Europe equal to more than twice their total capital; and many of these countries have neither the ability nor the intention to repay, placing the U.S. banking system in jeopardy. Early in September 1982, Third World leaders of the so-called Group of 24 (developing countries ranging from Algeria to Zaire and including Mexico, Brazil, Nigeria, and Argentina) issued a communique directed at the World Bank and International Monetary Fund. It warned that the collapse of the entire international monetary system and a worldwide depression were imminent. In desperation, the IMF took some emergency measures, but the international crisis has only grown worse, with several other countries joining Mexico on the brink of bankruptcy.[2]

Has Doom and Disaster Been Overdone?

The obvious seldom happens. Could it be that the disasters everyone fears and talks about will never materialize? If so, does the future actually hold something even worse? Or could it be very good? Under the present conditions, optimism seems a fool's dream. Yet there is a growing sense that good times lie ahead, and this contrary opinion is held by a number of very perceptive observers. They reject the almost-unanimous consensus of doom—not out of a commitment to optimism but based upon careful research. For example, *Reason* Magazine reporter Kelly Ross discovered that, contrary to popular reports, we're *not* running out of farm land.

Top researchers at Rand Corporation are predicting, in spite of much hand-wringing about spreading famine due to a "population explosion," that "declining birthrates [in the United States] and the resulting scarcity of young workers will usher in a boom time of low unemployment and huge gains in real wages."[3] The Rand group's surprising conclusion continues: "By the end of this decade, employers will be forced to institute huge wage increases to compete for dwindling numbers of young workers...wage hikes will outstrip inflation, resulting in significantly increased real incomes and purchasing power."[4]

The contrary opinion that good times lie ahead is shared by a growing number of experts. Robert Muller has been called "the philosopher of the United Nations and its prophet of hope."[5] Having served the United Nations for 33 years, he has "performed diplomatic missions all over the world and today is Assistant Secretary-General in charge of coordinating the work of the 32 specialized agencies and world programs of the United Nations."[6] Certainly one of the best-informed men in the world, Muller is convinced that "there will be no third world war between the big powers,"[7] but instead he believes we are headed for a "new age, a new world...a New Genesis, a true global, God-abiding political, moral, and spiritual renaissance to make this planet at long last what it was always meant to be: the Planet of God."[8] Though he claims to be a "good Catholic," his "God" is definitely not the personal God of the Bible, but an impersonal "basic cosmic force" residing within everyone and everything, "that impels us to respond to our evolutionary duties and...further ascent."[9]

His vision for a "new age" is shared by many other world leaders, and we will discover in a later chapter exactly what this means.

Herman Kahn, head of the Hudson Institute, a New York research organization dedicated to predicting the future, declares: "Even with all the problems we now face, mankind and the U.S. have a great future!" Disagreeing with the prophets of doom, Kahn recently predicted that "...many of the fears plaguing Americans today will be all but forgotten in coming years."

Based upon his painstaking research, Kahn predicts that: the population explosion will soon fizzle, with the birthrate dropping and the world population stabilizing at about 10 billion; the world is *not* running out of natural resources, since vast supplies lie untapped in space and in the earth's oceans; we have plenty of energy and will *never* run out of fossil fuels, since there is enough coal alone to last *hundreds* of years; in addition to nuclear power, there is also solar energy and thermal heat beneath the earth's surface in an almost-unlimited potential that we have scarcely begun to develop; all of the pollution problems that now seem so serious will eventually be solved; the inflation rate will drop below

5 percent and there will be a worldwide economic boom; computers will be the key to much of the above; and genetic engineering will make food plentiful and cheap by developing new edible plants that can be grown in saltwater.[10]

Bear Turns to Bull

In the midst of thickening worldwide gloom, the unbelievable happened in mid-August 1982. With unemployment in the United States at a post-World-War-Two record and still rising in Europe, Japan, and Canada, millions of Americans suffering from indigestion on a steady diet of gloom-and-doom were caught by surprise. Wall Street was shivering under a heavy cloud of overwhelmingly bearish sentiment. The highest percentage of investment advisory services in 40 years was direly warning that the stock market still had a long way to fall. Led by ace prognosticator Joe Granville, many experts were forecasting a worse crash than the one that shook the Street in 1929. The Dow Jones averages had been tracing out a series of new lows and looked as though they were heading over the cliff for sure...when suddenly the bear turned into a wild bull.

Exploding to the upside without warning and for no apparent reason, the market repeatedly broke volume and price records, catapulting the Dow ahead by 18 percent in a few never-to-be-forgotten days. Everyone was left gasping and the experts were dumbfounded, unable to explain or believe what had happened.

For months, domestic and world news had bred increasing pessimism. Hopes for a settlement following the Israeli invasion of Lebanon had sunk to a new low. In spite of the brave forecasts by the Reagan administration, the recession was worsening, unemployment was still inching higher, and bankruptcies were at a record rate, rivaling even the 1932 worldwide depression. High interest rates, which were squeezing the economic lifeblood out of the already-anemic veins of American industry, labor, and consumers looked to be heading back up again higher than ever. Then suddenly, without any warning, the news began sounding too good to be true. On August 18, 1982, the front pages of major newspapers around the country trumpeted headlines and unexpected stories that marked a turning point.

For example, page 1 of the *Los Angeles Times* carried lead articles with such titles as: " 'END OF SORROWS' NEAR, LEBANESE PREMIER SAYS"; and "STOCKS SET RECORD FOR ONE-DAY GAIN, Dow Leaps 38.81 Points In Wall Street Optimism Over Falling Interest Rates."

In what appeared to be a sudden and complete reversal of his previous position, Mark Skousen, a leading gloom-and-doomer, declared in a promotional mailer in August 1982:

> Contrary to much popular opinion, *President Reagan's economic recovery measures are going to start working— powerfully!* The investment climate will shift sharply before the year's end, and you will have the opportunity to make more money than you ever have before!
>
> Interest rates will drop. Stocks and bonds will come to the verge of a major bull market The economy will show surprising strength and may well lead us into a major boom! [emphasis in original].

Looking back now, August 1982 seems almost certain to be recognized by historians as one of the most dramatic and sudden reversals of the world economic and political climate in history. In the depths of the darkest valley of despair, the forgotten flowers of hope suddenly began to bloom once again—though the majority of people still couldn't detect their fragile fragrance. Oblivious to the continued bad economic news, the deteriorating relations with the Soviet Union, and the ecological collapse on the horizon, not only Wall Street but other stock markets around the world continued to climb higher.

The Thickening Gloom

Whatever the mysterious surge in stock prices was trying to say, few of the experts were willing to listen. Skepticism was as rampant as ever. Most financial prognosticators are still convinced that the unbelievable happenings on Wall Street have been a deceptive flash in the pan that will disappear in a puff of smoke and leave us more thoroughly disillusioned and worse off than ever. Their arguments are persuasive and their predictions frightening. An *Economic News Review and Financial Digest* mailer headlined "How To Survive The 1983 Currency Call-In" warned of the imminent collapse of the American dollar. The *McAlvany Intelligence Advisor* allowed a little more time before financial doom. It predicted that "the most massive" inflationary binge imaginable lies just ahead, which will culminate in "the most devastating inflationary blow-off in U.S. history...plunging this nation and the world into the Depression of 1987-1994."

The promotional mailer sent out in the fall of 1982 by Gary North's *Remnant Review* was no less explicit. Its warnings of economic and financial doom just ahead included the prediction that "President Reagan's economic policies will be completely scrapped as he gets blamed for the worst recession in recent history." The *McAlvany Intelligence Advisor* keeps its investors fully informed on events around the world that could affect their investments. Its recent warnings include the following:

> Third World debt is on the verge of wiping out dozens of America's largest banks.
>
> Terrorists in Africa are even now working towards dominating the world's supply of gold, diamonds and strategic metals.
>
> Soviet-trained agitators are surfacing once again on U.S. college campuses...for another round of anti-draft, anti-Reagan, anti-nuclear demonstrations—and they've promised to cause even more havoc than their predecessors in the '60s.

The Federal Reserve Board is quietly re-inflating the nation's money supply...guaranteeing another round of high inflation just around the corner.

The 'Gromyko Plan,' dormant during the early Reagan presidency, has once again shifted into high gear, virtually assuring the Soviets complete dominance of the Middle East oil fields by 1985.

The Fundamentalist Scenario

Over the last 20 years, fundamentalist writers and preachers have incorporated most of these grim forecasts into their interpretations of Scripture, fueling a growing interest in Bible prophecies about the "last days." Christians generally believe that the gloom-and-doom-financial-collapse-nuclear-holocaust-is-coming-scenario coincides with the "signs" that Jesus predicted would herald the nearness of His return. But is this really true? Perhaps we're overlooking something. Could the timing and sequence of events be different from what most Christians expect?

A worldwide economic collapse followed by the greatest war in history and a nuclear holocaust do seem to be prophesied in the Bible. These events are part of that period described in Scripture as the "Great Tribulation" prophesied for the "last days" that lead up to Armageddon. However, there are statements in the Bible about the "last days" that just as clearly speak of "peace and safety" and imply great prosperity. Understanding the timing of end-time events is clearly of primary importance: what comes when, and how?

The voices predicting a worsening of conditions in the months ahead, leading to economic collapse and World War Three, are so numerous, so well-qualified, and so persuasive that it seems foolish to adopt any other view. And so many events unfolding in the world today seem to fit neatly into the popularly believed scenario of impending disaster. For example, there are a number of sensational developments that Christians point to as evidence that the Antichrist is soon to make his bid for power. A huge computer in Europe, affectionately nicknamed "the Beast" by its creators, is supposed to be tied in already to the worldwide banking network in apparent readiness to fulfill the prophecies in Revelation 13 concerning the control of all buying and selling by the Antichrist. There are rumors that computer systems around the world have already been set up to read a mark on the forehead and/or hand that includes the Antichrist's number 666 just as the Bible predicts; and even that certain individuals have already received "by mistake" Social Security checks requiring such identification. These have been recalled hastily and replaced by the government with the embarrassed explanation that they were not to be issued "until 1984."

The alarmed voices warning of the imminent appearance of Antichrist, with Armageddon just beyond, have reached a crescendo. Others confidently proclaim, with full-page ads in major newspapers, that we are about to witness "the reappearance of the Christ." Who is right? Is it possible that both are wrong, and that the world is facing a great surprise?

A Contrary Scenario

Bible prophecy is often purposely clothed in double or obscure meanings and seemingly contradictory statements for important reasons. This is why it is so easy to succumb to the natural human tendency to color our interpretations of Bible prophecy by our estimate of what we think is going to happen, based on conditions and apparent trends in the world around us. Instead, we must be willing to let the Bible be its own interpreter. This is particularly difficult in a time when gloom-and-doom is so unanimously accepted among the experts on the future, both Christian and non-Christian.

If we can manage to close our ears to the voices of today's prophets and seers, then the Bible seems to be saying something else. Economic collapse and another great war do *not* seem to be the next events predicted in Scripture. In spite of appearances to the contrary in the world around us today, a careful examination of the Biblical description of the "last days" prior to the second coming of Jesus Christ seems rather to suggest that *boom, not bust, lies just ahead!*

Jesus seemed to place the time of His return in a period of unusual worldwide prosperity: "For the coming of the Son of Man will be just like the days of Noah...before the flood they were eating and drinking, they were marrying and giving in marriage...."[11] There was probably never a time in human history when everyone felt so secure in the enjoyment of peace and prosperity as just before the flood. The Laodicean church, which Bible scholars generally agree represents the church on earth in the "last days," is pictured as wealthy and in need of nothing[12]—hardly indicative of either a worldwide financial collapse or a nuclear holocaust.

In contrast to the gloom-and-doom and frightening forecasts of the vast majority of Christians and non-Christians alike, we shall propose "A Contrary Scenario": a coming new age of unprecedented peace and prosperity just over the horizon! However, there will be some startling surprises, necessitating great caution, all predicted in the Bible. As King Solomon warned long ago: "The complacency of fools shall destroy them."[13] The "prosperity teaching" so popular among evangelicals today could fit millions of professing Christians into the coming new age. Whether that is good or bad is a matter of opinion, and we will deal with this very carefully in the following pages.

If the Bible is true, then the coming new age of peace and prosperity could be the most dangerous period in human history, a time of mind-boggling deception that will be humanly irresistible. The Apostle Paul called it the great *delusion* and associated it with what he referred to as *the lie*.[14] What is this lie? And why should a new age of unprecedented peace and prosperity actually precipitate a holocaust of such proportions that the survival of the human race will take a miracle? That will become increasingly clear as we develop our *contrary scenario*.

2
Why the Optimism?

In his writings, H.G. Wells made a number of remarkable predictions that came true. It is therefore disturbing to note that in *The World Set Free*, he predicted the invention of the atomic bomb and the horrible destruction it would cause in a future war. There is a growing fear that such a war is inevitable. Even children seem to sense this. When peace educator Patricia Mische "interviewed children on their attitudes toward the possibility of nuclear war, she was astonished to find that 80% of her random sample expected a holocaust by the year 2000."[1] John Graham, former troubleshooter for the U.S. State Department, has said:

> I used to be a nuclear strategist for NATO. I can tell you that nuclear war is planned by a bunch of very ordinary, God-fearing, PTA-attending Americans. Planning nuclear war is as American as apple pie.[2]

The prestigious *Bulletin of the Atomic Scientists* has moved its famous Doomsday Clock to 1 minute before midnight, indicating just how late they believe the hour is in the countdown to a nuclear holocaust. Maurice Strong, first director of the U.N. Environmental Program, has stated: "The 1980s will be the most dangerous decade...the risks of war are growing." The world's stockpile of atomic weapons now represents destructive power equivalent to about 3½ tons of TNT for every man, woman, and child on earth! The development of ever-more-destructive nuclear weapons proceeds methodically behind the scenes. In America, experimental explosions of atomic devices are averaging about two per month. Hardly anyone notices. Announcement of America's thirteenth atomic explosion of the year occupied a mere six lines on page 4 of the *Los Angeles Times* of September 3, 1982, and read as follows:

20

A-TEST CONDUCTED UNDERGROUND IN NEVADA

YUCCA FLAT, Nev. (UPI) — U.S. scientists Thursday
morning conducted the 13th announced underground nuclear
test of 1982 at the Nevada Test Site, 74 miles northwest of Las
Vegas. The test, code-named "Cerro," had a maximum ex-
plosive force equal to less than 20,000 tons of TNT.

The Grim Facts

Like any other theory, our *contrary scenario* must take into consideration all of the facts. Even without a nuclear
holocaust, the world outlook seems extremely grim. Two-thirds
of the world's population has no access to safe drinking water
and sanitation.[3] Experts fear that the United States could suddenly face a similar crisis. A recent report to the federal Environmental Protection Agency (EPA) stated that "28,000
community water systems—43 percent of the total—were in
violation of federal health standards."[4] Wells supplying
municipal water systems are being closed down across America
by chemical pollution—a dozen in the Los Angeles area alone.

"Seventy percent of children in the insufficiently developed
Third World Countries (IDC's) are suffering from malnutrition. Between 10 and 20 million deaths a year...are directly
or indirectly attributable to starvation or malnutrition...[and]
earth's population is doubling now every thirty-five years...."[5]
"A billion people suffer from malnutrition and tropical
parasitic diseases."[6] Twenty-one African nations—nearly half
the African continent—are now suffering from severe food
shortages. About 440 million Africans—10 percent of the
world's population—have considerably less to eat now than
they had ten years ago; and 100 million Africans daily receive
less than the minimum food requirement. Assuring the starvation of that entire continent, an alarming number of African
nations has embraced Soviet-led Communism, which has a
proven history of destroying incentive and efficiency and reduc-
ing farm and industrial production where it takes control.

Addressing the Communist Party Central Committee in a major November 1982 speech, the late Leonid Brezhnev admitted that food still remains the number one Soviet problem.

In stark contrast to the days before the Communist revolution, when Russia used to export large quantities of grain, it now must import millions of tons just to feed its own people. The 1981 Soviet grain harvest, its worst in six years, was about 25 percent or 60 million tons below the official target called for in the latest revision of the current Five Year Plan.[7] America's farmers, by comparison, exported nearly two-thirds of their 1981 wheat production to feed other countries—and still had enough left over to provide U.S. consumers with bread and flour for three years.[8] However, America's farms are losing 4 billion tons of topsoil to erosion each year, which could have a devastating impact on already-inadequate world food supplies in the next decade.[9]

There seems little doubt that Americans will have to drastically change their way of living. The average person in the United States consumes an inordinate amount of water, energy, and food in comparison to the rest of the world. "To sustain a person in the United States over an average life span, 56 million gallons of water, 37,000 gallons of gasoline, 5½ tons of meat, 5½ tons of wheat, and 9 tons of milk and cream are required. In the poorer parts of the world, the level of consumption is only a fraction of such figures."[10] Such great discrepancies will not be able to sustain themselves in the coming new age—it simply won't be tolerated. And why should it be? The forces pushing for world socialism are growing stronger, and what moral arguments can be mustered against them?

Will the Crises Create a World Government?

When the grim facts are laid out, it is very difficult to keep from joining the followers of Howard J. Ruff, whom *Newsweek* has called the "dean of the Apocalyptic School of

Financial Advice." Ruff, whose *How To Prosper During the Coming Bad Years* has made him rich, selling more than 2.5 million copies, warns his 250,000 subscribers and his vast radio and TV audience "to flee the cities and hoard food and [gold and silver] bullion against the inevitable day of hyperinflationary reckoning."[11] It remains to be seen, however, whether those who are starving will allow the hoarders to keep to themselves the store of provisions they have laid aside. This may be why Mormons, whose teachings were largely responsible for the current "store-a-year's-supply" boom, include guns and ammunition in their storage program.

The Club of Rome, an exclusive association of 100 policymakers from 25 nations, has been warning of coming disaster for more than a decade. When 400 ambassadors, statesmen, scientists, industrialists, economists, and other leaders gathered for the Club's tenth anniversary, they were told that we have until 1988 at the latest for all nations to unite together in a new and wholehearted international cooperation, or else planet Earth is doomed! The U.S. presidential *Global Report 2000* described the "megacrises" of energy, pollution, population, soil, water, and various threats to humans and other species. It concluded on a solemn note:

> The only solutions...are complex and long-term...far beyond the capability and responsibility of this or any other single nation.
>
> An era of unprecedented cooperation and commitment is essential.

Forgetting the many other problems we face, the growing ecological crises alone demand a new era of worldwide unity if we are to survive. Will this desperate cooperative effort ultimately lead to a world government forced upon us by necessity? Pollution does not stop at national borders. What one country does affects the entire planet. The world's oceans are a clear example of the need for a central regulating body with more authority and power to enforce regulations than the United Nations seems to have.

A growing number of world leaders seems convinced that international cooperative attempts to solve the crises we face will gradually give birth to a new age of peace and prosperity. There are encouraging signs that world leaders are already yielding to grass-root pressures that are mounting from all sides. On June 15, 1981, 53 Nobel Prize winners issued an urgent appeal for "immediate [international cooperative] action to end world hunger."

In a rare show of unity, in October 1982 experts in 145 countries gathered to discuss what to do about the coming worldwide famine. The occasion was the declaration by the United Nations of October 16 as World Food Day, in recognition of the fact that 500 million people go to bed hungry every night, and that something drastic *must* be done, and *soon*.[12] More recently, the United Nations Committee for Development Planning issued a hopeful report with the optimistic title "World Economic Recovery and International Financial Cooperation." The document evidenced unprecedented unity among the U.N.'s 156 member nations, indicating that the threat of worldwide financial collapse has aroused a new spirit of unity and cooperation.

The World Can Be Fed

World Concern, a Seattle-based Christian relief organization, has demonstrated what can be done in one large refugee camp in Somalia containing 43,000 helpless and dying displaced persons. After meeting the initial emergency needs by bringing in food, medicine, and vital supplies, World Concern personnel began a training program. The refugees were taught to catch fish from a nearby river and plant crops—something these nomadic people had never done before. They were given the equipment and were trained to drill wells, make bricks, and build buildings. Many of them were trained to staff the clinics that World Concern had equipped and to meet the basic medical needs of their own people. This is an example of what could be done on a larger scale around the world.

Considering the tremendous productive capacity of the United States, especially its agricultural potential, no one need starve anywhere in the world. U.S. exports in 1980 "made up 84% of the world total of corn, 82% of soybeans and 45% of wheat."[13] The genius of American agricultural scientists has developed a method of irrigation that eliminates soil erosion; has doubled overall per-acre grain yields and tripled the yield of corn over the past few years; and by manipulating genes, "scientists say they can develop new, improved strains...that will withstand drought and disease better, be more tolerant of salt, require less fertilizer and provide more nourishment than crops now grown."[14] The equipment and methods that have worked seeming miracles on America's farms can be exported to other countries. In the meanwhile, we can produce more than enough to feed everyone who is lacking.

A Better Way to Deal with the Soviets

It makes little sense to punish the Kremlin by denying grain to Soviet citizens, since they have no means of bringing pressure upon their government to change its policies. It is also self-defeating, because it only increases the necessity for the Kremlin to tighten its hold, and at the same time it punishes the American farmer for Soviet policies. Nothing has revealed the weaknesses of Communism like the complete failure of collectivized farms—and the more food we sell them, the more fully that will be exposed to the whole world, and the better will be our relations with the average Soviet citizen.

Marxism was supposed to liberate the peasants and land from the tyrannical and exploitative grip of capitalism. "Collectivization" was the guaranteed magic formula for creating the Communist paradise through a proletariat brotherhood of cooperation free from the evils of competition caused by private ownership. Marxist theory was supposed to be the key to greater efficiency and productivity. But exactly the opposite has proved to be the case. The grand experiment that created the Communist world and has isolated it from the West has been exposed as an embarrassing debacle that carried a staggering price tag:

> Between late 1929 and 1935 [in the Soviet Union], 125 million peasants were uprooted from 25 million individual farms. In the process, 24 million people disappeared from the Soviet countryside: half fled to the cities, 3 million died of starvation in the Ukraine and the Volga Valley; millions more simply vanished into the Arctic, Siberia and China, many of them into forced labor camps.[15]

That was only the beginning. As Marxism strengthened its hold on Russia and spread to other countries, tens of millions more were uprooted, imprisoned, tortured, and murdered in the attempt to force them to adopt the Marxist way of life. The proof of the pudding is in the eating, and ever since the Communist revolution there has been less and less to eat in Russia. Although the Soviet Union cultivates far larger acreage than the U.S. and employs about ten times the number of farm workers as in America, Soviet collectivized agriculture cannot feed its own population! Without the capitalists to supply them with grain, the Communists would starve. It is obvious what this would mean if international Communism ever reaches its goal of taking over the world.

Due to the dismal failure of Marxism, China's new leaders are turning cautiously from collectivization to free enterprise out of dire necessity. Communist officials in Vietnam, facing the bankruptcy of their economy, now talk cautiously of allowing at least a limited return to private enterprise. The collectivization of land forced upon South Vietnam in 1975 after its surrender is now slowly being reversed in recognition of its failure. If this trend grows and spreads to other Communist countries, it could go a long way toward easing the tension caused by the enmity inherent in the old Marxist arguments against capitalism. This in turn could lead to a new age of cooperation between East and West and form the basis for serious negotiations leading to world peace.

Hopeful Steps Toward Disarmament

In an important speech in May 1982, President Reagan "called for cuts of almost 65% in the Soviet missile strength and 50% in U.S. forces—down to a common ceiling of 850 missiles each...[excluding] bombers and cruise missiles." In response, at the new strategic arms reduction talks (START) in Geneva before the mid-August recess, the Soviet Union offered to "cut Moscow's own missile and bomber force by 25% if the U.S. would cut its arsenal by 10%...."

U.S. analysts are divided in opinion over the Soviet proposal. "Some see it as a sign of serious negotiating intent by Moscow. Others consider it a sophisticated ploy to buy time until domestic and international pressures force the United States to accept a compromise the Soviets would find more favorable to them." The Soviet proposal would retain far more than the "limit of 5,000 warheads on both sides" called for by Reagan.[16]

Unfortunately, the Soviets have consistently broken their promises made in formal treaties, such as: Kellogg-Briand, Korean Armistice, Atlantic Charter, Yalta Conference, Potsdam Conference, SALT I and II, U.N. Agreement on Chemical Warfare, and the Helsinki Human Rights Agreement. Therefore, to make nuclear disarmament work, there must be some reliable means for monitoring compliance. The Soviets have persistently rejected any proposal for on-site inspection. This may now be meaningless due to new technology. American satellites over Russia, we are told, are now able to read a license plate on a car, and can track the movements of military personnel and supplies with amazing accuracy. Consequently, a workable nuclear disarmament treaty now seems feasible.

The idea that a practicable and lasting peace should be considered as a serious possibility seems to be taking hold. In an unprecedented move, "Congress is considering a plan to establish an entire school of disarmament—a National Peace Academy, modeled after West Point and the other U.S. military service schools." Calling themselves "Parliamentarians For World Order," 500 legislators from 24 countries have formed an international network to coordinate efforts aimed at halting the arms race and bringing about worldwide disarmament and permanent peace.[17]

The Growing Grass-Roots Movement for Peace

There is a growing and powerful grass-roots movement across the noncommunist world (such a movement is so far impossible in Communist countries) calling upon the major powers to agree to a nuclear freeze to be followed by nuclear disarmament. All levels of society are involved, from school children to world-renowned scientists. The rapidly-growing International Physicians Against Nuclear War, whose membership includes many world-renowned Russian, American, and European doctors, has stated that "the most serious disease facing mankind" is the growing threat of nuclear war. In a recent joint statement, they declared:

> We are involved because of our expertise in a new type of preventive medicine to ward off what could be the last epidemic.[18]

The subject of nuclear war and how to prevent it "has become one of the most popular new courses...[and] is creating a quiet revolution on American campuses."[19] At the 32nd Annual Pugwash Conference on Science and World Affairs, held in Warsaw during August 26-31, 1982, 97 Nobel Prize winners signed an appeal calling upon world powers to "freeze their nuclear arsenals and seek agreements to eliminate the danger of nuclear war."[20] Two months later, "nearly 900 members of the faculty and staffs at California Institute of

Technology and Jet Propulsion Laboratory signed a statement in favor of the nuclear weapons freeze.''[21] Only three days earlier, 26 organizations ''with a combined membership of 18 million formed a coalition to campaign for nuclear disarmament.''[22]

The growing and horrifying realization that World War Three, if and when it comes, is almost certain to unleash a nuclear holocaust has added a desperate sense of urgency to the international grass-roots nuclear disarmament movement. Large demonstrations demanding a nuclear freeze were held throughout the noncommunist world during the early months of 1982. Thirty-five million Japanese signed a petition for the banning of all nuclear weapons. In the United States, the nuclear freeze became the rallying point for the largest peacetime movement in American history. Thousands of groups are involved in what has become an international movement for peace that far exceeds in power and determination anything comparable in world history. The major problem with the disarmament movement is the fact that it exists only in the Western world. Consequently, if Western powers succumb to the pressures to disarm without negotiating comparable action on the part of the Soviets and Chinese, the peace movement could become the biggest trap in history.

The Bible very clearly prophesies a period of worldwide peace in the "last days." It also says that this "peace" will actually be a trap leading to the destruction of planet Earth! That should be a warning that extreme care is needed. However, world leaders who heed the Bible are in a very small minority. And the masses of ordinary citizens involved in the movement are so certain that worldwide peace, if it could be obtained, would be the answer to everything that they are largely deaf and blind to anything else.

3

A Colossal Trap?

The gathering momentum of the grass-roots movement for peace is a hopeful sign. The horror of the nuclear Sword of Damoclese hanging over all our heads has finally aroused a ground swell of antinuclear crusading. As actor Paul Newman, a member of the U.S. delegation to the first U.N. disarmament conference in 1978, declared at an October 5, 1982, pronuclear freeze press conference in Los Angeles: "There is no other issue that transcends this one."[1]

Rising to the desperation of the hour, millions of concerned citizens, celebrities, scientists, and respected leaders are forming action networks to bring massive pressure upon the major powers for nuclear disarmament. Their ranks include Thomas Watson, former chairman of IBM; William Colby, former director of the CIA; Clark Clifford, former secretary of defense; and many others of like stature. They constitute a new force that may well prove powerful enough to bring about a complete worldwide change in policies and direction. At a New York press conference in February 1982, dean of science fiction writers Isaac Asimov summed up the quiet anger and determination felt by growing numbers of activists when he declared:

> If there's one thing we know for certain, it is that if we do nothing, nothing at all, then disaster is certain to overtake us. We must do something![2]

The Planetary Initiative

The *something* Isaac Asimov referred to is called the Planetary Initiative for the World We Choose. Asimov was chairman of the committee which set up that press conference on February 8, 1982, in order to introduce this remarkable group to the world. Planetary Initiative is not only working for nuclear disarmament, but for a new world order of New

30

Age socialism. The ultimate goal is a one-world government based upon the premise that the only hope for survival of the human race is to create a new consciousness that transcends "narrow national loyalties" and embodies a new sense of "global citizenship." The Planetary Initiative widely distributes an elaborate *Organizing Manual* containing very sophisticated and detailed directions for setting up "Local Coordinating Councils" in a vast international network leading to a world congress in 1983.

Having its roots in the United Nations, the Planetary Initiative for the World We Choose was conceived in January 1981, when the "heads of five organizations joined together to cosponsor a major gathering of leaders from a broad spectrum of groups..." to work for a new and unified world order. "The cosponsors were from the Association for Humanistic Psychology, Club of Rome, Global Education Associates, Planetary Citizens [a U.N.-related organization—see below] and the United Nations Association of New South Wales. Seventy-five international leaders...met at the Stony Point Conference Center in New York...from mainstream church, political and social action groups, from human potential and new consciousness [New Age] organizations, from global-oriented academic research institutes...."[3] Goals of the Planetary Initiative include the following:

...to assist in development of a network for global cooperation among the numerous organizations and individuals addressing [planetary problems]....

A communication system equal to capturing this data...and relaying this information to network members and to the press will be developed...in preparing [for]...the culminating congress [in 1983]...involving the public in a constructive process illustrative of our capacity to choose and shape the human future....

The Planetary Initiative project will develop...an enduring network of individuals, local groups and global organizations...for contributing to the creation of a peaceful, just and humane world order.[4]

The Planetary Initiative is an outgrowth of Planetary Citizens, "which is in consultative status with the Economic and Social Council of the United Nations." Planetary Citizens, in turn, grew out of the 1970 Conference on Human Survival held at the United Nations in New York and hosted by then-Secretary General U Thant. One of the guiding personalities behind that 1970 conference was Norman Cousins, who "serves as Honorary Chairman of Planetary Citizens."

The Planetary Intitiative is an important part of the huge international New Age Movement, involving networks of thousands of organizations and millions of sincere people, all working for a new world of peace, harmony, and brotherly love. Since Marilyn Ferguson first documented the vast scope and power of this movement in her best-seller *The Aquarian Conspiracy*, the "conspiracy" has grown far larger. It may well hold the key to the future of planet Earth. We will have much more to say about this later.

A Trap?

Petitions demanding a nuclear freeze are circulating in over 100 noncommunist countries, but none in any Communist nation. Under that system, such petitions are considered provocation worthy of prison.

Consider the following examples taken from a 60-day period in the spring of 1982. Late in April, "seven European peace demonstrators unfurled a banner in Red Square calling for 'Peace, Bread and Disarmament.' Within two minutes they were bundled up by the KGB and whisked away."[5] On May 3, the bishop of Communist East Berlin "was moved to ask young East Berliners wearing disarmament arm bands to remove them."[6] On June 3, in Leningrad, "a small group of peace demonstrators (including U.S. peacenik Daniel Ellsberg of Pentagon Papers 'fame')" were summarily "towed out to sea."[7] Ten days later, "police sealed off a Moscow apartment where a fledgling disarmament group of 10 people were planning to meet. The group was dispersed as being 'provocative, anti-social and illegal.' The hapless leader of the group, Batovrin, was duly informed that 'the Soviet government and people are fighting for peace.' To date, his whereabouts are unknown."[8]

On the other hand, the Soviets are very much in favor of

peace demonstrations in the U.S. and Western Europe. Is this simple self-righteousness, or does it represent something more sinister? Communist front organizations have been involved in the nuclear freeze movement, including organizing demonstrations. Tass described the huge June 12 demonstration of nearly a million people in New York's Central Park as a popular expression of "resolute disagreement with the U.S. government's policy of war preparations."[9] The implication was, of course, that the Soviets are not at all involved in "war preparations"!

Popular demand by the man in the street for positive change was tried in Hungary, Czechoslovakia, Poland, and elsewhere; the tragic, oppressive, brutal results are known to the whole world. The sincere men and women involved in the thousands of grass-roots organizations, large and small, forming New Age networks working for peace around the world are to be commended for their concern and zeal. Many equally sincere persons, however, believe that if these groups succeed in forcing the U.S. to accede to their demands for a nuclear freeze, it may turn out that we have been led into a colossal trap.

The major argument against the freeze has been that it would lock the Soviets into their current position of superiority, leaving us vulnerable to nuclear blackmail. History supports the fears of those who believe that Soviet intentions are not compatible with peaceful coexistence. In 1977 President Carter was turned down flat when he proposed to President Brezhnev a freeze on the development, production, and deployment of nuclear weapons and a renunciation of the use of force in Europe. In order to show our good faith and to encourage the Soviets to follow our example, we made a whole series of significant unilateral cutbacks in our nuclear strategic forces. As a result of that, have we already walked into a trap, and is it in the process of being snapped shut on us?

A Frightening Clue to Soviet Intentions

In 1977 President Carter's administration canceled the order for 250 B-1 bombers that the Pentagon felt were urgently needed. Only in 1981 was this decision partially reversed by the Reagan administration, which ordered 100 B-1s. In 1978 the Minuteman III ICBM production line was closed, canceling 100 missiles, and that same year the production line was closed for short-range attack missiles. The following year 400 Hound Dog cruise missiles were deactivated. During President Carter's presidency there were significant delays and cutbacks in the production and deployment of ground-launched and sea-launched cruise missiles and air-launched missiles. The Trident submarine construction was cut back and the Trident II missile development was postponed. In the first two years of President Reagan's term of office, 10 Polaris submarines with 160 SLBMs were deactivated and the planned deployment of the MX was cut in half. Further, 54 Titan II missile launchers are scheduled for deactivation in 1983.

What was the response of the Soviets? Taking advantage of our cutbacks and delays during that period, the Soviets gained nuclear superiority through the most massive military buildup in history, which still continues at a frenzied pace. Obviously they are not after equality but superiority, and they will apparently not be satisfied with a significant advantage, but only with an overwhelming superiority. As Jimmy Carter's defense secretary, Harold Brown, remarked: "We build; they build. We stop; they build!"

In 1946, when the U.S. had sole possession of the atomic bomb, through its U.N. Ambassador Bernard Baruch it offered to share its nuclear secrets with the world for peaceful development of atomic power. This technology was to have been placed under the control of an international commission, which would supervise the destruction of all nuclear weapons then in existence and prevent their further production. This generous plan was vetoed at the United Nations by the Soviet Union, which was already deeply involved in stealing U.S. atomic secrets through its spy network with the help of the well-intentioned Ethel and Julius Rosenberg (and others), who apparently sincerely felt they were working for peace. If the Kremlin is really in favor of nuclear disarmament, 1946 would have been the time to vote for it. In fact, Soviet leaders have never swerved from the Communist goal of world domination; and it is clear that this has been the motivation behind their unrelenting drive to achieve overwhelming nuclear superiority.

A Deadlier Trap?

A hardheaded, realistic look at the world scene gives little cause for optimism. However, massive new forces are gathering momentum for positive change, spurred on by the desperation and lateness of the hour. U.S.-Soviet arms talks are in progress once again. After the recent death of Brezhnev, the swift ascent to power of former KGB Chief Yuri V. Andropov (acquiring the position of General Secretary of the Communist Party almost immediately) surprised Western observers and could be a good sign. The remaining leaders in the Kremlin are elderly and not in the best of health. Change is coming soon. Many observers fear that a new and younger Kremlin under Andropov's leadership will take an even harder line. However, this has not been the case with the new leaders in China, where many unexpected and encouraging developments are in progress. The same could happen in the U.S.S.R., confounding the experts.

Wall Street has been giving the world a most remarkable demonstration of experts being caught totally off guard by the impossible happening suddenly. Certainly the stock market isn't acting as though famine, depression, death of the dollar, and World War Three are on the horizon. It seems instead to be saying that peace and prosperity lie just ahead. Whether the market is accurately forecasting the future, as it often does, remains to be seen. At the very least, however, we have had a vivid demonstration of how quickly gloom-and-doom can turn to euphoria. That remarkable prophet H.G. Wells predicted a coming period of peace and prosperity with these intriguing words:

> A time will come when men will sit with history...or with some old newspaper before them and ask incredulously, "Was there ever such a world?"[10]

The coming peace and prosperity may carry some unpleasant surprises. Opponents of the nuclear freeze argue that it would turn into a trap, eventually handing the Soviets control of the world. Strange as it may seem, the coming new age of peace and prosperity could prove to be an even deadlier trap! According to the Bible, there is something far worse than

Communist control of the world: the Antichrist, not the Kremlin, will be taking over planet Earth!

Make no mistake about it—the Bible declares clearly that a new one-world government is coming. Appearing at first to be the beautiful solution to everything, it will eventually be unmasked as Satan's kingdom bringing utter destruction, but by then it will be too late to turn back. Will the New Age Movement be able to prevent this from happening? Or is the New Age Movement in fact part of a cosmic conspiracy to install the Antichrist? Is that what the Aquarian Conspiracy really is? We will confront these questions later.

How Will the Trap Be Sprung?

One of the major difficulties that must be faced by New Agers and by our own contrary scenario is the seemingly immovable set of national, ethnic, social, political, and religious barriers of today's world that stand in the way of the new one-world government. What could possibly unite a world that is now so divided? There are those who believe it will come about through a growing recognition of our common brotherhood as human beings, a realization of our "true self" that will transcend all else.

However, many Bible scholars believe that World War Three must occur first. From the ashes of horrible devastation, the Antichrist will presumably arise to rule a world desperate for the leadership of a genius able to pull everything together out of chaos. If this interpretation of Scripture is correct, then the next event in the prophetic timetable must be the Soviet attack upon Israel precipitating World War Three. Our "contrary scenario," however, disagrees with this viewpoint. Peace, not war, lies just ahead.

A number of important Scriptures seems to indicate that events will turn out somewhat as follows: the threatened worldwide financial collapse will metamorphose into booming prosperity; ecological disaster will cease to be a serious concern; the United States and the Soviet Union will move toward disarmament and cooperation; the threat of war in the Middle East will end; peace will reign all over the world, seemingly established firmly and permanently.

Nearly everyone will be convinced that a new age of unprecedented brotherhood, progress, peace, and prosperity has begun. The Bible indicates, however, that it will be a trap, a Satanic counterfeit of the promised millennium, a deceptive prelude to disaster. Just when earth's inhabitants—and especially the Israelis—are feeling most secure, all hell will break loose! Verses 2 through 4 in the fifth chapter of 1 Thessalonians seem to be saying this:

> For you yourselves know full well that the day of the Lord will come just like a thief in the night.
>
> While they are saying, "Peace and safety!" then destruction will come upon them suddenly like birth pangs upon a woman with child; and they shall not escape.
>
> But you, brethren, are not in darkness, that the day should overtake you like a thief.

It is difficult to accept this scenario, because World War Three seems to be the only catalyst that could reasonably prepare the stage for the Antichrist's ascension to power as world ruler. There is, however, another rather surprising possibility.

4
What About World War Three?

In August 1982 major newspapers around the world carried sensational articles quoting angry denials by Defense Secretary Caspar W. Weinberger that the United States was "planning a protracted nuclear war." This seemed to represent a dramatic and frightening departure from past official U.S. policy, which has always been based upon the belief that there are "no winners in a nuclear war."[1]

Upset by what he termed "inaccurate" reporting of American intentions, Weinberger wrote a letter to 30 U.S. newspapers and 40 foreign publications expressing his increasing concern "with news accounts that portray this Administration as planning to wage protracted nuclear war...."[2] His "correction of inaccuracies," however, left intact the central issue—that both the United States and the U.S.S.R. no longer consider a prolonged nuclear war to be out of the question, and both sides are preparing for that eventuality. The old concept of a swift knockout by a first strike has given way to the belief that a nuclear conflict could last six months or more. Weinberger blamed the Soviet Union for the new attitudes. The Soviets, he said, "appear to be building forces for a 'protracted' [nuclear] conflict," and therefore the United States has no alternative but to "keep pace."[3] None of this was good news for the average citizen in the U.S., the Soviet Union, or anywhere else in the world.

Carefully Planned Insanity

The Soviets have been planning civil defense for decades, building underground shelters to withstand nuclear blasts, and also equipping and stocking them. In the United States virtually nothing has been done to protect the civilian population in the event of war. This failure cannot be blamed entirely on our leaders, but is in large part the result of public apathy based upon two ideas that have dominated American thinking on this subject: 1) somehow nuclear war will be avoided; and 2) if not, then everything would be over quickly under the force of a devastating first strike, so why fret, plan, and spend for something that won't work anyway? For decades our policy was to have enough survivable retaliatory warheads so that the damage we could inflict upon the Soviets would deter them from attacking us.

This has all apparently changed within the past two years. Both sides have apparently adopted the insane delusion of "limited nuclear war" that would extend possibly for months. It takes no genius to recognize the inherent and irresistible temptation for the momentary loser in a "limited nuclear" war to escalate the nuclear involvement, thereby forcing his opponent to escalate...which would almost inevitably result in a full-scale nuclear war and the unimaginable holocaust that would produce. Nevertheless, the Reagan administration seems to be proceeding on this course.

Many observers feel that the idea of "limited nuclear war" that may last for months and which one side can eventually win is not only insane, but the most dangerous brand of insanity. Faith in this delusion could encourage one side or the other to start what it imagines will be "limited," and thereby begin an unstoppable chain reaction leading to the very holocaust we all dread and want to prevent.

Plans for the civilian population seem no less insane than those being made for the military. Having neglected civil defense worthy of the name, it is now almost too late to start. Moreover, the public still lacks either the will or the understanding to support the monumental construction project that would be required to build shelters. According to Tom Longstreth, a civil defense specialist for Defense Information (a Washington, D.C., think tank), the federal government plans to spend about 10 billion dollars on civil defense over the next five years, including the eventual construction of fallout shelters.[4] That sum, of course, would hardly start construction. The major portion of the government's belated plans calls for dispersal of the civilian population away from targeted areas. This is so clearly not feasible that the entire "Crisis Relocation" program seems like some surrealistic planned insanity.

The Edge of the Cliff

Soviet-American relations are currently at their lowest point since the days of the Cold War, in spite of President Reagan's recent offer to sell more grain to Russia and the continuation of the Strategic Arms Reduction Talks (START) in Geneva after the mid-August break. Plagued by severe economic problems at home and political troubles among its satellites, the Soviet Union was probably marking time under the direction of an interim committee while Brezhnev was chronically ill in the months before his demise. However, Yuri V. Andropov has emerged as Brezhnev's successor with apparent full control established in days instead of the years it has taken in the past for a change in Soviet leadership. This could mean that power is passing to a new group of leaders without the usual months and years of instability and jockeying for positions that creates uncertainty in foreign relations. The Strategic Arms Reduction Talks (START) are proceeding in Geneva—another good sign.

The Soviet military machine is generally believed to have at its disposal deadly laser weapons that are years ahead of U.S. developments. "The consensus in Washington is that the Soviets have already deployed the world's first operational ground-based beam weapon, and that they are going all-out to deploy space-based beam weapons....U.S. scientists long pooh-poohed the idea that such weapons were even possible, while the U.S.S.R. was busily using U.S. technology to solve those 'insoluble' technical problems of guiding beam weapons!"[5] U.S. intelligence only recently learned of "a new Soviet missile system that is zeroed in on American cities...involving three mobile missile regiments...equipped with (36) nuclear-tipped SS-16 solid-propellant missiles...with multiple warheads (MIRV)...an 8,000-mile range...designed to be fired at U.S. cities in three waves across the polar ice cap...from mobile launchers...in remote frigid areas near the city of

Perm...[where] military analysts have conceded that it would be quite easy for the Soviets to deploy the weapon in secret."[6]

The threat of nuclear war has been greatly increased by the superpowers' selling of advanced arms to the entire world. International arms sales have increased "from $100 billion in 1960 to $500 billion in 1980—*fifteen times higher than worldwide economic aid!*"[7] With the new high-technology weapons that are being amassed around the world, even small nations now have the capability of inflicting heavy losses upon the superpowers. The United States, U.S.S.R., China, Britain, and France are producing nuclear weapons. It is likely that India, South Africa, and Israel also have developed atomic arms. Within a few years, probably "an additional 20 to 25 nations will have the capability to produce nuclear weapons."[8] In fact, the necessary materials can be stolen and an atomic bomb manufactured with the know-how of a university graduate in physics. It would only take the right kind of provocation or even confusion to set off a chain of events that could lead to death and destruction on a worldwide scale that is hardly imaginable.

Prelude to World War Three?

Few analysts doubt that when it comes, World War Three will begin in the Middle East. The Israelis are more aware of this than anyone else, which makes their recent move into Lebanon seem all the more courageous. They acted to save Lebanon from total destruction and to remove the PLO in order to end their persistent and intolerable terrorist attacks upon Israeli civilians. Only political pressure from the United States prevented Israel from acting sooner.

Created by Egyptian President Nasser in 1964 and headed by Yasser Arafat since 1968, the PLO was driven out of Jordan by King Hussein's Bedouin Army in 1970 after it tried to take over that country. Fleeing to Lebanon, the PLO set up its headquarters in Beirut. Beginning in 1975 it seized territory and turned schools, churches, and apartments into armed fortresses. It accosted, raped, dismembered, and savagely terrorized Lebanese citizens.[9] At least 100,000 "Christian" Lebanese were brutally slaughtered, 300,000 wounded, and

500,000 forced to flee their homes as the PLO, later aided by the Syrian Army, expanded its military empire and turned Lebanon, once known as the Switzerland of the Mediterranean, into a perpetual war zone.[10] Under Soviet direction, the PLO camps in Lebanon became the training and operational center of international terrorism. This included all of the major terrorist groups, from the right-wing Baader-Meinhof Gang of Germany to the radical left-wing Red Brigade of Italy. Through the PLO in Lebanon, all of these international terrorist groups were financed, equipped, and goaded on by the Soviet Union.

The PLO brazenly went about its terrorism against Israel and the world, apparently certain that Israel would never invade Lebanon to destroy its operations for fear of retaliation by the surrounding Arab nations, particularly the Syrians, whose army had taken control of much of Lebanon in order to "keep the peace." Secure in this belief, on June 6, 1982, PLO terrorists attempted to assassinate the Israeli ambassador to Great Britain. Israel reacted instantly with air attacks against the PLO terrorist training camps in Southern Lebanon. Taunting Israel from its sanctuary behind Lebanon's borders—as though daring the Israeli Army to invade and thereby justify Soviet and Syrian intervention—the PLO bombarded Northern Israel with about 7000 rounds of Soviet-supplied heavy shells and rockets. This was the final straw. Israeli forces struck swiftly. With lightning thrusts they cut off and surrounded the PLO, preventing escape to the north.

Hesitant to engage the Israelis on the ground, in spite of their overwhelming numerical advantage in men and weapons, the Syrians decided to teach Israel a lesson in the air. In one of the largest and fiercest air battles in history, Syria put 200 MIG's into the sky to stop the Israelis, and about 130 Israeli planes engaged them. The result must have staggered and even frightened Syria's Soviet mentors and left them in a state of shock: 92 Soviet MIG's were shot out of the sky, killing 60 to 70 percent of Syria's best pilots, while not one Israeli plane was downed in dogfights! (One was lost to ground fire.)

A major purpose in Syria's occupation of Lebanon was to extend the Arab encirclement of Israel, tightening the noose.

Part of that process was the deployment of 23 of the latest Soviet surface-to-air (SAM) missile batteries east of Beirut. Israel's Prime Minister Begin had warned the Syrians to remove them or they would be destroyed. This had seemed like an empty threat. The SAM batteries were virtually unassailable, for any plane coming within range would be shot down. However, to the astonishment not only of the Syrians and Soviets, but American military experts as well, in one of the most spectacular accomplishments in modern warfare the Israelis suddenly wiped out every SAM missile battery without losing "a single attacking plane!"[11] This incredible accomplishment, which sent shock waves through the entire international military establishment, was the result of "an original Israeli invention."[12] There are rumors that Israel has so many other equally miraculous inventions up its military sleeve that its armed forces are confident they could defeat the Soviet Union if it ever attacks Israel, which they believe is inevitable.

Israel's lightning conquest of the PLO led to a most disturbing discovery: undeniable evidence that the Soviets have been seriously preparing to launch an all-out invasion of Israel. Even Israeli intelligence was shocked by the huge quantities of Soviet weapons held by the PLO in Southern Lebanon that were obviously not for their own use. Hidden away in basements, warehouses, and huge underground storehouses in PLO-controlled areas were enough modern Soviet arms to fully equip an estimated army of about 250,000 men! Obviously this weaponry was intended for Soviet troops to be brought into Lebanon secretly for a planned invasion of Israel. The Kremlin has apparently decided that the Arabs, after repeated failures, will never be able to destroy Israel, and therefore she must do it herself.

Unless some "miracle" changes the present course of world events, it is only a matter of time until the Soviet Union finds what it will then declare to be "unacceptable provocation" justifying its planned attack upon Israel. This will most certainly involve the United States and NATO. That World War Three will then develop into a full-scale nuclear holocaust seems almost inevitable, again barring some "miracle."

Is World War Three Armageddon?

The Bible speaks of a frightful battle called Armageddon, which will take place in Israel and result in the utter destruction of the armies of the world. Some Christians believe, that World War Three will occur 3½ to 7 years earlier than this, and that it will arise out of a Soviet attack upon Israel which will result in the almost-total destruction of the armed forces of Russia and her satellites and allies. Why do they feel that World War Three is separate from and must come before Armageddon? Because they can conceive of nothing except a greatly destructive war to prepare the world to accept the Antichrist as its ruler. Obviously Armageddon is too late for this, so there must be a great war before it.

According to this view, it is the destruction of the Soviet bloc's forces that leaves Western Europe as the greatest surviving power in the world, making it possible for a charismatic leader within this ten-nation confederacy—the Antichrist—to seize control and rule the world. The Antichrist's ascension to power is supposed to usher in a period of worldwide peace, which will later be shattered as God's judgment is poured out upon this earth during that period called the Great Tribulation. Finally Armageddon follows as the nations of the world, now recovered from World War Three, all converge in this great battle in the Middle East. Just as it seems that Israel will be destroyed, Christ returns from heaven to rescue her and set up His kingdom, with headquarters at Jerusalem.

Our "contrary scenario" is considerably different. With all due respect to the opinions of others, there seem to be many reasons why this interpretation outlined above doesn't fit the Biblical prophesies. Ezekiel 38:11,14 states clearly that the invasion will come during a time of peace, when Israel feels extremely secure and is not expecting any attack from anyone. This isn't even plausible as long as the Soviet Union and Arab nations continue to menace Israel. Clearly worldwide peace must be established *before* the Soviet attack upon Israel. This will only come about *after* the Antichrist takes control of the world. Therefore, the U.S.S.R.'s invasion of Israel and its total defeat by Israel and Western Europe can hardly be the means by which the Antichrist comes to power. In fact, there is no indication in the Bible that Israel and Western Europe allied together will defeat the Soviets and their allies. This will only be effected by the direct and miraculous intervention of Israel's Messiah.

Furthermore, this popularly accepted interpretation requires *two* attacks upon Israel and *two* great destructive battles in the Middle East. It seems clear, however, that there will be only *one* event fitting this description: Ezekiel 38 and 39, Zechariah 12, and Revelation 16:13-16 and 19:11-21 seem to be referring to *one* great battle on the soil of Israel, not to two. There are other difficulties with this popular view: 1) it requires a period of "peace and prosperity" between World War Three and Armageddon, but the length of time available— from 3½ to 7 years—hardly seems adequate; and 2) it leaves out China. Why wouldn't China move swiftly into Russia and take control there if the Soviet armed forces have been virtually destroyed and the Western Allies, though victorious, are themselves greatly weakened by the losses they have suffered?

Contrary Scenario with a Strange Twist

If we are to meet all of the criteria set forth in the Biblical prophesies, then not only Russia but also China must be neutralized. Moreover, this must happen *before* the eventual Soviet attack upon Israel. There will only be *one* attack, which will involve all of the armies of the world, including those of China. World War Three and Armageddon are one and the same event. The Antichrist will have already taken control of the world *before* this time. Israel and all the world will feel secure in a period of unprecedented peace and prosperity, a new age that many people will mistake for the millennium promised in the Bible.

We are left, then, with the necessity of finding an explanation for the Antichrist's ascension to power other than World War Three. How does he gain the allegiance of the entire world, including the Soviet Union, China, other Communist countries, and even the Arabs? The Scriptures don't spell this all out in detail, but there are enough hints to give us a fairly good idea of what is going to happen. As we look into this, we will see that events in the world today are accelerating swiftly in this very direction.

Our "contrary scenario" has a strange twist in it, yet it is so obvious that it seems amazing that it hasn't been recognized by everyone. The Antichrist will undoubtedly step into the vacuum caused by a catastrophic event that will dramatically shift the balance of world power. However, it will not come about through the destruction of the U.S.S.R., but through the sudden and mysterious elimination of the U.S.A. as a world power.

5

The Coming World Government

A ruthless, vicious, totalitarian government, saying all of the right things about peace, love, and brotherhood, will soon take control of planet Earth. Nothing can stop it. The United States, after its sudden and mysterious collapse, will be powerless, a mere pawn in the process. Will this be something that the fabled Trilateralists will bring about? No, the conspiracy is much larger than that and far too powerful for the Trilateralists to control.

Much of an alarmist nature has been rumored about a conspiracy among top political leaders in Washington to betray America's national interests. These men, all members or former members of the Trilateral Commission and/or Council of Foreign Relations (CFR), are said to be working hand in glove with certain highly placed Communist leaders in an international conspiracy to bring about a world government. Stretching from Washington to London, Paris, Bonn, Moscow, and Tokyo, this mysterious web of intrigue is alleged to include the wealthiest families in the world. Names like Krupp, Rothschild, and Rockefeller are mentioned along with the allegation that international bankers financed the Russian Revolution 65 years ago and have been backing both sides in every war since then.

There is no doubt some truth in such reports. However, the Trilateralists and CFR people are invariably referred to with exaggerations that seem to attribute omniscience and omnipotence to the "internationalists." Take, for example, the following statement from a fall 1982 promotional mailer for *The Spotlight*, the weekly Liberty Lobby newspaper:

47

The handwriting [is] on the wall...THE TRILATERALISTS ARE IN CONTROL. And it happened so swiftly, so cleverly...so well planned that even those of us who know the awful truth cannot help but marvel at their cunning....

Well before election day, the Rockfeller-led consortium of internationalists had a battle plan...operational in the event of President Reagan's election. And by midnight of election night, Ronald Reagan's policies and your vote were held captive by a faceless, anonymous group known as [David Rockfeller's] Trilateral Commission...a powerful, ominous force affecting the well-being of all American patriots....

Such reports have surrounded the "Trilateralists" with a terrifying mystique. Is there indeed a "faceless, anonymous" group so diabolically cunning and powerful that it can actually take control of any president of the United States the instant he is elected? Does this group really manipulate the president, congress, and cabinet like so many puppets? And does this hypnotic control extend to every nation on earth? That seems a bit too much to believe! If they indeed have the power to do so, one wonders why these internationalists haven't yet installed their puppet world ruler! Exaggerated reports like the above play into the hands of the internationalists by causing reasonable persons to doubt the whole idea of a conspiracy to set up a world government. That could be dangerous.

The Sincere Conspirators

It is a fact that members of several elite political organizations here and abroad are part of an international conspiracy to establish a world government. However, is that so bad? How else can there be a just and lasting worldwide peace? Surely a world government should not be considered evil, but the best hope for preventing a nuclear holocaust. Yet many object that it could only be established at the cost of freedoms that Westerners hold dear. It is assumed that the conspiring internationalists intend to distribute Western wealth among the poorer countries, forcing Communism on the world, which would destroy the world rather than save it. Just imagine the collectivization of America's farms! Who would feed the world then? Better to die instantly from a nuclear bomb than to die slowly by starvation, says the argument.

In several of his books, H.G. Wells seems to have anticipated with uncanny accuracy the steps leading to the coming world government. While proposing a worldwide benevolent socialism, he had no illusions about Communism, which he rejected with these words: "In practice, Marxism is found to...resort to malignantly destructive activities and...to be practically impotent in the face of material difficulties. In Russia, where...Marxism has been put to the test...each year shows more and more clearly that Marxism and Communism are digressions from the path of human progress....The one main strand of error in that theory is the facile asssumption that the people at a disadvantage will be stirred to anything more than chaotic and destructive expressions of resentment....We reject...the delusive belief in that magic giant, the Proletariat, who will dictate, arrange, restore and create...."[1]

Instead, he predicted that the new world order would be in the hands of "an elite of intelligent religious-minded people."[2] The religion of these sincere conspirators, as Wells laid it out and confessed it to be his own, was exactly what the Bible describes as the religion of the coming Antichrist! Few people will notice this, however, so intent will they be upon saving the world from nuclear holocaust. Their goals will be so sincere and seem so logical: that a lasting, genuine peace can only come through worldwide control over the nationalistic interests that otherwise compete for territories, resources, wealth, and power, and that create wars in the process. As H.G. Wells pointed out over 50 years ago:

> It is impossible for any clear-headed person to suppose that the ever more destructive stupidities of war can be eliminated from human affairs until some common political control dominates the earth....To avoid the positive evils of war and to attain the new levels of prosperity and power...an effective world control, not merely of armed forces but of the production and main movements of staple commodities and the drift and expansion of population, is required.
>
> It is absurd to dream of peace and worldwide progress without that much control....I am discussing whether our species...is to live or die.[3]

Raised to be an evangelical by his mother, Wells became

an apostate enemy of Christianity. A close friend of T.H. Huxley, Wells was an avid evolutionist and an atheist. Yet he had a religion, a belief that an elite of Godlike men would evolve in due time, "take the world in hand and create a sane order."[4] The world would be transformed through his apostate religion. It is doubtful that Wells realized that he was prophesying the fulfillment of a Biblical prophecy: "Let no one in any way deceive you, for...the apostasy comes first, and [then] the man of lawlessness is revealed, the son of destruction."[5] Many of the other Fabian Socialists besides H.G. Wells (such as George Bernard Shaw, et al) were apostate rebels from earlier Christian upbringings, and they did their best to promote a new world order based upon that apostasy. Wells, however, seemed to know that it would not come in his generation, but probably in the next:

> For my generation, the role of John the Baptist must be our extreme ambition. We can proclaim and make evident the advent of a new phase of human faith and effort.
> We can point out the path it has been our lifework to discover... 'Here,' we say, 'is...the basis for a new world.'
> ...saving the impact of some unimagined disaster from outer space, the ultimate decision of the fate of life upon his planet lies now in the will of man.[6]

The Open Conspiracy

The idea of a world government has been around for a long time. What is new today is the fact that almost everyone is coming to the same conclusion, and in the desperation of the hour millions of people are doing something about it. The Trilateralists, CFR people, and other internationalists are no longer the only ones working for a new world order. As H.G. Wells predicted, the "conspiracy" has now become an open movement involving hundreds of millions of "believers." Most of these "open conspirators," as Wells prophesied, have in mind a worldwide unity that will be built less upon government than the internationalists intend, and more upon a fundamental people-to-people relationship. That this could very well happen is being demonstrated by networks of thousands of groups of ordinary citizens already working together around the world in the new and powerful peace movement. Again it seems to have been anticipated by Wells, who wrote: "What we work toward is synthesis, and this communal effort is the adventure of humanity."[7]

Something important is taking shape—a huge, growing, grass-roots movement that is not so much political as it is religious though not in the ordinary sense. It is a new spirituality, a mysticism that is too big to be confined within the narrow limits of any religion. H.G. Wells predicted that this "new religion" would sweep away old institutions and usher in a new world order that would save the human race from destruction: "The conspiracy of modern religion against the established institutions of the world must be an open conspiracy...."[8] That the religion he referred to was Eastern mysticism and anti-Christian is clear:

> There was no Creation in the past...but eternally there is creation; there was no Fall...but a stormy ascent...if religion is to develop unifying and directive power...it must adapt itself....
>
> Man's soul is...part of a greater being which lived before he was born and will survive him. The idea of a survival of the definite individual...dissolves to nothing in this new view of immortality.[9]

The same belief that Wells expressed is now verified by physics, according to Fritjof Capra, forming the basis for his new world view. Ervin Laszlo, world order theorist and Club of Rome member, has declared that a "new age of global community is upon us whether we like it or not."[10] This seems to be the culmination of a process that has been going on for a long time, and is now accelerating to some apparent climax. Fritjof Capra says we are in a "crisis of perception."[11] Mark Satin has said, "...the world is being not just changed but transformed...the concept of the person is expanding...the spiritual, human potential, feminist and environmental movements" are the key to the new world order.[12]

Of great importance is the fact that increasing numbers of the world's top scientists are embracing this "new consciousness," because it seems to agree with the most recent discoveries and theories of science. Fritjof Capra, brilliant University of California at Berkeley research physicist, insists that "we are trying to solve the problems of our time by applying an out-dated world view, the mechanistic concepts of Cartesian-Newtonian science, which are no longer adequate." Arguing for a new planetary consciousness, Dr. Capra declared:

> We live today in a globally interconnected world...[requiring] an ecological perspective...a new vision of reality, a fundamental change in our thoughts, perceptions and values.
>
> The most severe consequence of this [outmoded world view] today is the ever increasing threat of nuclear war, brought about by an over-emphasis upon self-assertion, control and power...a pathological obsession with winning in a situation where you can't win any longer, because no one can win in nuclear war.
>
> ...the world view of modern physics is holistic and ecological. It emphasizes the fundamental inter-relatedness and interdependence of all phenomena.[13]

Global Consciousness

The space program in particular has contributed significantly to this growing sense of "planetary consciousness" that Dr. Capra and so many others are speaking of today. Our landings on the moon gave us a new view of "Spaceship Earth," as it is being called. As a result of his trip to the moon on Apollo 14, for example, astronaut Dr. Edgar Mitchell had a mystical experience of the unity and sacredness of all life. Abandoning the outer-space program, he joined the millions searching within themselves for the True Self (God) in "higher" states of consciousness. Since then he has become a popular lecturer at the large Unity Church in West Palm Beach, Florida, a New Age center that practices and promotes the apostate "modern religion" that Wells predicted would one day take over the world through an "open conspiracy."

Growing numbers of leading clergymen, such as Theodore Hesburgh, President of Notre Dame, and James Parks Morton, Dean of New York's Episcopal Cathedral of St. John the Divine (both strong supporters of the Planetary Initiative), are advocating and working toward a new age "planetary society." This goal of the huge New Age Movement is pursued by thousands of grass-roots groups linked around the world by "networks." They expect a new world order to emerge out of a transformation of individual consciousness to a "higher state" (unity consciousness) that expresses universal love and oneness with all life based upon Muller's "all-pervading force"—i.e., the alleged "God" within all. As John Graham, a leader in Planetary Initiative for the World We Choose, has said: "It's [human] consciousness...that has to be reached, all the way to the White House...to transform consciousness."[14]

This new "global consciousness" was clearly reflected in the international contents of that gold record attached to Voyager I and II space vehicles, on which was recorded a message to any intelligent life that might come across it in space. A statement was included from President Carter, which reflected not only his sympathy with the global goals of the CFR and Trilateral Commission, but an even larger dream:

> This Voyager spacecraft was constructed by the United States of America...a community of 240 million human beings among the more than 4 billion who inhabit the planet Earth...still divided into nation states, but...rapidly becoming a single global civilization.
> We cast this message into the cosmos...a present from a small distant world....We hope someday, having solved the problems we face, to join a community of galactic civilizations.

The Aquarian Conspiracy

Beginning with the drug movement in the 1950's that moved into Eastern mysticism in the 1970's, untold millions of Westerners have had a mystical yet extremely real experience of "unity consciousness" just as Edgar Mitchell did on Apollo 14. Whether it came under psychedelic drugs, transcendental meditation, or other forms of Yoga and Eastern mysticism, this powerful "realization" of oneness with all life and with the universe itself has become a compelling force preparing the way for a new world order transcending narrow nationalistic limits. It would not be too much to say that a mystical "one-world consciousness" is sweeping planet

Earth in preparation for the coming world ruler.

It is interesting that when H.G. Wells wrote of the "open conspiracy" that would eventually establish the new world order, he declared: "This is my religion...the truth and the way of salvation....It is astir already in many intelligences...an immense and hopeful revolution in human affairs...."[15] There is overwhelming evidence that what Wells predicted is happening at last, that it is not a chance phenomenon, and that it is already much too big for the Trilateralists to control.

Millions of people today sincerely believe that this "Aquarian Conspiracy," as Marilyn Ferguson has called it in her best-selling book of that name, is being engineered by mysterious, invisible intelligences who have been guiding human destiny from behind the scenes since the beginning. Again H.G. Wells hinted at this in 1901, when he wrote: "It is as if a hand had been put upon the head of a thoughtful man and had turned his eyes about from the past to the future."[16]

Mediumistic dictations received in a trance state or via automatic writing have convinced many serious, well-educated followers of various Eastern gurus and spiritualist cult leaders that these entities are "ascended masters" or "masters of wisdom"—allegedly highly evolved past inhabitants of earth, members of our own race, who have moved on after death to "higher planes" of existence. The writings of Helena Petrovna Blavatsky, early leader of the Theosophical Society, contained many references to these entities, whom she sometimes referred to as "the Great White Brotherhood." Hitler believed fanatically in them. Elizabeth Clare Prophet, known as "Guru Ma," claims to be in constant telepathic contact with them today, and the many followers of the Church Universal and Triumphant, which she heads, base their lives upon alleged dictations from these so-called Ascended Masters or Masters of Wisdom.

Are "E.T.'s" Involved?

On the other hand, a number of highly qualified scientific investigators have become convinced by the evidence that these mysterious and as-yet-elusive entities are highly evolved inhabitants of other planets (E.T.'s), who placed us here and have been monitoring our evolutionary progress ever since. In this view, the increased UFO activity of recent years is an apparent indication that these "guardians" of our destiny believe we are almost ready for their return to take visible control over the next step in our development—a quantum evolutionary leap to a "higher consciousness." After so many years of supposed sightings, but nothing tangible in hand, the average person has probably grown weary of UFO stories and written it all off as a delusion. Supposedly the Air Force and other government agencies, having concluded that UFO's were a figment of overactive imaginations, closed the book years ago on any further investigation. That view, however, has been exposed as a blatant lie by, of all things, a recent Supreme Court ruling that was only briefly reported on the back pages of a relatively few newspapers:

FILES ON UFOs CAN BE WITHHELD, HIGH COURT SAYS

Washington (AP) — The Supreme Court Monday refused to order the National Security Agency to disclose what it knows about unidentified flying objects.

The court, without comment, let stand a ruling that the agency's files on the subject do not have to be made public under the Freedom of Information Act.

A group calling itself Citizens Against UFO Secrecy had sought all the executive-branch agency's documents relating to UFOs. The agency released some information but withheld other data.

In November, the U.S. Court of Appeals in Washington upheld a trial judge's ruling that the disputed information must remain secret because it "clearly relates to the most sensitive activities" of the agency.

The U.S. Supreme Court is much too busy to protect nonexistent or unimportant information. It is clear that the government knows something about UFO's that it refuses to tell. Despite rumors about little green E.T.'s on ice and wrecked UFO's in Air Force warehouses, it seems more likely that the information we have is beyond the ability of any government on earth to cope with or to fully comprehend. Something real is out there, but it seems to be more spiritual than physical. There is sufficient evidence, which we cannot cover here, to indicate that UFO's are just part of a larger conspiracy.[17]

The Mysterious Plan

Whether one calls these elusive entities "space brothers" or "masters of wisdom" seems irrelevant. No matter what identity they assume, the mode of operation and the message they communicate is basically the same: they are going to guide us into a new world order of peace and brotherhood based upon the essential perfection of our "Higher Self" and the oneness of all life. Even among ordinarily skeptical scientists, there is a growing belief in the existence of these mysterious "guardians." Of even greater significance is the fact that alleged telepathic communications to select disciples from these "masters of wisdom" over the past 100 years—and more recently from so-called "space brothers"—have anticipated the present awakening of "global consciousness" with startling accuracy. There is considerable evidence that these beings, whatever one calls them, have in fact orchestrated the "consciousness revolution." The similarities are too close for coincidence between "The Plan" that H.G. Wells laid out in detail in 1928 in *The Open Conspiracy* and information received from the "masters," such as in the following "dictation":

> The Plan is concerned with expanding human consciousness...it will reveal to man the true significance of his mind and brain...and will make him therefore omnipresent and eventually open the door to omniscience.
>
> The implementation of this Plan has been the objective of all esoteric training given during the past four hundred years....Humanity needs to realise that there IS a plan, and to recognise its influence in unfolding world events...expansions of consciousness...into which Aquarius is hurrying mankind....
>
> The Plan is concerned with re-building mankind....as human beings begin to take the higher initiations...the true nature of the divine Will will be grasped....
>
> The Masters are working according to a Plan...which will demonstrate a large measure of world unity...marked by universality...that aims at expanding human consciousness...founded in love and...goodwill....[18]

One of the remarkable factors that forces us to regard "The Plan" as something more than fantasy is the obvious conjunction existing today between these mystical states of consciousness, alleged telepathic communications about the coming new world order, and the recent development of computer technology that suddenly makes "The Plan" possible on a practical basis. It seems quite clear, for example, that we are moving rapidly toward a cashless society. This has only recently become possible through today's computer technology, and was not feasible even a few years ago. Eventually every transaction will be by credit card alone. With only one credit card for each person, government-issued and number-controlled, "The Plan" will be well on its way to implementation.

Convergence of Prophecy and Technology

Recent developments in computer technology have made the next step in "The Plan" possible: to create an international electronic network that will give a gas station attendant, cashier in a restaurant, or store clerk anywhere in the world instant access to a central computer network telling him whether a particular credit card is good at that moment for the amount of a given purchase. This developing system has many obvious advantages that can't be argued against, including: elimination of the loss of billions of dollars from forged, stolen, or bad checks; elimination of the millions of muggings and bank and store robberies; elimination of countless hours spent in making deposits in banks, cashing checks, and approving credit.

Having all transactions for each "planetary citizen" computerized under a single credit card number is clearly the next step toward a cashless society with its many undeniable advantages. The one obvious problem remaining will be the card itself: how can it be safeguarded against accidental loss, forgery, or theft? The only real solution will be exactly what the Bible predicted 1900 years ago, when it warned of the coming Antichrist: every person must have indelibly impregnated into his or her body an identifying number readily accessible to a scanning device, thus eliminating altogether the credit card and its inherent shortcomings. The Apostle John wrote:

> And he causes all, the small and the great...to be given a
> mark on their right hand or on their forehead...that no one
> should be able to buy or to sell, except the one who has the
> mark....[19]

Of course, the mark will be invisible except to the scanner;
and the logical place is just where the Bible predicted 1900 years
ago: on the hand or forehead. The Bible specified that this
mark would be a number which the Antichrist would use to
regulate international and local commerce and finance. The
fact that something which modern technology has only recently
made possible was described with such accuracy 1900 years
ago might be considered a "lucky coincidence" were it not
for the hundreds of other Bible prophecies that have already
come true. The odds against all of these being the result of
chance are so astronomical that it would require far more faith
to believe that than to believe that God inspired the writers
of the Bible.

This transformation has been quietly taking place and will
probably be completed over the next few years. Nothing will
stop this process now. We have gone too far down the road
in that direction to turn back. It is too logical and its benefits
are too great for people to pay any attention to Biblical warnings about an alleged Antichrist. That will be passed off as
coincidence.

What should concerned persons do—those who don't wish
to participate in the Antichrist's new order? There seems to
be no prohibition in the Bible against participation up to the
point where the final credit card must be turned in and the
number on it transferred to hand or forehead. There is *one
way* to escape this situation altogether, which we will explain
later. Otherwise it will be either the wrath of God for those
who take the mark or else death at the hands of the Antichrist's
minions for those who don't!

> ...as many as do not worship the image of the beast
> [Antichrist] [will] be killed....
> If anyone worships the beast and his image, and receives a
> mark on his forehead or upon his hand, he also will drink of
> the wine of the wrath of God....[20]

Why the Delay?

All of the advanced technology necessary to complete the process now exists, and most of the actual electronic equipment is already in operation. The plans have been laid; yet there is a delay. Why? If the general public knew all that is being planned, they would raise a storm of protest. Therefore the process is being carried out very quietly and slowly. Even so, the consequences that are already obvious are frightening, and Christians in particular have begun to sound the alarm. Among the general public there is also an instinctive fear of the awesome power of electronic control. The system is being implemented cautiously, one step at a time, in order to prevent a general protest. We are like the proverbial frog in a pot of water that never jumps out because the temperature is raised so slowly that the frog cooks to death without recognizing the danger.

At the present time there is no indication either from the Bible or world events that the Antichrist is already exerting his insidious influence from behind the scenes. A computer-controlled, cashless society will probably be in existence before he seizes control of the world. For how long before, we don't know, but it will probably be in existence only a matter of weeks or months, not years. Only after the Antichrist takes over will the last credit card be eliminated and the mark on hand or forehead be required. The world leader who puts that final stage into effect will be identifying himself very definitely as the Antichrist.[21] When that happens, it will be too late for anyone to escape except by death!

In the meanwhile, the delay seems to fit Bible prophecy. Paul wrote that the Antichrist would not be able to make his move to take over the world until God allowed it to happen: "...he who now restrains [him from being revealed] will do so until he is taken out of the way."[22] The inference seems to be that the Holy Spirit present in the followers of Christ around the world is the Restraint that prevents a premature emergence of "the man of lawlessness...the son of destruction."[23]

At times of great crisis and turning points in history, the majority opinion is often and perhaps nearly always wrong.

This fact alone suggests a contrary scenario. However, we must build the scenario cautiously, carefully weighing all of the evidence and trends in relation to Bible prophecies. Each piece must fit the puzzle. The way this particular piece (i.e., the cause of the delay) fits will become clear only in a later chapter. There we will see its relationship to the sudden elimination of the United States as a world power.

Before getting to that, however, it is necessary to piece together several other factors. A world government is coming soon. Nothing can stop it now. However, the nuclear holocaust cannot be unleashed until *after* the Antichrist assumes world control and establishes peace and prosperity for a time.

We face not only a coming world government, but also a coming world religion. In the space age, it must have the endorsement of science. What could this religion be?

It takes no great genius to realize that if the Bible calls its leader the Antichrist, then this religion must be antichristian. However, Jesus Himself warned that this man would pretend to be the Christ, and that his masquerade would be so clever and convincing that it would "mislead, if possible, even the elect."[24]

From what the Bible tells us, it is clear that the coming world religion will appeal to everyone: to the members of all religions and even to atheists, materialistic scientists, and psychiatrists. At the same time, it will seem to be Christian. So far, at least, it sounds somewhat similar to the "positive Christianity" that Hitler claimed to be establishing in Germany and intended for the entire world.[25]

6
The New Age Movement

A new kind of revolution is quietly taking over planet Earth. Unlike the Russian Revolution and other violent uprisings that installed new governments in the past, this revolution will conquer without guns. As New Age Movement leaders would say: "The new politics is involved more with...getting in touch with our 'Higher Self,' more with mysticism than violence...." It is a "consciousness revolution" that is preparing planet Earth to recognize and receive the coming world ruler, whom the Bible calls the Antichrist. Rejecting Biblical prophecies and the whole idea of an Antichrist, H.G. Wells saw the consciousness revolution as something good, a positive and open conspiracy that would save the world from destruction. In this connection, he made another startling prediction:

> The Open Conspiracy is the natural inheritor of socialist and communist enthusiasms; it may be in control of Moscow before it is in control of New York![1]

We will discover later why this seemingly incredible prediction by Wells makes sense. First of all, however, it is necessary to understand that the coming new world order is actually a religion, though it often wears a political mask. Its millions of sincere participants have adopted an ecumenical faith that will form the basis of the coming world religion: belief in the oneness of all life and in themselves as part of the Universal Self or Consciousness. They fervently believe that an awakening of brotherhood and love will usher in a new age of peace, prosperity, and incredible progress. As evidence of this, they point to a new and worldwide phenomenon that was first ignited by the drug culture and then expanded through the spread of Eastern meditation techniques in the West: the emergence of a new "planetary consciousness" in human beings. As Mark Satin has said:

61

Planetary consciousness recognizes our oneness...with all life everywhere and with the planet...the interdependence of all humanity....

Planetary consciousness sees each of us as "cells in the body of humanity," as Planetary Citizens.

...we are beginning to see the emergence of a new *collective* consciousness.[2]

The Aquarian Network

Marilyn Ferguson has called this movement *The Aquarian Conspiracy*. Many others agree with her in identifying the new age as the Age of Aquarius. New age thinking involves a new "openness" to one another, to ourselves, to nature, to a universal "Force" pervading the whole cosmos—which produces an awakening of unimagined powers of the mind. Playing an important role in the new age, astrology is based upon a belief in this interconnectedness, which determines personality and destiny depending upon the date and location of one's birth in relation to certain heavenly bodies. Like Hinduism, upon which it is based, the Aquarian Conspiracy claims to embrace all beliefs, all religions, on the premise that all is one. Dealing with the question "Is nuclear war in our future?" New Age astrologer Virginia Kay Miller declared:

...the world is in the midst of a massive upheaval.

...many people believe that humankind is on the verge of an evolutionary break-through and we are standing on the threshold of a New Age.

Called the "Aquarian Age," it will bring about a new world order in which individuals will realize their true spiritual being and their interconnectedness with all life.

To survive...as a planet, we must...develop the Aquarian consciousness, which recognizes that we are all linked together as members of the human race and as inhabitants of planet Earth.

We must network....[3]

"Network" is a New Age code word that refers not to radio or television but to the thousands of groups around the world that are all working toward the realization of this "interconnectedness" of all life through the establishment of a world government. Many of these networks expect the United Nations one day to function as the "central nervous system" in the new world order. This new planetary consciousness is shared by many leaders, who often express their belief in almost-mystical terms. Robert Muller, Secretary of the U.N. Economic and Social Council and an avid networker, has said: "This old planet and the human species on it are [like]...a big brain whose neurons are multiplying incessantly, encompassing everything from the individual to the planet, to humanity and the universe....The world brain is already so complicated ...new interconnections are being created so rapidly...[it] is a new biological phenomenon, one of the most momentous ones in the earth's history....The U.N. is a system of central universal organs...."⁴ It is this interconnectedness of planetary consciousness that New Age networks express visibly around the world. As the authors of *Networking: The First Report and Directory* declared:

> We went looking for networks, and we found Another America....
>
> In the end, we found that we had mapped a significant American subculture with values oriented to human transformation and global peace.⁵

Networks are composed of hundreds and sometimes thousands of groups. There are "New Age caucuses...trying to work for New Age-oriented change-and-transformation from within our already established social, cultural, economic and professional organizations and institutions...[such as] the Social Change Network of the Association for Humanistic Psychology...."⁶ There are "New Age business and professional organizations...[such as] the Transpersonal Association...the Holistic Health Organizing Committee...[and] the Association for World Education. New Age discussion groups are springing up across the country: the Political Science Committee of the Institute for the New Age and New Age Feminism ...The Institute for the Study of Conscious Evolution is investigating the relevance of 'transpersonal consciousness and conscience' for the 'survival and evolution of the species and the planet.'...New Age education groups...propagate...New

Age ethics and values in an almost infinite number of ways. ...[There is] the Naropa Institute...the Hunger Project, Planetary Citizens, Movement for a New Society" and a host of others.[7] The list is almost endless.

Planetary Conspirators

Marilyn Ferguson, apparently with all seriousness, insists that the New Age Movement "is not a new political, religious, or philosophical system. It is a new mind—the ascendance of a startling world view that gathers into its framework breakthrough science and insights from earliest recorded thought."[8] It is hard to imagine how a world view could be neither philosophical nor religious! In fact, the New Age Movement is both. "Insights from earliest recorded thought" is a euphemistic way of referring to ancient occultism. The "new mind" that Ms. Ferguson speaks of comes about through acceptance of basic Hindu philosophy, which is the cement that holds together the otherwise seemingly disparate views of this new world religion. And it *is* political, for the common goal is a new world order, a world government.

The Association for Global Education, Cooperation, and Accreditation declares: "Only by the birth of global consciousness within each individual can we truly achieve transnationalization."[9] Such an ambition used to be the private heresy of a secret clique of infamous elitists of the ilk of Trilateralists and CFR people. Now it is the declaration of faith of millions in the New Age Movement. As the Servers' Network has declared, we are indeed witnessing the "emergence of a new universal person and civilization."![10] The normal loyalty to the nation of one's birth is being overturned in favor of "planetary citizenship." That this is being advocated by sincere persons under the duress of the dire emergencies we face and in order to save our species from extinction is not doubted. That anyone could deny the political nature of the Aquarian Conspiracy, however, is beyond comprehension.

Paradoxically, most of the energy, time, and attention expended by those in the New Age Movement is directed inward, getting "in touch with themselves" in order to find out who they really are, getting "in touch with their feelings." How could this narcissism become the basis for universal brother-hood and global consciousness? It is based upon the experience of "unity consciousness" that comes through drugs or TM and other forms of Yoga and Eastern meditation, leading to the Hindu belief that atman (individual soul) is identical with Brahman (universal soul). New Age global consciousness and interconnectedness is based to a large extent upon a denial of the Judeo-Christian God of the Bible in exchange for the belief that we are all "God." This is ancient Hinduism, yet it is be-ing accepted today as nonreligious modern science. By a hand-ful of naive fanatics? No, by millions of well-educated sophisticates.

The range and scope and influence of the New Age Move-ment is worldwide and truly awesome. No one lays it out as well as Marilyn Ferguson:

> The Aquarian Conspirators range across all levels of income and education...schoolteachers and office workers, famous scientists, government officials and lawmakers, artists and millionaires, taxi drivers and celebrities, leaders in medicine, education, law, psychology....
>
> There are legions of conspirators...in corporations, univer-sities and hospitals, on the faculties of public schools, in fac-tories and doctors' offices, in state and federal agencies, on city councils and the White House staff, in state legislatures...in virtually all arenas of policy-making in the country.
>
> ...the conspirators are linked...by their inner discoveries...an unlikely kind of conspiracy...their *lives* had become revolu-tions...a personal change began...re-thinking everything....
>
> They have coalesced into small groups in every town and institution. They have formed what one called "national non-organizations."...millions of others who have never thought of themselves as part of a conspiracy but sense that their ex-periences and their struggle are part of something bigger, a larger social transformation that is increasingly visible if you know where to look....
>
> There are tens of thousands of entry points to this conspiracy.[11]

What New Age Movement?

Of course, not everyone takes the New Age Movement

seriously. Some deny that it even exists. "What New Age Movement?" is a common remark. While almost everyone will have noticed the words "New Age" appearing with increasing frequency, not many people recognize the coherent pattern involved, and fewer still understand what the words really mean, much less their great importance in shaping the future of humanity and this planet. In fact, many New Agers are scarcely aware of the full implication of their involvement in the movement. And because the movement is more an organism than an organization, many people would vehemently deny that they are involved at all.

Most people outside the movement who recognize its existence sincerely believe that it is limited to a few visionaries whose impact upon society will be very minimal at most. Nothing could be further from the truth! Suggesting that the New Age Movement may in fact exist "largely in Marilyn Ferguson's head," Stanford University history professor Paul Robinson criticizes her *Aquarian Conspiracy* as "an exercise in mindlessness" that obliterates "most of what our civilization has achieved" in its "thoughtless pages." He accuses her of using a style of thought that "is wholly uncritical, an abdication of the powers of the mind...."[12] If there is such a movement, Robinson condemns it and Ms. Ferguson soundly with this scathing rebuke:

> To dream of endless transformation is to remain an intellectual child....
>
> Ferguson's book and the people it describes betray a psychological immaturity and a contempt for the mind that are truly chilling.[13]

Robinson's harsh judgment is a typical materialist denunciation that recognizes only the rational aspects of the brain and rejects as deception or delusion the apparent paranormal powers of the mind that are axiomatic to New Agers. Considering Robinson's rationalism a hindrance to personal growth and progress, however, the New Age Movement is far more concerned with the *transpersonal* or so-called *transcendent* powers of the mind—those seemingly supernatural or Godlike powers that the Yogis, shamans, witch doctors, and voodoo priests have always manifested. Materialistic science has traditionally viewed psychic phenomena with suspicion and skepticism. Within the past few years, however, ESP, psychokinesis, telepathy, clairvoyance, and other such powers have been scientifically demonstrated beyond any reasonable doubt. Therefore, the New Age belief in these "powers of the mind" simply cannot be dismissed as "mindlessness" in the cavalier manner with which Robinson attempts to write them off.

Far from being guilty of "a contempt for the mind," the New Ager worships mind, convinced by scientific experiment and his own experience that the universe itself is a great Mind, which his own mind is a part of and can tap into through "altered states of consciousness." He believes that minds not only can move and bend and otherwise affect physical objects at a distance, but that ultimately he can create his own reality with his mind. In calling this "an abdication of the powers of the mind," Professor Robinson betrays his own naivete' and lack of knowledge concerning the underlying belief system behind the New Age Movement. To catalog such beliefs as intellectually childish is to ignore the fact that many of today's most brilliant scientists, including not a few Nobel laureates, are convinced that the New Age view of mind is correct. Their position must be taken seriously, not ridiculed; and the evidence must be examined carefully, which we intend to do.

First of all, however, we need to understand that the New Age Movement is based upon beliefs that have always been regarded instinctively by the human race as witchcraft and demonic. Whether the old categories of "good" and "evil" should now be dropped in the New Age vision of the Oneness of All is a question that we will consider carefully. In that regard, we agree with Robinson that Ferguson and other New Agers, while perhaps not "wholly uncritical," have been too easily convinced that the "mind powers" they seek are desirable. In fact, these may not be "mind powers" at all—at least not the capabilities of *human* minds! Our "contrary scenario" proposes an explanation for such powers that has been overlooked or disdained by the New Age Movement; yet we expect to show beyond reasonable doubt that it is the *only* explanation that fits all of the facts.

Whether real or imagined, and whatever the explanation, through "altered states of consciousness" paranormal "mind powers" have been experienced by millions of people in the West under stimulation of drugs, Yoga, hypnosis, Eastern meditation, etc. These experiences of alleged "mind powers" seem so real that all of the rational arguments or ridicule of a Paul Robinson have little effect on New Agers.

As a result, the Hindu monistic view of reality has become the predominant world view in the West today. This is true in science, medicine, psychology, sociology, education, politics, and business. It is certainly the case with feminism, which is in the forefront of the New Age Movement.

The Women's Movement

In universities across America, a new group of courses called "women's studies" has come into existence within the past decade. There are "women's studies departments" in our colleges and "centers for feminist therapy" in our cities and suburbs. The national attention that was given to the Equal Rights Amendment and the almost-daily publicity concerning "women's rights" has given women a new confidence in themselves and a new prominence and power in politics. The ERA campaign failed to reach its 1982 goal of an amendment to the United States Constitution, but the major force behind the movement was spiritual, not political, and is still gaining momentum. The Women's Movement is one of the most important parts of the New Age Movement. It is at the heart of the consciousness revolution that is sweeping the Western world. As Fritjof Capra has said:

> Now from the earliest times of Chinese culture, the yin was associated with the feminine and the yang with the masculine....Feminists have repeatedly pointed out that the values and attitudes favored by our culture are those of patriarchal cultures...the most severe consequence of this imbalance today is the ever increasing threat of nuclear war....
>
> Like the Cartesian paradigm, patriarchy is now on the decline. And I believe that the rise of Feminist awareness is one of the most important aspects of the emerging new vision of reality.[14]

Closely related to transpersonal psychology, the New Age Movement involves "getting in touch with yourself...with your feelings...getting into yourself...finding out who you really are...accepting and loving yourself...getting in tune with your 'Higher Self'...learning to *be* yourself." These are not just catch phrases, but serious goals for those in the movement. And when women "get in touch with themselves," they find that they are *very* special, the key to the survival and destiny of our species. Feminine spirituality plays a leading role in New Age transformation of the individual and society.

Many of those involved in the Feminist Movement may sincerely believe it is a political crusade to gain equality with men. In fact it is more than that: it is also a spiritual movement based partly upon a reawakening of "goddess consciousness," and its real goal is matriarchy, not equality. One major spiritual force behind some aspects of the feminist movement is witchcraft, which is based upon the power of female sexuality derived from a mystical relationship with "Mother Nature" and "Mother Earth."

Take, for example, the Women's Conference held in Southern California during April 24-25, 1982. Its title was "Women: The Leading Edge of the New Age." Declared Linda Barone, the feminist therapist who organized the conference: "The New Age will allow us to experience a sense of wholeness, a sense of connectedness with nature" (i.e., Mother Nature).[15] Any witch would immediately recognize the significance of that statement. However, for those who don't know that "nature religion" is witchcraft, the movement often spells it out more clearly. On March 15, 1982, 11 leaders in the Women's Movement held a planning meeting at the West Los Angeles Center for Feminist Therapy. One of the brochures available that day to be handed out to potential participants in the April Conference was from the Universal Goddess Center, Inc., and stated:

> Nineteen-eighty-two is the year for revolution in religion, higher education and New Age learning, in which the holistic, interconnected nature of reality is widely recognized...[and in which women are encouraged] to express their "new" spirituality—which is the oldest on earth.

As any witch will proudly inform you, the oldest spirituality on earth is Wicca or witchcraft. Who would suspect that *new* spirituality means *oldest* spirituality, or that *higher* states of consciousness are really *lower* states, sinking ever deeper within the "Self"? The New Age Movement employs words and phrases that seem to mean one thing but actually mean something entirely different to insiders. "Self-transcendence" is really "subscendence." "God" in the New Age is the pantheistic god of ancient paganism, the All of Hinduism, and *not* the transcendent God of the Judeo-Christian Bible. Thus "transcendental meditation," which is pure Hinduism posing as science, is a deceptive label that really means the opposite: *subscendence* ever deeper into oneself. The "new" psychic powers being verified in some of our top laboratories today, from Princeton to UCLA, are really the *old* occult powers that Yogis, shamans, witch doctors and voodoo priests have always exhibited. "New Age" is a euphemism for "old occultism." And this is nowhere seen more clearly than in the "new spirituality" advocated by many leaders in the Women's Movement.

Goddesses of the New Age

A large and typical "Women's Spirituality & Healing Conference" was held October 22-24, 1982, at Los Angeles Valley College in North Hollywood, California. One of the popular seminars that weekend was titled "Introduction to Goddess Consciousness and the Craft." One would have to be very naive not to know that "the Craft" is *witchcraft.* Included in that workshop were discussions of "goddess consciousness... nymph, maiden, crone; the Sacred Wheel; politics of women's celebrations; how do spells and rituals work?" Other seminars included "Pathways to Your Inner Light" ("meet your own spiritual guides, and discover the light within...harmonize your mental, physical, emotional and spiritual levels of beingness through hypnosis and meditation"); "Medicine Wheel Magic" ("you will learn how...a medicine wheel...can become a valuable spiritual resource for you and how you can build one for your own use"); "How to Enjoy the Present by Experiencing Past and Future Lives"; "Women's Spiritual Journey:

Loss and Recovery of 'God' " ("We will explore paradigms for this transformation to wholeness, found in the Sumerian myth of the goddess Inanna..."); "Female Erotic Power and Orgasmic Responses"; and "In The Beginning Was the Goddess." The brochure described this last seminar as follows:

> In this workshop, women will discover their own lost heritage by exploring ancient concepts of deity as "goddess." Although the great Mother Goddess was worshipped everywhere in the world for more than 100,000 years *before* the concept of male gods emerged in human consciousness, She is little known [today].
>
> More than 200 slides of images of various aspects of the universal Goddess will be shown, their psychological and spiritual ramifications for our lives and for our time will be discussed, and the positive benefits of incorporating into our value structure a feminine image of the divine will be explored.

Under the heading "GODDESSES OF COMING NEW AGE PROBE THE MEANING OF IT ALL," *Los Angeles Times* staff writer Elizabeth Mehren reported on the March 1982 gathering of leaders in the Women's Movement mentioned above.[16] Among those present was Charlene Spretnak, who declared: "Women's spirituality exposes revisionist history and reveals the truth about our past." As for the future, she said, "I believe that women are the teachers in society's transformation into the New Age."[17] Past-lives therapist Jean Whitaker, transpersonal psychologist Jackie Holley, and former cloistered nun Patricia James, now the guru and director of the Awareness Ashram in Echo Park, Los Angeles, were there explaining the importance of the Women's Movement in the New Age. Martial arts instructor Beth Austin spoke of the "internal balancing of energies, the spiritual, mental, physical and emotional aspects of self, through...meditation."[18]

Malka Golden-Wolfe, founder of the Universal Goddess Center in Malibu, California, and former aide to Los Angeles Mayor Tom Bradley, declared in no uncertain terms that "the healing of the planet depends upon women." She explained that through going "deeper into myself" she discovered the "guru and the teacher and the mother within all of us."[19] The goals of the movement are pretty well summed up in a recent

590-page book of feminist writings edited by Charlene Spret-nak, *The Politics of Women's Spirituality* (Anchor Books/Doubleday, 1982), which a reviewer described in part as follows:

> The particular brand of spirituality championed in the book as the hope of the world is the ancient goddess worship that characterized a supposedly bygone Golden Age of matriarchal rule.
>
> Goddess worship, paganism, Wicca, and witchcraft are all names for a form of natural religion that is centered around the mystery, sexuality, and psychic abilities of the female.
>
> The book is a clarion call to women to regain their natural power and to overthrow the global rule of men. The authors' starting point for the re-establishment of female dominance is in bringing an end to Judeo-Christian religion.[20]

The New Age Movement professes a broad-minded openness to all religions, but its basic underlying philosophy represents a carefully calculated undermining of Judeo-Christian beliefs. It bears a remarkable resemblance to the apostate world religion that H.G. Wells claimed as his own and predicted would one day take over the world. It also fits the description of "The Plan" for establishing the new world government that is described in various psychic communications from alleged E.T.'s and ascended masters. There is one more connection: the New Age Movement fits the description of the Antichrist's religion—a rejection of the Judeo-Christian God and the declaration that Self is God.

All of this seems far too much to be a coincidence. Consequently, our "contrary scenario" tentatively identifies the New Age Movement with "the apostasy" that the Apostle Paul predicted would immediately precede the Antichrist's takeover of the world in a bold rebellion against the Judeo-Christian God and against the moral absolutes which the Bible attributes to Him.[21] For this reason the Antichrist is described in the Bible as "the man of lawlessness."[22]

Since the apostasy is preparing the way for a counterfeit Christ, we would expect it to hide its rebellious antagonism against Judeo-Christian beliefs under a deceptive cloak of euphemisms. In fact, this is one of the most fascinating characteristics of the New Age Movement: its use of code words and phrases that sound innocent or even orthodox, but which mean something else to the insiders. Is this just another coincidence?

7
Truth or Lie?

As we have already seen, the New Age employs euphemisms in order to disguise the religion behind it. Words like witchcraft, spiritism, animism, and voodoo still have "bad vibes" and connotations of ignorance and superstition. "Traditional" sounds so much better: it has an aura of broad-minded acceptance of "native" cultures without judging them; and getting back to one's roots is currently in vogue. For those who are still struggling to shake off Judeo-Christian morality learned in childhood, the euphemism "traditional" covers a multitude of sins.

As a means of easing the burden on modern health-care systems, the World Health Organization (WHO) of the United Nations has given official approval to "traditional healers" around the world. In Bulawayo, Zimbabwe, for example, Dr. Bingara Tshuma, "a consultant traditional healer who shares a medical center with two conventional, Western-trained doctors, straightens his animal skin headdress, removes his shoes, inhales snuff through both nostrils and wills himself into a hypnotic trance."[1] He then calls upon his spirit guide to advise him. "People who come here have a choice between the *nganga* [traditional healer] or the doctors," says Babra Sibanda, a registered nurse who owns the Zimbabwe Medical and Traditional Practitioners' Center. "But the *nganga* is the busiest of our consultants. Even whites choose to go to him."[2] There are about 8000 licensed "traditional healers" in Zimbabwe alone, who "pass on their secrets—and their spirits—from father to son or mother to daughter, and claim to be able to cure most illnesses."[3] To New Agers, "spirits" is a "native" word for the "mind powers" that lie within us all.

74

Euphemistic Exorcism

It is not merely the word "traditional" that exorcises witchcraft and spiritism of its old demonic connotations. Witchcraft and shamanistic powers, which have always been instinctively recognized as *demonic*, are today called *psychic* and are accepted even by science. Under the new labels, leading scientists (who formerly rejected witchcraft and spiritism as pagan superstition) are now "discovering" real power in "traditional" techniques.

Zimbabwe's deputy health minister, Dr. Simon Mazorodze, has said, "These traditional healers have a lot to teach us, especially in the field of mental health."[4] A recent "experiment at the All-India Institute of Mental Health in Bangalore found that Western-trained psychiatrists and native [traditional] faith healers had a comparable recovery rate. The most notable difference was that the so-called 'witchdoctors' released their patients sooner!"[5] This should not have been surprising. Long before this test was conducted, world-renowned research psychiatrist E. Fuller Torrey in his book *Mind Games* declared: "The methods of Western psychiatrists, with few exceptions, are on the same scientific plane as the methods of witchdoctors." If "all is One," as New Age consciousness tells us, then evil is good, God and Satan are One, and everything there is can be found within the Self. Therefore, as Danish physician Dr. Halfdan Mahler, director-general of WHO, declared:

> Nothing should be sacrosanct simply because we have been led to believe that it is witchcraft.[6]

"Alternative" is another popular New Age euphemism. "Alternative medicine" is considered to be the "new wave" in health care. In reality it is mainly a return to the old methods of pagan occultism, involving a "realignment of psychic forces" within the body through such occult techniques as acupuncture, reflexology, and Yoga, along with diagnostic practices out of the occult, such as vitamin kinesiology, radiesthesia, and pendulum diagnosis. Like a placebo, these things work only if one believes they will. Thus they are related to the mysterious "mind powers" of the New Age. We will analyze "mind powers" in a broader context later.

Then there are "alternate" lifestyles, another euphemism for homosexuality or lesbianism or free sex, which is supposed to remove any connotation of "sin" or immorality. The word "lifestyle" itself is a euphemism that frees New Agers of any moral restraint. Whatever way of life one chooses to adopt is simply a "style" that can be changed like hair or dress styles without any moral implications, or so one is led to believe.

The Abolition of Man

New Age educators use the term "values clarification" as a euphemism in our public schools to hide their deliberate rebellion against moral absolutes. "Clarification" of values is generally calculated to do away with Judeo-Christian morals by denying that there is any absolute standard available for measuring moral values. Obviously, if there is no objective measurement, then the very word "values" becomes meaningless. Certainly it has no morality attached to it. In rejection of the Judeo-Christian moral absolutes taught in the Bible (that derive from the personal Creator-God), "values clarification" encourages the student to look within himself for "inner guidance." The only thing that matters is how the student "feels" about a situation. Above all, he must be "true to himself" and not succumb to the pressure of the opinions of others, the taboos of society, or religious standards. What is actually happening, however, is that the unsuspecting student is being conditioned to accept New Age values! And in most cases the parents are just as unsuspecting of what is really happening to their children in the process of public school education.

In his fascinating book *The Abolition of Man*, C.S. Lewis referred to an elementary school textbook of his day which was supposed to teach English to school children. However, it was in reality a calculated attempt to undermine a belief in any moral values outside the individual's own preferences and feelings. It was also designed to condition the unsuspecting students to accept the "values" presented in the textbook. What C.S. Lewis had to say about that particular children's textbook in his day is of even greater importance with regard to hundreds of similar but more dangerous New Age textbooks in the 1980's:

> The very power of [the authors] depends on the fact that they are dealing with a boy; a boy who thinks he is "doing" his "English prep" and has no notion that ethics, theology, and politics are all at stake.
>
> It is not a theory they put into his mind, but an assumption, which ten years hence, its origin forgotten and its presence unconscious, will condition him....
>
> The authors themselves, I suspect, hardly know what they are doing to the boy, and he cannot know what is being done to him.[7]

Much like the book that C.S. Lewis describes above, but far more persuasive and dangerous, Dr. Beverly Galyean's *Language From Within* is supposed to be a Confluent Education "handbook" for teaching English in today's public schools. In reality it has far less to do with English than with philosophy and religion. Says Dr. Galyean, "Confluent Education has as its goal to educate teachers in Gestalt Awareness theory and practice, and to research the results of teachers using these Gestalt strategies in classes."[8] One wonders how many parents would object if they knew that their children were guinea pigs in a government-funded psychotherapeutic experiment to test Gestalt theory! Galyean also says, "Confluent Education is the deliberate attempt to merge thinking and feeling into one integrated process."[9] Without realizing what is being done to them, the students are conditioned to look to their feelings for guidance. This is a very dangerous conditioning process. Dr. Galyean's own peculiar religious beliefs are being taught in public schools, where religion is not to be introduced.

Dr. Galyean's book instructs teachers in how to carefully condition their students to accept and experience Galyean's own religious beliefs. If Christianity were being taught in public schools under a similar guise, it would be promptly thrown out. Certainly the ACLU would be up in arms. However, Galyean's Confluent Education and other similar New Age education techniques are accepted in public schools and backed by government funds, even though they condition the students to accept the basic religious beliefs of Hinduism. Very few parents or students recognize what is happening. This conditioning process that is going on in our public schools across America was described well by C.S. Lewis:

> The process which, if not checked, will abolish Man, goes on apace among Communists and Democrats no less than among Fascists. The methods may (at first) differ in brutality. But many a mild-eyed scientist in pince-nez, many a popular dramatist, many an amateur philosopher in our midst, means in the long run just the same as the Nazi rulers of Germany.
>
> Traditional values are to be "debunked" and mankind to be cut out into some fresh shape at the will (which must, by hypothesis, be an arbitrary will) of some few lucky people in one lucky generation which has learned how to do it.
>
> The belief that we can invent "ideologies" at pleasure... begins to affect our language.[10]

Guided Imagery

The language that Dr. Beverly Galyean's Confluent Education conditions the students to accept "from within" is euphemistic and New Age to the core. Children are led into contact with "spirit guides," but Dr. Galyean cautions teachers that it is best to call them "imaginary" guides or "wise persons" in public schools. Typical of the method that Galyean and other New Agers teach and which is being widely used in public schools today, beginning in kindergarten, is the following suggestion to be intoned by the teacher:

> Close your eyes and relax. I will lead you in a guided fantasy.
>
> Imagine...a very beautiful valley....Ahead of you is a mountain...you have magic powers so climbing...is easy...at the top...look into the sun and as you do the face of a very wise person slowly appears.
>
> You...ask..."What must I do to find happiness in my life right now?"
>
> The person answers....Listen to this person speaking...you may...engage in a conversation.
>
> When you feel finished with your conversation, come back to us here in the room. Write an account of what was spoken between you and the wise person.[11]

Similar methods are being used by medical doctors, such as Dr. Irving Oyle of the University of California at Santa Cruz; and the "psychic guides" that appear in the imagination literally cure impossible medical problems that have defied all other treatment.[12] Fundamentalist Christians believe that these "guides" are spirit beings of great evil and deception, similar to the demons that impersonate spirits of the dead in seances.[13] Although psychologists generally reject this belief, they have no better explanation for the psychic phenomena that often develop spontaneously and the evil that can suddenly arise out of what seemed at first to be so good. Elmer and Alyce Green, who have been involved in biofeedback research at the Menninger Foundation in Kansas since 1964, warn against the dangers involved in developing contact with "imaginary" guides. New Age public schoolteachers are either unaware of or ignore the warnings. Here is one of the many cases the Greens cite:

> ...a woman wrote that after her husband had taken the [mind-training] course, one of his "imaginary psychic advisers" unexpectedly began speaking to him without being asked.
>
> The adviser explained that he was God and that for spiritual reasons the wife also must take the course.
>
> When she refused to do this, "God" told him to get a divorce. She and her teenage sons were unable to influence her husband.
>
> He also developed some other peculiarities.[14]

Abuse of the imagination plays a large part in Confluent Education, because Galyean and other New Age educators are convinced that the students can create their own reality with their minds. Although Galyean sincerely believes that we are each God and therefore have within us all knowledge and wisdom, she adopts the euphemisms "intuition" or "universal consciousness" to hide any religious connotations. Her presentation of Hinduism is usually not recognized as religion, because guided imagery seems so "natural." And what could be more "natural" than getting in touch with yourself? As that master occultist Rudolf Steiner, founder of Anthroposophy, said years ago:

And here's my vision: the creation of a deeper, fuller human being...having a full knowledge of Self...and ultimately connected with all humanity.[15]

New Age Education

Maria Montessori, founder of the world-famous Montessori schools, was a forerunner of New Age education. Rejecting the imposition of wisdom from outside, she wanted to free students to be guided by the "inward teacher." She was convinced that this would produce a "New Man...able to direct and to mold the future of mankind."[16] Rudolph Steiner, "whose educational philosophy is embodied in the worldwide network of Waldorf schools...defined the Waldorf approach as...the art of awakening what is actually there within the human being."[17] Well-known educator Jack Canfield states the essence of New Age education in similar terms: "The next step in the transformation of education will be to nurture and value the emergence of what exists innately within the student."[18]

Jack Canfield's New Age education manual, *100 Ways to Enhance Self-Concept in the Classroom*, was "recently used in a federally-funded teacher education program in Connecticut....Maureen Murdock's meditating and guided imagery programs" are another example of New Age religion being promoted in our public schools at taxpayers' expense.[19] The 1982-83 "Holistic Education Network L.A. Conference Series," held at California State University at Los Angeles, advertised the following speakers and subjects: Beverly Galyean ("holistic learning...extra sensory perception, mind synergy"); Barbara Clark ("a host of New Age strategies...to optimize classroom instruction with students, pre-kindergarten to graduate level"); Gay Hendricks ("centering and transpersonal education...learning to love yourself"); Joyce Chapman, Director of the New Age School in San Diego ("holistic approach...to remain true to your higher self").

Heavily involved in the Planetary Initiative for the World We Choose, the Association for Humanistic Psychology is an integral part of the New Age Movement. Since humanistic psychologists are classical atheists, one would assume that their organization would be very antireligious. However, New Age Hindu occultism is being introduced into our public schools by humanistic psychologists—all in the name of science, of course! For example, the May-June 1979 Education Network newsletter of the Association for Humanistic Psychology suggested that public school teachers incorporate the following highly religious activities into their daily routine:

> The students will: do yoga each morning before class; interpret their astrological charts; send messages via ESP; mind project; astral project; heal their own illnesses; speak with their "Higher Selves" and receive information necessary for joyful living; lift energies from the power chakra to the heart chakra; practice skills necessary for color healing; hold an image of themselves as being perfect; receive advice from their personal [spirit] guides; merge minds with others in the class to experience the collective consciousness of the group.

In *The Bridge at Andau*, James Michener relates how escapees from Hungary during the 1956 revolution told him they would stay up all night if necessary to deliver their children from the Communist lies they had been taught that day at school. Parents in America have failed to do the same, unaware of what is happening to their children. While they have slept, Hinduism has been seductively presented to their children as New Age education. Some parents may be happy to have their children converted to Hinduism in public schools. Many others, however, would be very unhappy if they knew this were happening!

The New Age Movement has a stranglehold on our entire society. Its most strategic work is in the public schools. It is teaching our children that they are gods, and that the only authority they need follow is the "inner light" of their "Higher Self." New Age educators are deliberately trying to bring about a transformation of thinking, morals, world view, and personal identity in public schools across America. It is not honest for them to hide the religious nature of their beliefs behind euphemisms. Jack Canfield speaks in glowing terms of "the essential Self that is evoked in New Age education...the High Self." He adds:

Each person's essential Self knows why it's here and what it needs to learn to further its Soul-purpose. The role of New Age education is to facilitate that inner unfoldment. Not to impose values and meanings from the outside.[20]

Truth or Lie?

Whether they know it or not, what Canfield, Galyean, et al are teaching is basic Hinduism. In Hinduism, the goal of Yoga is "Self-realization," to "realize" that one is "God." This is the "truth" that is offered to the one million pitiful creatures who live today in the streets of Calcutta, where they were born and will die, suffering unspeakable poverty, misery, and disease. What salvation does Hinduism offer them? That by the practice of Yoga they can achieve a "higher" state of consciousness, where they will "realize" that the physical universe, including their abject misery, is an illusion (maya) and they are really gods. This is the "ancient wisdom" we have received with open arms from the gurus and Yogis who have brought it to America! Hinduism has turned India, in spite of its vast natural resources and manpower, into one of the poorest and most suffering countries on earth. It could do the same to America, if we continue down this path.

New Age leader John White, author of more than 200 articles in such prestigious periodicals as *Readers' Digest* and *Science Digest*, declares: "Our present world situation is a crisis of consciousness...the solution...very simple: change consciousness."[21] *The Next Whole Earth Catalog* declares: "We are as Gods and might as well get good at it...." In explaining the basis for her philosophy of New Age education, Beverly Galyean states:

Once we begin to see that we are all God, that we all have the attributes of God, then I think the whole purpose of human life is to reown the Godlikeness within us; the perfect love, the perfect wisdom, the perfect understanding, the perfect intelligence, and when we do that, we create back to that old, that essential oneness which is consciousness.

So my whole view is very much based on that idea...the system of confluent education as I work with it is totally dependent on that view, because my whole philosophy is that learning is...looking within and discovering what information is inside you....[22]

In his famous poem, "The Immortal Friend," world-renowned Hindu philosopher Jiddu Krishnamurti sets out on his "guided imagery" journey to find that same "wise person" that American students are being conditioned to seek. Krishnamurti eventually finds his "friend" in the same place that students in America's public schools are finding theirs—within. The closing lines of the poem express the essence of Hinduism and the New Age:

> My search is at an end.
> In Thee I behold all things.
> I, myself, am God.

That is either the most important truth, the greatest discovery one can make, or else it is the most cruel hoax, the most blatant and destructive lie in the universe! The promise of godhood is first found at the very beginning of the Bible, in Genesis chapter 3. It is the offer that Satan, speaking through a serpent,* makes to Eve. According to the Bible: this was the Lie of lies that destroyed Eve and her descendants; the human race has never escaped its seductive influence in the thousands of years since then; and this lie will be at the heart of the Antichrist's religion that he will use to unite the world and bring peace and prosperity for a time, before all hell breaks loose on planet Earth.

Marilyn Ferguson, Beverly Galyean, and the other New Age leaders mentioned above would vehemently deny that what they teach is a lie or at all related to Antichrist. We do not question their sincerity or their motives. We must, however, examine the facts. Hinduism teaches that the god Vishnu periodically, at times of great crisis, reincarnates once again upon earth as the avatar or Savior for that age. Many New Agers are expecting the Age of Aquarius to produce its Savior also,

---

* For a discussion of the historicity, scientific validity, and meaning of the serpent in Genesis 3 and in modern society, see Dave Hunt, *The Cult Explosion* (Eugene, Oregon: Harvest House Publishers, 1980), pp. 109-15.

a great world leader bringing peace and prosperity to planet Earth.

The Spirit of the New Age

The Hebrew prophets also spoke of a coming Messiah, and religious Jews still await Him today. Christians claim that He has already come: they call Him Jesus Christ, and believe that He is personally returning to earth very soon. In spite of the fact that the Bible identifies a denial of Jesus with the spirit of Antichrist, New Age teaching denies that Jesus is the one and only Christ. Instead it speaks of the "Christ Spirit" or the "Christ consciousness" that temporarily reincarnated into Jesus of Nazareth between His baptism and crucifixion, and has allegedly reincarnated once again in another man, the coming world ruler. Benjamin Creme, who claims to be his John the Baptist, calls him "Lord Maitreya," and declares that he is living in a Hindu-Pakistani community in southeast London, England. A recent classified ad in a New Age periodical declared:

VENTURA COUNTY [California] WELCOMES CHRIST MAITREYA!
Join us in cultivating the Principle of Sharing locally and worldwide. New World Central, New Age networking headquarters.[23]

Many Christians are convinced that the Antichrist is alive on earth today, waiting in the wings for the curtain to be raised on the next act. Is he "Lord Maitreya"? What about the coming "world ruler," who, according to Jeane Dixon, was born at 7:00 A.M. EST on February 5, 1962, and who, she says, will unite the entire world in a new Christianity?

The Bible specifically states that the Antichrist will sit in the temple of God and declare himself to be God.[24] There seems little doubt that the declaration of one's own godhood is central to the philosophy underlying the New Age Movement. It would therefore not be overstating our case to say that the spirit of the New Age is the spirit of Antichrist, and that it is gathering awesome power and influence in today's world.

But what of the Antichrist himself? In order to face that question and further develop our "contrary scenario," it will be necessary first of all to examine the messianic myth.

8

The Myth
That Wouldn't Die

One of the most fascinating discoveries that any serious investigator of the occult eventually stumbles upon is the fact that the same messianic content, heavily flavored with Eastern mysticism, dominates all communications received from alleged "higher intelligences" by occult means. This is true whether the messages come from "spirit guides" or from "space brothers," and whether they are received through Ouija boards, by automatic writing, in seance or other hypnotic trance, on a drug trip, or in TM or other forms of Yoga. The evidence seems to point inevitably to a central intelligence behind all psychic-occult phenomena. Even UFO's seem to fit into this pattern. Brad Steiger wrote:

> I have been engaged in UFO research since the 1950s, and I have come to the conclusion that, throughout history, some external intelligence has interacted with *Homo sapiens* in an effort...to communicate to our species certain basic truths....
>
> ...an evolved Intelligence, whose manifestations we have been mistakenly labeling our "gods," has been challenging us, teaching us, and preparing us to recognize fully the "god-self" within each one of us.[1]

Here we have it again: the ancient promise of godhood. The recognition of "the 'god-self' within"—which Steiger himself believes—is associated in the Bible, as we have already seen, with Satan and Antichrist. That fact, however, seems to concern very few of those who have adopted this Hindu-occult philosophy. They are so convinced by the reality of their experiences that nothing else can influence them.

Like their American counterparts, a number of Soviet scientists are convinced that "higher intelligences" have long had a continuing interest in our world. They theorize that astronauts from advanced civilizations in other parts of our galaxy, visiting earth in the past, inspired many of the stories about "gods" in the scriptures of earth's major religions. Dr. Vyacheslav Zaitsev, one of Russia's top space scientists, thinks Jesus of Nazareth was a cosmonaut emissary from another planet; and in this light, the "coming of God to earth" was a "genuine cosmic occurrence." Such theories have caused speculation that the increased UFO activity of the past few decades is part of the "signs in the skies" associated with the Messiah's "second coming" that is predicted in the Bible.[2]

Rejecting the theory that Jesus was an ancient astronaut, Christians believe the Biblical account: that His birth in Bethlehem—*not* a spaceship—brought Jesus to this earth. Increasing numbers of Westerners, however, are adopting yet a third idea: that Jesus of Nazareth was a reincarnation of the "Christ Spirit" that lived also in Buddha, Confucius, Mohammed, Zoroaster, Krishna and many other great religious leaders. This concept has a special appeal for people who are looking for ways to unite all religions. Syncretism and ecumenism are two of the major goals of the New Age Movement, which has its own prophecies about the coming new world order of peace and prosperity.

Prophecy, Precognition, and Crises

Not very many years ago, few non-Christians were interested in such ideas as the second coming, the Battle of Armageddon, the Great Tribulation, and the end of the world. "Prophets" were laughed at. Few educated persons took seriously the idea that future events could be predicted. This attitude, however, has gradually changed. Although they are almost always wrong, a host of previously unknown psychic seers has made enough accurate predictions to convince Mr. and Ms. Average Citizen that visions of the future are not necessarily all phony. And today's broad-minded approach makes it possible to believe in prophecy without attaching any religious meaning to it. It's just part of nature. Or is it?

Modern science has recently stunned the skeptics by giving solid verification of prophecy. Known today as "precognition," the ability to foresee the future is accepted by scientists around the world as just another amazing "mind power" for which there is no real explanation at present. We will examine the possible explanations in a later chapter. Some of the most interesting demonstrations of precognition have occurred in the laboratories of Stanford Research Institute during "remote viewing" experiments. In these tests, a computer picks at random a point somewhere in the world, giving only its latitude and longitude. Amazingly, certain psychics have been able to describe the unseen site with considerable accuracy. This ability is called "clairvoyance." More amazing, however, is the fact that several psychics were able to describe the site *before* the computer picked it![3]

Psychic research is extremely dangerous, because it seems to open the mind to alien influences that create an undesirable effect, which used to be called "demon possession." In laboratories around the world today, white-smocked investigators are verifying psychokinesis, telepathy, and other mysterious "mind powers" that until very recently were the sole province of Yogis, voodoo priests, witch doctors, and spirit mediums, and were laughed at by science as self-delusions. Predictions by well-known psychics have increasingly involved the theme of a hoped-for Messiah, who will bring lasting peace and prosperity to earth.

Skeptics argue that times of crisis have always produced a revival of the messianic myth, and that today's renewed interest in the second coming is simply a psychological reaction to the overwhelming problems now faced by humanity. There is no doubt some truth in this allegation. Nearly every century in the past has produced a number of persons who claimed to be the Messiah. However, there are at least 100 times as many would-be Messiahs on earth today as at any other period in history. Is this just another coincidence? On top of this, there is a growing sense of expectancy in both scientific and religious circles that some apocalyptic event is soon to occur.

Signs of the End?

The very crises that our modern world now faces, which presumably create a climate favorable for the rise of Messiahs,

were predicted in detail by Jesus of Nazareth as signs that
would signal the approach of his second coming: "wars and
disturbances...great earthquakes, and in various places plagues
and famines...terrors and great signs from heaven."[4] This particular prophecy has been dealt with often and in detail by many
writers and lecturers. There is something else, however, that
Jesus said would herald the nearness of His return and the end
of current human history. This was the very *first* sign that Jesus
mentioned to His disciples when they asked how to recognize
the "last days." Therefore, this "sign" must be of special
importance.

> And Jesus answered...Take heed that no man deceive you.
> For many shall come in my name, saying, I am Christ, and
> shall deceive many....
> For there shall arise false Christs, and false prophets, and
> shall show great signs and wonders, insomuch that, if it were
> possible, they shall deceive the very elect.[5]

Critics have tried to explain away Christ's declaration that
wars, pestilence, earthquakes, and famines would signal the
"last days." They have called this a "lucky guess" that hit
upon the inevitable result of a cooling earth, exploding population, and stagnating social order. But there is no explaining
away the prophecy that just prior to his second coming religious
deception would be rampant on the earth, and that it would
specifically involve apparent miracles performed by *false prophets* and *false Messiahs*. The odds against *many* in the year
1982 claiming to be Christ are so astronomical as to be beyond
calculation.

The religious leaders of Israel sternly rejected Christ's claim
that He was the Messiah foretold by the Hebrew prophets.
They were determined to kill Him and to make certain that His
name would be forgotten, apparently unaware that in buying
His betrayal and crucifying Him they were fulfilling exactly
what their own prophets had said would be done to the
Messiah.[6] Though great crowds had followed Jesus at first,
His popularity had quickly waned. Nevertheless, Jesus had the
audacity to predict that in the last days, when nations would
be seeking a superleader to rescue the world from destruction,

such a man would be thought of as a *Messiah*, taking that title from Jesus Himself.

Within a week of making this seemingly foolish prediction, Jesus was summarily executed in disgrace, hanged naked on a cross between two thieves. Rejected by His own people Israel, condemned as a criminal by Rome, forsaken by His tiny band of followers (who scattered in fear), and His grandiose claims apparently exposed as fraud, that should have been the end of the Nazarene. But it wasn't. Three days later His grave was empty; and with a boldness they had never known before (which was itself presumptive evidence for what they claimed), His formerly timid and inarticulate disciples began to declare with arresting power that Jesus the Christ had risen from the dead and had been seen and handled by them. This created such a dramatic and upsetting awakening throughout Palestine that both the Roman rulers and the Jewish religious leaders would have given almost anything to be able to produce the "stolen" body in order to prove that this revolutionary movement called Christianity was based upon a fraud. However, they were never able to produce a body. The best they could do was to spread rumors that didn't fit the facts.

And today there is no explaining away the fact that 1900 years after Jesus made these remarkable predictions, including the promise that He Himself would one day return at a time of great deception, the messianic myth is more alive than ever. Hundreds of millions of people in today's modern space-age world are literally watching, waiting, and hoping for the second coming—and the very signs that Jesus gave would seem to indicate that the day is near. Even millions who are not Christians are hoping for a "Messiah." And in almost everyone's mind, that title is associated primarily with Jesus of Nazareth, just as He predicted.

A Cosmic Conspiracy?

It is fascinating that so much of the literature involving UFO's has messianic overtones, including specific references to Christ. Alleged UFO contactees widely scattered around the world continue to receive messages about a coming Messiah, which are so similar that coincidence must be ruled out. The emergence of scores, perhaps hundreds, of UFO cult groups within the last two decades, all preaching a similar Cosmic Gospel, along with the enthusiastic response of the public to such films as "Close Encounters" and "E.T.," are evidence of a growing belief and interest in the inevitability of contact with beings not of this earth.

For example, the Solar Light Retreat in Central Point, Oregon, publishes transmissions allegedly received from a space being, which are very similar to the entire New Age philosophy. There is talk of man's "divine Self within" that must be developed through a secret knowledge given to initiates, which in turn will aid their cosmic evolution to godhood. The Christ Consciousness or Christ Spirit is also mentioned often, together with the promise that spirit beings are soon to "descend in vast numbers to planet Earth" in a cosmic second coming.

The Mark-Age MetaCenter in Miami, Florida, has published voluminous teachings received from the space brothers: about the God-Self within, known as the Christ or I-Am Self; that God is not personal, but a Force of which every atom and person is a part. The fact that there is a consistent theme and that it is so similar to New Age thinking argues forcibly for a conspiracy directed by some central intelligence. There is a persistent messianic overtone consistent with the core of the messianic myth in all ages. And there is increasing emphasis placed upon a common prophecy that "the second coming of the spiritual world ruler" of planet Earth is very close at hand.

Typical of the saucer-cult Messiahs is Allen-Michael Noonan, who claims to have been commissioned by Venusians from the twelfth dimension to "help save the world." Leader of the One World Family, Noonan claims to be in telepathic contact with extraterrestrials (E.T.'s), who will eventually establish God's kingdom on this earth through spread of the Everlasting Gospel. According to Noonan, "Galactic Beings...have a great plan to intervene directly into affairs here to bring on an artificial tribulation in order to insure the success [of world unification]." Noonan claims to be God and the Messiah promised in the Bible. Amazingly, he calls his followers "Agents 666," a number that the Bible assigns to the Antichrist!

The natural inclination would be to write off Noonan and

the many other Cosmic Messiahs representing various UFO cults as self-deluded pretenders or deliberate hoaxters. But it isn't that simple. There are serious questions involved, which deserve more than cynical dismissal. What is the explanation for the recent emergence of so many widely scattered groups who all claim to be in touch with E.T.'s? How is it that UFO cults in different countries, speaking diverse languages and unknown to each other, have received basically the same messages and in the same manner?

We must either believe that large numbers of individuals widely scattered around the world have independently and co-incidentally, in defiance of the laws of probability, all had the same hallucinations, or we must admit that a common outside source has been communicating with all of them concerning a planned takeover of this earth by "higher beings." We are forced to consider seriously the possibility that intelligent beings beyond earth have a selfish interest and purpose in preparing earthlings to accept a personage they would like to install as their world ruler. Though it sounds like something right out of science fiction, this theme is so consistently predominant among the messages allegedly received from UFO's that it cannot be dismissed as mere fantasy.

Is there a conspiracy of cosmic proportions to foist a so-called Messiah upon the world? Could the ultimate motive be to control the human race? How and why? And what relation, if any, does all of this bear to that remarkable prophecy that Jesus made about many false Messiahs coming in the last days in His name? How can one be protected from the deception that Jesus specifically warned would accompany this profusion of would-be Messiahs?

The Plot Thickens

The current rash of messianic claims and expectations is not by any means confined to UFO cultists. There is a definite tie-in with the Age of Aquarius and a well-documented relationship between UFO's and the occult. Antichristian investigator John Keel has observed: "The manifestations and occurrences described in [occult] literature are similar, if not entirely identical, to the UFO phenomena itself. Victims of demonomania [possession] suffer the very same medical and emotional symptoms as the UFO contactees."[7] A U.S. Government publication produced for the Air Force Office of Scientific Research has noted the same relationships. In the preface of the 400-page volume, on the basis of researching thousands of UFO articles, books, and other publications, senior bibliographer Lynn E. Catoe had this to say:

> A large part of the available UFO literature is closely linked with mysticism and the metaphysical. It deals with subjects like mental telepathy, automatic writing, and invisible entities, as well as phenomena like poltergeist manifestations and "possession"....
>
> Many of the UFO reports now being published in the popular press recount alleged incidents that are strikingly similar to demonic possession....

Astrologers and psychics had long predicted that on February 5, 1962, a new Messiah would be born. Heralding the prophesied birth of this world ruler, who would bring peace at last to earth, all eight planets were in the sign of Aquarius, something that had not happened in nearly 2000 years. This "sign" in the sky was supposed to mark the birth of the Age of Aquarius, long awaited by mystics and occultists.

Shortly before dawn on that special day, Jeane Dixon, the psychic seer of Washington, D.C., had what she called the "most significant and soul-stirring" vision of her life. Mrs. Dixon saw a long-dead Pharoah and Queen Nefertiti at his side striding toward her. The queen was holding out a baby as though offering it to the world. Jeane recalls reverently: "The eyes of the child were all-knowing...full of wisdom and knowledge."[8]

As she watched in fascination, Jeane saw the child grow to manhood, and a small cross that formed above him began to expand until it "dripped over the earth in all directions. Simultaneously peoples of every race, religion and color, each kneeling and lifting his arms in worshipful adoration, surrounded him. They were all as one."[9] Mrs. Dixon believes that the Messiah was reincarnated into the world as a babe at the time of her vision. She says he will "bring together all mankind in one all-embracing faith...the foundation of a new Christianity with every sect and creed united...the world as we know it will be reshaped and revamped into one without wars or suffering."[10]

But Jeane's experience is far from unique. In recent times similar prophecies have come from other mystics and psychics. Though differing as to the exact date of his birth, there is surprising agreement among persons of widely varying beliefs that such a man—some call him the Antichrist, others call him the Messiah—is probably alive on the earth right now biding his time. Moreover, for the first time in history, in obvious fulfillment of Christ's most remarkable prophecy, there are literally hundreds of persons living on earth today who claim to be the Messiah. Some of them number their followers in the millions.

Through a worldwide publicity campaign, the human race has recently been called upon to receive as the Christ a man who bears almost all of the classic Biblical marks of the Antichrist. Full-page ads in major newspapers around the world on the weekend of April 24-25, 1982, announced, "THE CHRIST IS NOW HERE," and confidently predicted that he would make himself known publicly "within the next two months." That date passed without the much-heralded "Reappearance of the Christ," but the Tara Centers that placed the newspaper announcements explained that the delay was only because the consciousness of the human race was not quite right, but that "Lord Maitreya" definitely would make himself known soon.

How can one tell the true Messiah—if there is one—from the Antichrist? Which prophets are to be believed? Is the messianic myth that has so long been a central theme of science fiction as well as religion about to be realized at long last? Are we on the verge of the second coming? Or is the whole idea of a messiah an escapist syndrome that surfaces periodically at times of great human crisis? Whatever the answers, these no longer seem to be idle wonderings, but questions of the utmost importance.

The Myth That Wouldn't Die

The persistence of the messianic hope is a phenomenon that cannot be waved aside. As one recent writer, though doubtful of all Messiahs, has said, "To call messiahs devils or heretics explains nothing. To dismiss them as mad or deluded is too easy."[11]

The gullible and enthusiastic have always been prone to follow a variety of Pied Pipers, but not the same old worn-out lie century after century. Therein lies a peculiarity of the Messiah syndrome that cannot be explained away: it has refused to die in spite of the history of shattered hopes and broken promises. Why? It is not enough to say that the human race has a peculiar weakness for this particular "myth." If so, then we must explain that weakness. What is its basis?

Critics have often scoffingly said that the idea of God becoming man to save humanity is found in many religions, as though this would discredit the concept. On the contrary, if a variety of conflicting religions adhere to a similar mythology in spite of cultural barriers and the isolation caused by language differences, the probability must be very strong that some common seed of truth lies hidden in the "myth." What is it?

Assuming that the messianic hope *is* a myth without substance, then why hasn't modern man with all of his sophistication been able to free himself from this groundless tradition, if that's all it is? Apparently that isn't all it is. Its source appears to be outside of the human imagination, psyche, or subconscious.

C.S. Lewis believed most fervently that the Biblical teaching about the Messiah was fact. Calling it a myth, could not explain away the myth itself.

> ...where is the epicureanism of Lucretius, the pagan revival of Julian the Apostle...the dogmatic materialism of the great Victorians? They have moved with the times. But the thing they were all attacking remains.
>
> The myth (if one insists upon calling it that—of God becoming man and dying for our sins)...has outlived the thoughts of its defenders and of all its adversaries.[12]

Tracing the Myth to Its Source

Skeptics have attacked the Bible's teaching about the Messiah as not unique, claiming that it was borrowed from pagan religions. Then from whom did the pagans borrow it? Such arguments go around in circles and lead nowhere. In actual fact, the Biblical teaching concerning the Messiah is radically different in several vital points from every other messianic tradition: specifically, the Biblical Messiah is God who became man (without ceasing to be God) in order to die for our sins, and was resurrected (not reincarnated), remaining forever the same, and who is coming again. In contrast, the pagan or occult Messiahs are often men on their way to godhood, or one of the gods reincarnating again and again (such as the Hindu avatars). And of course none of them dies for our sins, but assigns a path of good deeds or ascetic practices whereby his disciples can escape "bad karma." There are definitely two sources of the messianic myth: one for the Hebrew and Christian prophets, and another for every other religion. It also seems quite clear, from the evidence, that *neither* source is human.

How can we say that? In spite of differences, the messianic hope is so widespread and so persistent that it must originate with an intelligence or intelligences capable of spreading the concept in the following manner: 1) to peoples of every language anywhere in the world; and 2) continuously throughout the entire history of the human race. That much is indisputable from the evidence we have.

There is scarcely an ancient culture or religion of any kind where the idea did not persist that "someday...in the appointed time...when the gods ordained," a ruler would arise who would bring everlasting peace to the whole world. For example, an Egyptian prophecy from the twelfth dynasty concerns a man who "shall bring cooling to the flame...a shepherd of all the people...[who will] smite evil when he raises his hands against it."[13] Comparable hopes were held in such widely separated lands as Greece, Africa, and India. The universality of similar beliefs is an indisputable fact not only of history but of today's world as well.

Worldwide communication was not humanly possible in centuries past. Yet the messianic myth was always widespread. Clearly, then, the "myth" has no human source. There are four possibilities that remain: 1) God; 2) Satan; 3) E.T.'s, and; 4) the Universal Unconscious. The New Age is satisfied with either numbers 3 or 4.

If there is a real Satan, then from his point of view, it is immaterial whether humans believe numbers 3 or 4 to be the source, since either of them is a substitute for God. We can also say that neither 3 nor 4 could be the *only* source of the myth, since it has two versions that are diametrically opposed. And since the only opposition to either 2, 3, or 4 could come from number 1, then it seems clear that the God of the Bible exists and is indeed the source of Biblical prophecies and teaching about the Messiah. The corollary would be that all messianic traditions that oppose the Judeo-Christian teaching have their source in the enemy of the God of the Bible, Satan himself.

And the Antichrist?

In spite of the overwhelming evidence, the New Age denies that Jesus is the Christ. As we have already seen, this denial is the primary identification of the spirit of Antichrist.[15] Benjamin Creme tells us very boldly that the Christ he is promoting, Lord Maitreya, is *not* Jesus, thus clearly identifying the spirit that motivates him and the Tara Centers that paid for those full-page ads. Jesus, says Creme, was reincarnated, apparently several times (*not* resurrected), after His crucifixion and presently lives in a Syrian body 640 years old.

According to the Aquarian Conspiracy, the new world of peace and prosperity will be brought about through a transformation of *consciousness*. This is the key to human evolution; and parallel to this is the teaching that the only thing that made Jesus the Christ for His day (i.e. during that lifetime) was that he had attained to a "higher" state of consciousness called "Christ Consciousness." According to New Age thinking, we all have the potential to attain this state and thus to become "Christed ones." Although the Human Potential Movement founded by Abraham Maslow generally does not refer to our potential as "Christ Consciousness," the same basic concept is contained in the slogan "Human potential is unlimited."

One can hear the hollow echo of this impossible dream reverberating across primordial space and time, and then through the corridors of human history: "I will be like the Most High!"[15] This is the description given of Satan's downfall by the Prophet Isaiah. No greater self-delusion can be imagined: how many "Most High's" can there be? Yet humanity eagerly bought this lie—and not just Adam and Eve, but their billions of descendants, including those on planet Earth today in this new age.

Like venom infecting the whole human race, the serpent's lie in the Garden can be traced down through occultism, preserved in its most virulent form in numerous secret societies: from Hinduism and Tibetan Buddhism to the Gnostics and Rosicrucians, Theosophists and Hitler's own Black Knights of the SS Order. This messianic myth promises that a superman who fully demonstrates the Christ Consciousness (infinite human potential) will one day take control of the world. He will capture the imagination, allegiance, and worship of all humanity, because he will be at once the embodiment of New Age theology and the living proof that we can all attain godhood if we follow him.

There is a great deal of information in the Bible about the Antichrist that seems to be receiving remarkable verification in our world today. Before moving on to that, however, let's take a brief look at several representative false prophets and false Messiahs throughout history to see how they compare with Jesus of Nazareth, and whether there is any consistency in the contrast.

9
Violence, Mysticism, and Secularism

The Bible claims that its prophets were inspired not by E.T.'s visiting planet Earth but by God the Creator. Such a claim should not be accepted without examining the evidence to see whether it is true or false. The most specific prophecies about God coming to earth to save mankind and to bring everlasting peace are found in the Hebrew Scriptures of the Old Testament. The very word *Messiah* comes from the Hebrew language. *Christ* is the Greek translation of *Messiah*, which literally means "the anointed one."

According to the Torah, the Jewish priests were to be anointed with a uniquely compounded oil, symbolizing the Spirit of God coming upon them with special power and authority for their appointed tasks. Hebrew prophets and kings were also to be anointed in a similar manner. The Messiah, as *The Anointed One*, was to function as all three: prophet, priest, and king—God incarnate. He would come twice: the first time He would come meekly, and as a result He would be rejected;[1] the second time He would come in power to execute judgment upon the earth, and only then would He establish peace.[2]

The Hebrew prophets agreed that the Messiah would be one of King David's descendants; yet David called the Messiah his Lord,[3] which was not the manner in which he would address any of his purely human offspring. The rabbis were unable to answer Jesus when He asked them why David called the Messiah, his son, "my Lord."[4]

The Hebrew prophets had made it clear that the Messiah would be God Himself entering the human race in space, time, and history as the unique God-man[5] in order to die for our sins.[6] Isaiah declared that this One who would establish

98

everlasting peace would not only be "a child born...a Son given," but that he would also be "the mighty God, the everlasting Father."[7] This concept of the Messiah being God incarnate is so widespread among the world's religions that its denial by Orthodox Judaism, Jehovah's Witnesses, and Islam is the exception rather than the rule.

Early Jewish Messiah Candidates

With the messianic myth so widespread and persistent, it is not surprising that down through the centuries many great leaders have claimed to be the very world ruler that the prophets foretold, come at last to bring peace to the earth. Judah the Maccabee was one of the earliest Jewish candidates for the role of Messiah. In 165 B.C. he cleansed the temple in Jerusalem from the defilement that Antiochus Epiphanes had caused three years earlier through sacrificing a swine and placing a statue of the god Zeus on the temple altar. A brilliant strategist and inspiring leader, Judah led his people to stunning military victories against their Syrian rulers. Many began to believe that Judah the Maccabee was the Anointed One and that the time of Israel's deliverance from all enemies and leadership over the world had come at last. However, Judah was not descended from King David, as the Messiah had to be, but from a line of Aaronic priests. His death in battle in 160 B.C. was not at all like a "lamb submitting meekly to slaughter," as Isaiah had predicted.[8] King Herod had the last of the Maccabean line executed in 37 B.C., ending the hope for the millennium to be established at that time.

In 4 B.C., Simon, one of Herod the Great's slaves, declared himself to be king, raised an army, burned down the royal palace, and plundered the treasury. He was soon caught and beheaded by the Romans. Next Judas of Galilee, who headed a band of armed robbers, became a great folk-hero messiah until his career too was cut short by the long arm of Caesar's legions. Theudas, who proclaimed himself to be the Messiah around 45 A.D., likewise enjoyed some military success against the Romans, but eventually he was killed also. His head was displayed in Jerusalem as a warning of the fate that awaited those who might be tempted by messianic delusions and promises.

Jesus of Bethlehem and Nazareth

Judea and all of what had once been Israel were firmly under Roman hands when Jesus was born in Bethlehem at about 4 B.C. Micah the Prophet had designated this small town as the place of the Messiah's birth.[9] However, because He grew up in Nazareth of Galilee, most of His contemporaries were not aware that Jesus had in fact been born in Bethlehem of Judea. A meeting of the Sanhedrin would later be convinced that Jesus was an imposter by the argument: "Search and see that no prophet arises out of Galilee."[10]

Mary and Joseph—and perhaps a few close relatives—knew that Mary had been a virgin when Jesus was born; but they kept that incredible fact a secret to ponder in their own hearts. After the birth of Jesus, Mary had a number of children by Joseph, thus losing all claim to be called thereafter "the Virgin Mary."[11] A virgin birth is required by the Judeo-Christian Scriptures: only with God as his father and a human mother could the Messiah be the "only begotten of the Father," the unique God-man. In Hinduism, however, both of the avatar's parents can be human since everyone is God anyway, and the only difference in Hinduism or the New Age between those who know they are God and those who don't know is the state of their minds or consciousness.

The Old Testament contains more than 300 prophetic references to the coming Messiah that were fulfilled in the life, death, and resurrection of Jesus.[12] Sixty of these are considered to be major prophecies. If we eliminate 12 of these as within the power of Jesus and/or His disciples to deliberately fulfill, that leaves 48. Professor Peter Stoner calculated the odds to be 10^{-157} that 48 such prophecies could be fulfilled *by chance* in Jesus Christ. In probability theory, it is generally agreed that any odds smaller than 10^{-50} are the same as zero. Since 10^{-157} is 10^{107} (that's a 1 with 107 zeros after it) smaller than 10^{-50}, we can safely say that the fulfillment by Jesus of these 48 specific prophecies proved conclusively that He is the Messiah.

Some critics and skeptics have "explained" the detailed fulfillment of the messianic prophecies in Christ's life and death as a series of fortunate coincidences. The impossible odds refute this. Others have credited Jesus Himself and/or His disciples with cleverly contriving to have the prophecies come true. This was the thesis, for example, of *The Passover Plot*. Certainly the manner and place of His birth, the specific amount of money the rabbis paid for His betrayal, the failure to break His legs on the cross in direct contrast to established custom, the soldiers gambling for His clothes, and the spear wound inflicted after His death are examples of prophecies fulfilled that Jesus could hardly have arranged. Nor did His disciples have either the money, prestige, or courage to influence any of these events, much less all of them.

The greatest weakness in such an argument is an obvious moral one. To say that Jesus wasn't the type to indulge in such deliberate fraud is an understatement. And though we may not have such complete confidence in His disciples, it is ludicrous to imagine that 11 cowards who were afraid to stand up for what they believed was right would suddenly get the moral courage to die for what they knew was a deliberate fraud!

A Hindu Jesus?

From the time we see Jesus in the temple in Jerusalem astonishing the Pharisees with His wisdom and knowledge as a boy of 12, we are told nothing more of him in the New Testament until He reappears at the age of 30 to begin His public ministry. Most Bible scholars are convinced that this silence in the Scriptural record is deliberate. Its purpose is apparently to indicate that during those 18 years Jesus did no preaching or miracles, but lived as a seemingly ordinary, though sinless, teenager and maturing young man.

Various non-Christian sources, however, such as *The Aquarian Gospel* and Edgar Cayce's "Information" via trance, claim that during these unreported 18 years Jesus was living among the Essenes and studying in various mystery schools in Egypt and under gurus in India. Spirit dictations in seances also attempt to establish this link between Jesus and other religions. The obvious purpose is to strip Him of His uniqueness, which is attacked by all non-Christian religions. However, there are three major problems with this view: 1) sources of alleged "spirit" or "space brother" dictations, which betray themselves as clearly demonic by other things they say and the evil effects they produce, almost with one voice echo this Essene-Egyptian-Indian theory; 2) there is not one scrap of historical evidence to support it; and 3) the New Testament record unquestionably contradicts it.

The four Gospels clearly imply that Jesus remained in Galilee during these so-called "missing" years. He was well-known in His hometown of Nazareth not only as "the carpenter's son"[13] but also as "the carpenter."[14] This certainly implies that Jesus not only had worked in the carpenter shop as a boy assisting His father, but after His father's death had carried on the family business, perhaps assisted by younger half brothers (James, Joseph, Simon, and Judas)[15] so that He had become known as "the carpenter." We know also that it was customary for Jesus to read the Torah (the sacred Hebrew Scriptures contained in large scrolls) in the synagogue at Nazareth: "And as was His custom, He entered the synagogue on the Sabbath and stood up to read. And the book of the prophet Isaiah was handed to Him."[16]

There is no indication that Jesus had ever been absent from Nazareth for any extended period of time, much less that He had gone away to any mystery school or foreign land that would explain His teaching, authoritative manner, or miracles. On the contrary, the people in Nazareth were astonished that He suddenly began to teach[17] and travel about Galilee with great crowds following Him. To them, this was a scandal. They treated Him with a contempt born of familiarity, which seems to indicate that they had a long-standing and continuous acquaintance with Him—again negating the idea that he had been off studying in foreign lands. Had He studied for years in India, for example, He would have been famous on that count alone. We are clearly told, however, that His fame began after His baptism and return from the 40-day temptation in the wilderness, and not upon His return to Galilee from studying abroad.

Furthermore, everything that Jesus said and did contradicts the theory that he had sat at the feet of a guru in India. Every guru who comes from India (Maharishi Mahesh Yogi, Paramahansa Yogananda, Swami Muktananda, et al) always refers to his own guru as his source of authority, the one who commissioned and sent him. In Hinduism everyone, including the gurus themselves, must have a guru. Yet Jesus never referred to His guru, but declared that His "Father in heaven" had sent him—a term, that neither the gurus nor the rabbis used or liked. The gurus all boast of the years of ascetic practices—Yoga and austerity, perhaps in a Himalayan cave—that they have gone through in order to achieve godhood or Self-realization. Jesus, on the other hand, was always God.[18] Though truly God, in love He had become a man in order to die for our sins; He was not a man who had achieved godhood through Self-realization. The gurus are all vegetarians; Jesus clearly was not. He fed the multitude with fish more than once;[19] He directed Peter to go to the lake and catch a fish;[20] on at least two occasions He helped the disciples to make a huge catch of fish in their nets;[21] He ate fish himself;[22]\and He partook of the traditional passover feast, for which a lamb had to be killed and eaten.[23]

There are and have been thousands of gurus, but the Bible claims that Jesus Christ is absolutely unique. Benjamin Creme and other New Agers regard Jesus as just one son of God among many, declaring that we are all sons of God. The Bible, however, calls Jesus the "only begotten Son of God" at least five times.[24] Steve Scott points out a number of other differences between Jesus and the gurus that give the lie to the whole idea of His having studied in India:

> The *Guru Gita* [says]: "The water with which the feet of the Guru are washed is the sacred drink. The remains after Guru's meal are the proper food."
>
> ...some of the real differences start to show. Jesus...points out that all who are thirsty should come to Him to drink the "living water" that He can provide. He says nothing about washing His feet in it first. In fact...He knelt and washed the feet of His followers.
>
> ...the fellowship of the last supper in which Jesus *shares* a common cup and a common loaf, [is] a far different picture than the one painted by the Guru Gita, which insists that eating the Guru's leftovers will somehow enhance your spirituality.

...Jesus' statements...[declare] the exclusivity of salvation through Him: "I am the way, and the truth, and the life; no one comes to the Father but by me" (John 14:6).[25]

A Meek, Crucified Messiah?

Unlike other messiahs of this era, Jesus never tried to lead a rebellion against the Roman oppressors. Instead of mounting a fiery stallion to lead an invincible army, He had ridden humbly into Jerusalem on the colt of a donkey, just as the Prophet Zechariah had also foretold.[26] Jesus taught that the kingdom of God could not be established by force of arms. Every man must choose for himself whether or not he wanted to be a part of it. God's kingdom would be based upon love, and His disciples must even love their enemies.

To the average Judean, ground down by Caesar's legions, such talk seemed like so much pie-in-the-sky nonsense. The Roman oppressors were the only thing they wanted to be "saved" from by their Messiah. In contrast, Jesus declared that the real problem lay in their hearts. Until men had been reconciled to God through accepting the Messiah's death for their sins, they could never live in peace with one another. Military might could only create a false peace that would never last. Of course, His meekness made His claim that He was God seem ludicrous. Who could believe that *God* would allow Himself to be crucified!

Had Jesus lived in India, His claim that He was the I AM[27] (Jehovah-God in the Old Testament) would scarcely have caused a raised eyebrow, much less gotten Him crucified, for Hinduism teaches that everyone is God. To the Jew, however, this is the ultimate heresy. It was this claim of Jesus to personal deity that led to His execution. "You, a mere man, are claiming to be God"[28] was the accusation leveled against Him. For this blasphemy the Sanhedrin demanded the death penalty. It seems a miracle that in their religious zeal they did not vent their hatred by stoning Him to death, as they had tried to do to Him several times before and would do to Stephen only a few weeks later. Instead, they obeyed Roman law, which denied to them the power of capital punishment, and delivered Jesus to Governor Pilate.[29] Although Pilate knew that Jesus was innocent, he condemned him in order to please the Jews. Thus that long-misunderstood prophecy that the Messiah would be crucified, made hundreds of years before crucifixion began to be used, was remarkably fulfilled.

The fact that they were able to kill Him so easily was taken as proof by His executioners that Jesus was an imposter. However, His willingness to die was one more evidence that He was indeed the promised Messiah. Isaiah had prophesied that the Messiah would be "led as a lamb to the slaughter" and would willingly take the death penalty upon Himself in payment for the sins of the whole world.[30]

Convinced by their Leader's apparent impotence that He couldn't have been the Messiah, and stunned and shamed by His death as a common criminal, Christ's disciples fled for their lives and went into hiding. Three days later, however, the tomb was empty in which the body of Jesus had been placed and carefully guarded by soldiers. During the next 40 days, according to the written testimony of eyewitnesses, Jesus visited His disciples on several different occasions, ate with them, carefully demonstrated to them that He was indeed alive from the dead, gave them final instructions, and then ascended into the sky as they watched until He disappeared from their view in a cloud.

The final argument of doubters and skeptics—apart from their assertion that a resurrection is impossible—is based upon the undeniable fact that Jesus failed to establish peace upon earth. Yet the Hebrew prophets declared that the Messiah would reign in a kingdom of perfect peace. Consequently, Jesus could not have been the Messiah, according to this argument, no matter how many other prophecies He managed to fulfill. Careful reading of the Hebrew prophets, however, seems to indicate that the millennium was not to be established until the second coming of the Messiah.

Secular Messiahs

The secular world has its messiahs too. There were three in the last century, whose influence was so great that they deserve recognition: Darwin, Marx, and Freud. The exact reverse of the Biblical Savior who brings men to God, secular messiahs lead their followers away from Him. It is not hell they save us from, but heaven.

Darwin rescued us from the moral obligation of pleasing a Creator-God. If all happened by chance and proceeded under the impetus of self-existent laws, then there is no God nor any need for one (unless we ask ourselves, "How can there be laws without a Lawgiver?"). However, a sense of moral accountability to God and the desire to know Him could not be the product of natural selection or survival of the fittest. Moreover, prayer to and worship of a nonexistent God, rather than aiding survival in the jungle, would hasten extinction.

Marx carried Darwin's theory to its logical conclusion. Belief in God and the Bible were not only unexplainable by natural selection but were dangerous hindrances in the evolutionary process. Religion was the enemy of progress, unspeakably vile, to be stamped out ruthlessly for the good of the species. Why this pernicious tendency hadn't already been eliminated by natural selection remained a mystery that Marx could not understand. No matter. The proletariat would take care of that by intelligently assisting the evolutionary process. A communist paradise would result (though that word was troublesome, having a religious origin!). If we were products of nature, why did we long for something better than nature?

Strongly attracted to Darwinism, Freud applied it to human behavior in his attempt to understand what was abnormal. Of the three forces which he theorized made up human personality, only the first two, *id* and *ego*, could possibly be explained by evolution or natural laws. The *superego*, representing the dictates of conscience, was admittedly *idealistic* as opposed to what Freud, Marx, and Darwin would consider *realistic*.[31] *Conscience* also carried unfortunate religious implications.

Heavily influenced by the anti-Christian writings of Feuerbach,[32] Freud hated religion as much as did Marx. Following the unproven mechanistic dogma of his teacher, Brucke ("No other forces than the common physical-chemical are active within the [human] organism"),[33] Freud built his system of psychoanalysis upon a medical-biological model of man. Though he regarded religious beliefs as a neurosis to be expunged by psychotherapy, Freud became a religious guru himself.[34] Since the beliefs of all three of these secular messiahs, by their own theories, could be no better than the product of chance evolutionary developments in their brains, we have good cause to question their validity.

"Scientific" Religion for the New Age

Science has come a long way since the days of Darwin, Marx, and Freud. In spite of the diligent scouring of planet Earth and much scratching and digging, the simple fact remains that the vast quantity and variety of fossils unearthed have contradicted instead of supported Darwin's grand theory. Today, evolution is still accepted by the majority of scientists, but dozens of theories have replaced Darwin's original thesis, some of them contradicting others, and not one having sufficient scientific evidence to support it. The entire theory of evolution is in a shambles, with its adherents frantically seeking some ingenious inspiration to explain away the lack of evidence and multitude of contradictions. Darwin merely brought to modern science an old belief that had been in occultism and mysticism for thousands of years, in which every species has always had its avatar in the process of cosmic evolution upward to godhood.

A blind faith in some imagined and unproved evolutionary force that will eventually evolve humans into gods (the dream of Nietzsche and inspiration of Hitler) is the secular religion of many scientists today. Based upon the unsubstantiated, speculative belief that evolution on other planets could have been in process for billions of years longer than here on earth, well-known astonomer Robert Jastrow expresses the faith of many other scientists when he declares that "science assures us" that beings exist out there who are "as far beyond man as man is beyond the worm."[35] He adds: "They are creatures whom we will judge to be possessed of magical powers when we see them. By our standards, they will be immortal, omniscient and omnipotent."[36] So even hard-core, materialistic science has its gods. The relationship which this faith of science bears to ancient occultism, Eastern mysticism, and the New Age is obvious.

Marxism has been a scourge such as nothing ever experienced

before it on this earth: it has been responsible for the murder of at least 120 million human beings and the subjugation of countless millions more to the living death of slavery and mind control. The "paradise" that Communism has proudly produced is today surrounded by Iron and Bamboo Curtains, walls, electrified fences, mine fields, watchtowers, searchlights, and roaming dogs and guards. Strangely, none of this is necessary to keep outside anyone attempting to gain admittance to this Communist dream world! It is all to prevent the workers themselves from fleeing this supposed "workers' paradise"—which they would do by the tens of millions if they were ever to be given the momentary freedom to vote with their feet. After 65 years of trying to prove that God does not exist, there are about 100 million Christians in the Soviet Union and about 80 million in China, plus millions of Muslims, Buddhists, and other believers in assorted gods.

And Freud? The religious faith he bequeathed to the world has probably destroyed even more lives than Marxism. Yet it has more disciples today than ever before. Most of these unfortunate guinea pigs have been lured into its elaborate and endless mazes by the false advertisement that it is scientific—a blatant lie that has been repeated so loudly and so often that not only the unsuspecting public but the psychologists and psychiatrists themselves have begun to believe it. Proliferating like a deadly cancer spreading through society, the numerous competing denominations of the religious cult of psychology and psychiatry involve hundreds of conflicting schools of thought that contradict each other. Martin L. Gross has called Freud's deadly legacy "the major agent of change" in modern society.[37] "Its experimental animals," says Gross, "are an obliging, even grateful human race" whose members "as never before" are "preoccupied with *Self.*"[38] Humanistic and transpersonal psychologies have integrated the theories of Darwin and Marx even more thoroughly with the occult. As we have already seen, the Human Potential Movement, which these two modern schools of psychology spawned, with its worship of Self and Self's "infinite potential," is at the heart of the New Age Movement.

A host of incredible discoveries has changed the scientist's view of himself and the cosmos. The universe has come to be regarded more like a great thought than a giant machine; and the exploration of consciousness (inner space) through altered states has become the new frontier of science, far more challenging and exciting than the exploration of outer space. Science has moved on, like the messianic myth itself, in the direction of Hinduism. As Mark Albrecht and Brooks Alexander have said:

> Science itself is being dragged kicking and screaming into the realm of parapsychology. Ultimately, the sheer weight of masses of psychic evidence and experience, the likes of which the world has never seen before, will cause the alteration (or collapse) of science as we know it.
>
> The emphasis on data and facts will give way to the exploration of "consciousness" (i.e. subjectivity) as a means of controlling reality; psychic phenomena, especially UFOs, will receive the imprimatur of scientific respectability.[39]

Today we are witnessing the formation of a new worldwide religion based upon a marriage between science and Eastern mysticism. "The Plan" that H.G. Wells wrote about and believed in has moved into high gear under the direction of the "higher intelligences" that are orchestrating it. Whoever these entities are, they are believed in under many names by millions of people whose intelligence, education, and social standing spans the whole spectrum of the New Age Movement that Marilyn Ferguson described so well. They are believed in by such men as Robert Muller (already referred to), Assistant Secretary-General of the United Nations, who puts them in the same category as Christ and calls them "outer-space emissaries."[40] They are so firmly believed in and followed by Donald Keys, founder of the Planetary Initiative for the World We Choose and a consultant to the U.N., that he has dedicated his book *Earth At Omega* to these ascended masters or spirit guides, whom he calls "my mentors."[41]

Something is happening on planet Earth that is moving very rapidly and is far beyond the power of the Trilateralists or CFR people to control. It seems evident that this world is in the final stages of preparation for the Antichrist. However, before coming back to the Antichrist, who is probably alive on planet Earth today, three very fascinating and important "messiahs" from the twentieth century are of particular interest in the further development of our contrary scenario.

10

Preparation for Delusion

One of the major purposes behind the U.S. space program is the search for E.T.'s, which most serious scientists today are convinced exist, in varying stages of evolutionary development, on billions of planets scattered throughout the universe. Like Robert Jastrow, the vast majority of scientists assumes that evolution has produced many creatures out there somewhere whose mind powers would seem supernatural to us. The celebrated Israeli psychic, Uri Geller, believes that highly evolved E.T.'s from another planet, acting as special agents for the "controllers of the universe," have chosen him as their ambassador to earth. They are channeling psychic powers through Uri as intermediary in a plan to gain our confidence and direct our further evolutionary development.[1]

When Stanford Research Institute was making its documentary film about him, Uri Geller complained that most psychologists insisted upon attributing his psychic powers to his subconscious. Uri explained that the source of power was not his mind but in other minds out there tuned toward him every second, whose bidding he must do. Far from ridiculing this seemingly outrageous idea, the SRI scientists involved in the tests admitted that they had long suspected that E.T.'s were behind psi phenomena, but had not been able to prove it.[2] There is grave concern as to the identity, motivation, and goal of the E.T.'s involved—and whether or not they may have the psychic powers to take over our minds if they wish to do so.

A brilliant medical scientist with scores of patents to his credit, Andrija Puharich brought Uri Geller to the attention of Western science. Puharich's experiences with the entities that are using Uri Geller have left him puzzled and helpless. Referring to these E.T.'s, Puharich has said: "We're pretty low creatures compared to the kind of stuff they're dazzling us with...are they going to take us over?" He was concerned by the apparent ability of a group of entities that refers to itself as "IS" to control his mind to the extent of causing him to "experience" things that could not possibly have happened. Almost in despair, Puharich declared:

> These two days' events numbed me. Sarah and Uri experienced one sequence, and Ila and I experienced another, in the same time frame...that is real in my mind to this day.
> ...the four of us had had an experience imprinted on our minds by what could only be the agency of IS...given the existence of IS, I could never again know which of my experiences were directly imposed upon me by IS and which were not.
> I have never been so deeply shaken in my life as when I realized the full implication of this power of IS.[3]

Psychological Conditioning for Deception?

One of the most disturbing elements of UFO phenomena has been the fact that contactees very often become disoriented, lose segments of time, experience altered states of consciousness, and develop the classic symptoms of demon possession. With impeccable scientific credentials and one of the world's top ufologists, Jacques Vallee has concluded after 20 years of investigation that UFO's may be psychologically programming us for some ultimate deception that is too horrible even to imagine as yet.[4] The deception may actually go far deeper than Vallee or almost anyone else dares to suspect. Alleged abductees almost never have a conscious memory of the experience. How do they learn of their "abduction" aboard a UFO? Nightmares and psychological problems cause them to seek psychiatric help. In the process of being regressed back in time under hypnosis, the "memory" of the "abduction" is uncovered by the therapist. Whether UFO cultism is myth, magic, or madness, its high priests are psychiatrists, and the religious ritual they employ is *hypnosis*.

One reason for calling hypnotherapy a *religious ritual* is the fact that it produces mysterious effects that leave any investigator who approaches it as science thoroughly puzzled: 1) under hypnosis administered by psychiatrists, persons who have never had any contact with UFO's can be stimulated to "remember" UFO abductions that conform in detail to those described by supposed genuine abductees;[5] 2) hypnosis also leads to spontaneous "memories" of past and future lives, about one-fifth involving existence on other planets;[6] 3) hypnotic trance also duplicates the experiences common under the stimulation of psychedelic drugs, TM, and other forms of Yoga and Eastern meditation;[7] 4) hypnosis also creates spontaneous psychic powers, clairvoyance, out-of-body experiences, and the whole range of occult phenomena;[8] and 5) the experience of so-called clinical death is also produced under hypnosis.[9]

Two conclusions that most investigators find very distasteful seem nevertheless to be inescapable: 1) there is a common source behind all occult phenomena, including UFO's, that seems to be intelligently and deliberately orchestrating a clever deception for its own purposes; and 2) hypnosis, or the power of suggestion, is at the very heart of this scheme. If this hypothesis is rejected, then nothing makes sense. The researcher is then left, like Professor Alvin H. Lawson of California State University at Long Beach, to mutter: "The nature of the stimulus here is a very spooky thing!"[10]

In light of the above, it is very disturbing to notice the growing acceptance and use of hypnosis under a wide variety of labels and variations in almost every area of society today, including medicine, psychiatry, business, and education. Is it possible that the current proliferation of hypnosis in its many modern forms is part of a process to prepare humanity for some much larger deception? The disturbing fact that deception is an integral and inescapable part of hypnosis has recently been recognized officially by the courts. Yet it is still used by many so-called Christian psychologists.

Professor of psychology Charles Tart reported the results of his study of hypnosis with an intelligent, well-adjusted, 21-year-old college student named William. The connection between hypnosis and Eastern mysticism became clear. At varying depths of the hypnotic trance, William described experiences that are identical to the cosmic consciousness and self-realization induced by yogic trance. He experienced first of all a deep peace, then detachment from his body, then release from identity with his own small self to merge with the universe and the feeling that he is everything and has no limitation upon what he can experience or become: i.e., God-consciousness "in which time, space, and ego are supposedly transcended, leaving pure awareness of the primal nothingness from which all manifested creation comes."[11]

Hypnotic trance opens the subject to exactly the same source of delusion that is experienced in TM and other forms of Eastern meditation, which is the same as that experienced under drugs. Based upon years of research, two well-known authorities on hypnosis, medical doctor William Kroger and psychologist William Fezler, warn against being "confused by the supposed differences between hypnosis, Zen, Yoga and other Eastern healing methodologies. Although the ritual for each differs," say Kroger and Fezler, "they are fundamentally the same."[12] In their excellent booklet summarizing the latest findings on hypnosis, which everyone ought to read, Martin and Deidre Bobgan declare:

> Compounding the word *hypnosis* with the word *therapy* does not lift the practice from the occult to the scientific....
>
> The white coat may be a more respectable garb than feathers and face paint, but the basics are the same. Hypnosis is hypnosis, whether it is called medical hypnosis, hypnotherapy, autosuggestion, or anything else.
>
> Hypnosis in the hands of a medical doctor is as scientific as a dowsing rod in the hands of a civil engineer.[13]

Hypnosis: The Courts and Society

The darling of criminal investigators and secret weapon of supersleuths, hypnosis has been widely used in law enforcement.[14] It was hypnosis, for example, that broke the famous Chowchilla, California, kidnapping case: under hypnotic regression, the bus driver was able to "remember" the license number of the kidnappers' vehicle, though he had no conscious memory. In the 1980's, however, hypnosis is being exposed as a charlatan and expelled from the courts. The Supreme Court of California recently "barred the use of virtually all testimony from witnesses who have been hypnotized in an attempt to refresh their memories."[15] This follows similar rulings by the supreme courts in Arizona and Minnesota; and other states, such as Maryland, seem sure to follow soon.

What could be wrong with hypnosis, this tested and honored technique that is so widely used in psychotherapy and accepted as a valid tool of medical science by the American Medical Association? Why rob the police of a weapon that has cracked so many cases? In its decision, the California Supreme Court cited "an 'overwhelming consensus' among experts... that hypnosis-induced testimony is frequently unreliable... [because] the technique...could result in creation of 'pseudo-memories or fantasies.' "[16] Contrary to the confidence expressed by experts for years, it has been discovered that "hypnosis is just as likely to dredge up false information as true accounts of past events...[and] individuals can and do lie under hypnosis."[17] One of the foremost experts on hypnosis, Bernard Diamond, professor of law and clinical psychiatry, states that "hypnotized persons graft onto their memories fantasies or suggestions deliberately or unwittingly communicated by the hypnotist"[18] and thereafter cannot differentiate between the original factual memory and the hypnotically produced alteration. Moreover, in the *California Law Review*, Professor Diamond insists that hypnosis is so rooted in deception that it is *impossible* to prevent distortion and fabrication from entering in.[19] How could one then rely upon a psychiatric "therapy" that utilized hypnotically induced "memories"?

This is not, however, the worst problem with hypnosis. There is another mysterious factor that sheds further light on the spontaneous production of psychic powers and "memories" of UFO abductions, clinical death, Yoga, and drug trips. Hypnosis restores "memories" of actual facts that, strangely enough, *were never known*. The popular "rebirthing" is one example. In this process, the subject is regressed back into the womb to discover traumas suffered there which are allegedly still causing psychological problems. Validity of this hypnotherapy is seemingly supported by the fact that the subjects describe in factual detail their births, including persons present, clothes worn, instruments used, conversations, and surroundings. The source of this data could hardly be the brain, however, since a newly born baby could not understand conversations taking place at its birth. Moreover, even if it could, as the Bobgans state, "this all flies in the face of the well-known, neurological, scientific fact that the myelin sheathing is too underdeveloped in the prenatal, natal and early post-natal brain to store such memories."[20]

The obvious implication is that *other minds* (E.T.'s) are using the hypnotic trance to implant a factual "memory" that never existed in the subject's brain. Whoever these entities are, they are somehow familiar with what happened at the birth in question, and have their own reasons for assisting the psychiatrist and his patient in restoring a "memory" that never existed. This conclusion is distateful to materialists, who instead dream up fantasies about language ability existing in genes and memories being stored in some mysterious "inner mind."[21] The following case, however, involved a memory that could not possibly have existed in the genes or inner mind and demands the admission that it was implanted by some intelligence that was able to use the hypnotic trance to its own mysterious ends.

> Following a murder in Joliet, IL last year, an eyewitness who was unable to recall the face of the murderer was hypnotized by a police force hypnotist. Although the crime had occurred at night and the witness had been almost 100 yards away, he was able under hypnosis to zoom in on the murderer's face and identify him as a former classmate.
>
> The suspect was brought to trial on the basis of the eyewitness identification and might have been convicted, had not an ophthalmologist testified that, under conditions like those on the night of the murder, accurate resolution of images was impossible beyond 30 feet.[22]

In this case, the witness never saw the murderer's face with his physical eyes. There was, in fact, no visual imprint on the brain to be recalled. What was the source, then, of the "memory" that was brought forth under hypnosis? There is no indication that it was produced by suggestion from the police hypnotist. It would have been thrown out of court on that basis. It was the fact that physical identification had been impossible that convinced the judge that something was not right. This case seems to fit the pattern of hypnotically induced, nonexistent "memories" of UFO abductions, drug trips, astral travel, clinical death, and birth.

Clearly these "memories" have a common nonhuman source whose deliberate purpose has been to convince humanity that "all is one," that the universe is a living organism, a great Mind of which we are all part, and that human consciousness is the link to all knowledge and power. The only alternative to this Eastern mystical view is found in the Bible: that there is not just one great Mind, but many individual minds, each with the power of choice. E.T.'s are not humanoids, but either angels or demons: the former serving God, the Creator, the latter having rebelled against Him to follow Satan. The philosophy promoted by the phenomena that hypnosis produces is exactly what the Bible attributes to Satan. This identifies the E.T.'s as demons. Rejecting that idea as mere superstition, the New Age prefers to accept without question the implanted suggestion. Indeed, suggestion in a variety of forms has become the panacea of the New Age, from psychotherapy, positive and possibility thinking, and autosuggestion self-improvement tapes and techniques to mantras, chanting, and creative visualization that is believed to produce whatever one really wants.

The Suggestion Messiah of the New Age

Of all the false messiahs of recent times, none seems less likely than Emile Coue'. Yet few people have played a more important part in the preparation of the world for the Antichrist than the almost comic "originator of the psychotherapeutic system called Couéism."[23] Involving "frequent repetition of the formula, 'Every day, and in every way, I am becoming better and better,'"[24] Couéism was the modern forerunner to self-help and other New Age groups and beliefs that are proliferating at an almost unbelievable rate across the United States in the 1980's and even infiltrating the church.

While working as an obscure pharmacist in Troyes, France, around the turn of the century, Emile Coue' "observed his patients receiving from certain drugs beneficial effects that could not be ascribed to the medicines. That led him to believe that it was the power of 'imagination' that effected the cure."[25] This discovery launched Coue' into a study of hypnosis around 1901, with special interest in the apparent therapeutic effects of self-hypnosis. The modern applications of hypnosis have their roots in "Mesmerism." However, it was Coue' who carried Mesmer's theory to its logical conclusion and thereby laid the foundation for the New Age.

Franz Anton Mesmer received his medical degree from the University of Vienna. His doctoral dissertation, "Influence of the Planets," carried the astrology of his day into medicine, attempting to show the influence of a "planetary force field" upon human bodies and thus health. Learning in 1774 that a Jesuit priest, Father Maximilian Hell, one of Maria Theresa's court astrologers, was performing remarkable cures with magnets, Mesmer quickly recognized a logical application of his thesis. As Szasz says, "Magnetism, originally a property of some ferrous metals, became, in Mesmer's mind, an omnipresent force."[26] To Mesmer it seemed logical that the manipulation of this force with magnets could hold the key to curing all disease. He soon discovered, however, that he really did not need to wave magnets over his patients' bodies; he could achieve the same results by using only his hands. Mesmer explained this as a biological force called "animal magnetism," a term he coined in 1775.[27]

The similarity is obvious between Mesmerism and the New Age belief that the manipulation or realignment of psychic forces within the body's alleged "chakra system" is the key to healing, knowledge, and power. The connection between Mesmerism, Couéism, Eastern mysticism, and astrology is clear. The New Age application of this "ancient wisdom" has been neatly expressed by W. Brugh Joy, medical doctor turned guru:

> The *chakras* are the centers for these energies, both inside the body and immediately outside it. Known for thousands of years in Eastern philosophy, the chakras [are]...inextricably associated with...the various states of awareness.
>
> Tapping these energies is fire, and the consequences...can be psychosis, aggravation of neuroses, acceleration of disease processes and suicide.
>
> But the awakening into certain states of consciousness can bestow gifts of such value that they are beyond price, gifts such as the mastery of any or all of the psi phenomena, healing

powers not yet recognized by conventional Western science and deep serenity and knowledge of life.

That the chakra system exists is beyond doubt....But no one, not one person, knows what it actually is or all of its aspects, and no one has ever known, despite attempts over thousands of years to master this knowledge.

My tentative belief is that the chakra system is...capable of being directed by thought and capable of converting matter into various forms of energy, and vice versa, transcending the constraints of time and space.[28]

Autosuggestion for Self-Mastery

After years of diligent study and experimentation, Coue' perfected his system of "self-mastery." He is generally credited with coining the word "autosuggestion," which he popularized in his lectures and his book *Self-Mastery Through Conscious Autosuggestion*. "Stressing that he was not primarily a healer, but one who taught others to heal themselves," the French pharmacist "claimed to have effected organic changes through autosuggestion."[29] This was in contrast to Mesmer, who, unaware of the power he had uncovered, specifically avoided anything except psychosomatic problems.

One of the earliest pioneers of the free clinic concept, Coue' seemed to be genuine in his concern to help others. In 1910 he set up a free clinic in Nancy, France, to practice his now-perfected system. The results were so phenomenal that Coue''s fame spread across Europe and even to America. In 1920 he set up a clinic in New York. During his speaking tours of the United States and Europe, "even the largest lecture halls could not contain the enthusiastic crowds, thronging to see the master himself repeat the famous words: 'Every day and in every way, I am becoming better and better.' "[30] This "chant of the devotees of Emile Coue'...was sweeping the nation in the 1920s."

Preaching remarkable "powers of suggestion," the Messiah of the New Age had arrived before his time. In spite of the cure of so many serious ailments by the power of "suggestion" that Coueism effected throughout the Western world, Coue''s "system" eventually fell into disrepute.

Couéism failed because it was taken to be exactly what its originator claimed: a "system." As Coue''s followers forgot to *believe* what they were saying and chanted the magic words more and more mechanically, the cures became less and less, until no one believed anymore.

Had Coue' only lived into the New Age, he would have seen himself fully vindicated in the adoption of hypnosis by the American Medical Association and its growing use by psychologists and psychiatrists. The old master would be pleased, too, to see in the 1980's a host of self-improvement techniques based upon the very same "power of suggestion" that he was convinced could cure anything: "positive thinking," "possibility thinking," self-hypnosis tapes by the thousands, numerous salesmanship and management success seminars used by both Christians and non-Christians, positive mental attitude (PMA) seminars, est (Erhard Seminars Training), Lifespring, Silva Mind Control, Alpha Level Training, biofeedback, guided imagery, creative visualization, Confluent Education, psychotherapies by the score, and an almost endless list of other New Age self-improvement techniques.

Seeing Mesmer's "universal force" as mental rather than physical, Coue' recognized that the secret of "animal magnetism" was very simple: *suggestion*. This idea has been revived today through drugs and Eastern mysticism as the "consciousness revolution" that ushered in the New Age, and it has been popularized by George Lucas, a devout believer in and evangelist of Mesmer's Force, through his Star Wars series of movies. Whereas Mesmer publicly declared that "he could help only people suffering from nervous disorders and no others,"[31] Coue' demonstrated that the power of suggestion has no such limits. The New Age is a revival of Coue''s adaptation and extension of Mesmer's limited theory: that human potential is *unlimited*, because the mind through suggestion can accomplish and create anything that it believes it can. Or can it? Could this be a delusion deliberately created by *other minds* from another dimension?

A Placebo-Prone Generation

Whether it is a sugar pill, a saline solution, or whatever,

a placebo's composition makes no difference at all. Its power is in the *suggestion* that is made to the patient at the time it is given. Whatever the patient "believes" the placebo is supposed to do will become his experience. A placebo can poison as well as cure. It works about 50 percent of the time. Modern science has no explanation for it. We only know that the secret of the placebo is the same power of *suggestion* that creates factual memories that never existed and produces psychic powers and mystical experiences, and that those who fall most easily into deep hypnosis receive the greatest benefit from placebos.

For all the good that this strange quirk of the human mind produces, there are two troublesome facts associated with it: as Dr. Joy admits concerning the chakra system, 1) no one on earth knows how *suggestion* works, and 2) it can be very dangerous. Placebos can kill as well as cure. The strangest part is that so many New Agers are willing to play around with alleged "mind powers" that are beyond comprehension and potentially deadly. Could it be that certain "other minds" out there are not only deceiving Uri Geller and Andrija Puharich, but everyone else who plays this same game? The bait on the hook is clearly those "gifts of such value that they are beyond price" that so excite Brugh Joy and other New Agers. Our *contrary scenario* will eventually demonstrate that the purpose behind this deception is to prepare the world for the Antichrist.

The basic placebo mentality lies at the heart of the New Age: it does not matter *how or why* something works—only that it does work. This is the case for the numerous New Age self-improvement techniques being used in medicine and psychiatry and PMA success methods that we have already referred to, for which there is no scientific explanation, yet they are accepted as "scientific" simply because they "work." It is Couéism's "power of suggestion" revived with a vengeance and turned loose upon today's society on a scale that would make Coué's chest burst with pride! In an age when science has replaced God, the endorsement of the power of suggestion by science has opened our generation to the very deception that Christ warned would precede His second coming.

The significance of today's revival of Couéism under

various new labels can hardly be overstated. New Age thinking rests upon a childlike faith in the "power of suggestion" to transform consciousness, to cure disease and environment, and eventually to produce a new world of peace and prosperity. This attitude has spawned a generation of placebo-prone individuals with unprecedented vulnerability to deception (ideal for the coming Antichrist to take advantage of) and programmed to accept as truth any lie that can be "experienced" subjectively.

Called "the yoga of the West," biofeedback has become one of the new darlings of science, yet it has been demonstrated that false biofeedback data also produce the same results. Some experts who use it confess that "biofeedback may be the ultimate placebo."[32] Psychotherapists and Christian psychologists and preachers resort to flattery, distortion, and lies in order to convince the patient that psychotherapy is working and/or that they are worth so much that God loves them. In group therapy, total strangers tell each other that they love them or how wonderful they are, simply to build up their "self-esteem." It is one big charade of feeding placebos to ourselves and to each other. The famous humanist psychologist Carl Rogers has said, apparently in all earnestness: "Objective facts are quite unimportant. The only facts of significance are the feelings which the client is able to bring into the situation."[33]

The entire Human Potential Movement is based upon the belief that there is unlimited power and wisdom within the human psyche that can be released by suggestion and visualization. As a generation, we seem to be seeking the ultimate placebo: a way out of the human dilemma, an escape from the threat of ecological and/or nuclear holocaust through a change in consciousness. Will this be our ultimate downfall? The magic key to the New Age transformation of consciousness that is being popularly pursued today is the *subconscious*. It is therefore extremely disturbing, for example, in a lengthy brochure offering self-hypnosis tapes to cure or accomplish almost anything, from bust and personality development to accelerated learning and personal happiness through suggestion and the power of the subconscious, to read that:

[The] subconscious...stubborn[ly] insists on believing everything it sees or hears....

...the subconscious...is unable to make judgments. It cannot distinguish between right and wrong, good and bad, true and false.

It willingly accepts as an absolute fact everything that is fed into it...and then tries to impose its will upon our lives, based on what may be completely false information.

The subconscious is just too powerful for us to control.

Amazingly, after telling us the above—that the subconscious cannot be trusted at all—the brochure bases everything it promises upon the "power of the subconscious"! It goes on to explain that the subconscious can be made to work for us through hypnosis, and there are no limits to what positive suggestions can accomplish if properly directed to the gullible unconscious part of our minds. Eastern mysticism as practiced in TM and other forms of Yoga is one of the most powerful deceptions exerted by autosuggestion upon the alleged subconscious. In spite of all objective evidence to the contrary, the delusion that "all is one" and that Self is God is readily accepted and experienced in deep yogic trance. It is this further extension of Mesmerism and Couéism that the Hindu and Buddhist gurus brought to the West. One of the most important gurus in this century was a young Brahmin from India, whose story is very instructive.

The Theosophical Society

Several decades before H.G. Wells wrote about it, "The Plan" formulated by "higher intelligences" to install a world ruler was known to other writers, among them Helena Petrovna Blavatsky and Annie Besant. "Revelations" of "The Plan" through psychic means began shortly after the founding of the Theosophical Society in New York City on November 17, 1875, under the leadership of Helena Blavatsky and Colonel Henry Olcott. The teachings of Theosophy, often called the Ancient Wisdom or the Wisdom Religion, combine Gnosticism and the mysticism of Egypt, India, and China with certain elements in the philosophies of Plato and Plotinus. This spiritual smorgasbord is very much on target with the E.T.'s' ultimate goal: to combine all religions into one all-embracing creed that everyone can accept, thus preparing the way for the Messiah for all religions.

A spirit medium and a loose-living adventuress, Madame Blavatsky was one of the early advocates and practitioners of free sex. In addition to the blatant opposition to Biblical morals which she picked up from "higher intelligences" that she contacted in trance, Blavatsky also absorbed their hatred for the cardinal Biblical doctrines. After writing her viciously anti-Christian *Isis Unveiled*, she authoritatively defined Theosophy's beliefs and goals in *The Secret Doctrine*, which later held a strange fascination for Adolf Hitler and Sirhan B. Sirhan, the assassinator of Robert F. Kennedy.

Through reading *The Secret Doctrine*, in 1889 Annie Besant—a chief spokesperson for the Fabian Socialists and one of several women with whom George Bernard Shaw was entangled at the time—was converted to yet another cause. She became an immediate and enthusiastic Blavatsky disciple.[34] A highly talented, energetic, and emotional person, Annie had gone from one cause to another: from the rejection of her earlier evangelical faith, to a desire to become a nun, to involvement in the Oxford Movement and the mysticism and sensual imagery of high church ritual. A disastrous marriage to a dominating clergyman brought embittered rejection of all established religion, especially Christianity. Obsessed with a desire to prove that salvation was *not* through the death and resurrection of Jesus Christ for man's sins, as she had once believed, Annie Besant became a powerful influence in laying the foundation for the apostasy predicted in the Bible.[35]

The Annie Besant Revelations

Madame Blavatsky died in 1891 and Annie Besant became president of the Theosophical Society in 1907. Together with the homosexual clergyman C.W. Leadbeater, codirector of the society, Mrs. Besant developed further applications of Darwin's theory to karma and reincarnation, similar to the theories that Edgar Cayce and Teilhard de Chardin would also promote. The acceptance of Darwin's theory was one of the early moves of science into Eastern mysticism, which had always taught "cosmic evolution" of animals and men upward to oneness with God. Evolution is also "verified" under hypnosis.

Years before "past lives therapy" would become popular with psychiatrists in the West, Mrs. Besant "clairvoyantly" explored her past lives and allegedly discovered that in one of her previous reincarnations—as a large monkey—she had died in the process of saving the lives of the Buddha-to-be and his family. Because of this heroic, karma-improving deed, the Besant-monkey had become human at the moment of its death, thus taking a giant step in its upward evolution toward ultimate union with the Absolute.[36]

Through her practice of Yoga meditation, similar to TM, Mrs. Besant also had revelations of the future. It was "revealed" to her in 1909 that the Messiah was a young Brahmin disciple of Theosophy named Jiddu Krishnamurti. Annie prophesied that the "World Teacher, or 'Guiding Spirit of the Universe'—described as the invisible head of every religion"—would manifest itself by taking "possession of Mr. Krishnamurti's body."[37] This would be the *Ascended Master* or *Christ Spirit* that had allegedly taken possession of the body of Jesus of Nazareth during his life upon earth.

Krishnamurti was identified as the latest in a long line of alleged reincarnations of the Christ Spirit. The crux of his mission in the world, in preparation for the new world government to follow, would be to "combine all religions into one new, worldwide religion."[38] The similarity to Jeane Dixon's vision of a messiah who will "bring together all mankind in one all-embracing faith...with every sect and creed united" is obvious. In fact, upon this point there seems to be near-unanimous agreement among all occultists. The acceleration of the apparent fulfillment of this long-standing plan through the present New Age Movement is all the more significant in view of the fact that this is exactly what the Bible predicts for the "last days" just prior to Christ's return visibly and in judgment.

Mission Impossible

In 1911, 6000 delegates of the order of the Star in the East, listening to Krishnamurti, suddenly heard "another voice...of wondrous sweetness and power ring out through his lips," and Krishnamurti, "spoke in the first person as a god." According to a news report, some of the delegates "bowed down to worship him." At the moment of this miraculous change in his voice, "a great coronet of brilliant, shimmering blue appeared above his head," witnessed by the stunned onlookers.[39] There were other equally convincing supernatural signs in the presence of large crowds.

Preparations for ushering in the new Messianic Age proceeded, with Krishnamurti tutored by Leadbeater and Besant. In 1926, Mrs. Besant brought this "chosen vessel" to the United States. Already widely acclaimed in Europe, where he had been hailed as the "leader of a new civilization," Krishnamurti needed only a favorable reception in the world's most powerful and influential nation to launch the New Age.

However, as his ship pulled into New York harbor, Krishnamurti's occult powers suddenly and mysteriously left him. He had come to America to oppose historic Christianity, particularly its teaching about sin, repentance, judgment, and forgiveness through the death and resurrection of Jesus the Messiah, just as Vivekananda, founder of the Vedanta Society, and many others had done before him. Apparently that faith was still held by so many people in this country that it stripped Krishnamurti of the psychic power that had so impressed thousands in other parts of the world.

"Even on shipboard in New York harbor, Krishnamurti complained of what he called the electrical atmosphere intensity of New York and said he doubted that he would be able to meditate successfully there." Without the proper altered state of consciousness he achieved through Eastern meditation, Krishnamurti apparently lost touch with the spirit entities (E.T.'s) that guided him and gave him his occult powers. *The New York Times* reported that Krishnamurti became almost incoherent during an interview aboard ship. Instead of manifesting any miraculous abilities, he came off as "a shy, badly frightened, nice-looking young Hindu."[40]

Plans for Krishnamurti to speak in New York were canceled. In Chicago for a convention of Theosophists, he complained of the "bad atmosphere conditions" in America that he blamed for his loss of power. His planned national tour canceled, Krishnamurti went into seclusion. With Mrs. Besant's death in 1933, Jiddu Krishnamurti seemed to lose all memory of his association with the Theosophical Society and began to expound his own version of Eastern mysticism. His books are still very popular in the West today.

A Fascinating Connection

Apparently the "Ascended Masters" had not prepared America thoroughly enough, causing their plans to be aborted at that time. In the years since then, however, those behind "The Plan" have done their work well. The "atmosphere" in America has become so agreeable for occultism that today millions of Americans practice the very same Eastern meditation that Krishnamurti found impossible in the United States only a few decades ago. In altered states of consciousness, Americans and Europeans are receiving psychic communications from the same E.T.'s who have been in touch with Yogis and witch doctors for centuries. Today's Yogis are Nobel prizewinners, psychiatrists, physicians, sociologists, university professors, business leaders, and politicians—all part of the huge New Age Movement that syncretizes Mesmer's hypnosis, Coue''s powers of suggestion, and Freud's unconscious (id) into a new world religion that draws heavily from Eastern mysticism.

Designed around a snake formed into a circle, the symbol of the Theosophical Society provides a fascinating link with a more recent and important false Messiah. The serpent's head and tail (yin and yang) meet behind a *swastika*, the symbol that most people associate with Hitler's Nazism. Banned from public display in Germany by the allied forces of occupation, the swastika is still prominent on temples throughout the Orient, where it has been a sacred symbol in Buddhism and Hinduism for thousands of years. Hitler's connection with these religions—symbolized by his adoption of the swastika—is more than incidental.

The false Messiah who made the swastika infamous was a very serious devotee of black magic, which has its roots deep in Hindu and Buddhist philosophy. He was also the master of mass hysteria created by hypnotic powers of suggestion. Claiming to be the Messiah, he came the closest to being the Antichrist of any other figure in history. Before proceeding further, it will therefore be necessary to turn our attention to Hitler, to see what we can learn from him that will influence the development of our *contrary scenario*. The astonishing phenomenon of Germany's messiah is very instructive in helping us to understand the progressive steps in the preparation of the world for the ultimate delusion that is hastening upon us.

11
Hitler,
The Almost-Antichrist

We have already noted that the Bible says two incredible things about the Antichrist: that he will unite the entire world 1) politically, and 2) religiously. In fact, it is prophesied specifically that "all who dwell on the earth will worship him."[1] Worship implies religion. The leading Nazis were all convinced that National Socialism was a new religion that was destined to rule the world and establish a new age. Hitler said, "Whoever sees in National Socialism nothing but a political movement doesn't know much about it...we shall wash off the Christian veneer and bring out a religion peculiar to our race."[2] Dr. Ley, head of the Nazi Labor Front, declared, "Our faith...is National Socialism, and this religious faith does not tolerate any other faith alongside itself!"[3] It was clear that "Rudolph Hess's religion replaced God with Hitler"[4]—exactly what the whole earth will do with the Antichrist. French academician Louis Bertrand, a convert to Nazism, exulted in his newfound Messiah:

> What sovereign, what national hero, has ever been acclaimed, adulated, adored and worshipped as has [Hitler]...this little man in the brown shirt...followed by his cortege....
> This is something altogether different from mere popularity, *this is religion!*
> In the eyes of his admirers, Hitler is a prophet, the partaker of the divine![5]

Had it not been for a few miscalculations, Hitler could conceivably have conquered the world. Although he failed in that grandiose ambition, he was *worshiped* if ever man was. That is what gives Hitler special significance for our analysis: the fanatical, blind submission that most of Germany gave to him, embracing with wild enthusiasm his most insane whims. Germany's fawning, mindless adulation of Hitler would seem to offer an instructive example of the very kind of worship which the Bible predicts the whole world will give to the Antichrist. As William Shirer, author of *The Rise and Fall of the Third Reich*, and an astute observer who saw it all happen, wrote in his diary at the time:

> Today, as far as the vast majority of his fellow-countrymen are concerned, he [Hitler] has reached a pinnacle never before achieved by a German ruler.
>
> He has become—even before his death—a myth, a legend, almost a god, with that quality of divinity which the Japanese people ascribe to their Emperor.[6]

What Source, This Dark Power?

There is no normal explanation for the staggering mystery that was Hitler: an inept and bumbling ex-corporal with obsessive delusions, rising out of obscurity to make the entire world tremble. Bewildered historians have asked the question: "How could a man so ignorant, so enslaved by stupid dogmas, have achieved such practical success?"[7] Yet this comic figure with the bobbing mustache and frantic gestures outmaneuvered the world's leaders time and again with his insane boldness, conquered Europe with ridiculous swiftness, and held the destiny of nations in his mad grip. There is neither political, psychological, nor other ordinary answer to the enigma that was Hitler.

What was the mysterious source of the irresistible seduction with which this deluded Messiah dragged millions into destruction in his wake? When it came to swaying a huge audience, a nation, the world, no human was Hitler's equal. During his speeches, he was like a medium in a trance. Afterwards, like a medium who has been drained by the spirits, Hitler would collapse, deathly pale and exhausted, and it would take several drafts of beer to revive him. Impounded by Allied intelligence after the fall of Berlin, the personal diary of Joseph Goebbels, who became Nazi Minister of Propaganda, reveals the hypnotic influence that Hitler exerted upon him when they first met:

He is the creative instrument of fate and deity. I stand by
him deeply shaken...recognize him as my leader....He is so deep
and mystical...like a prophet of old.

With such a man one can conquer the world...my doubts
vanish....Germany will live! *Heil Hitler!*[8]

It may be true that Goebbels was an unstable neurotic, ripe
for hero worship. But why was this unlikely "little man in the
brown shirt" the one who completely mesmerized him? And
what of the multitude of other men with strong wills and
brilliant minds who were also swept relentlessly into this
maelstrom of evil just as suddenly and completely? After
meeting Hitler in 1941, the historian Benoist-Mechin declared
in awe: "...his eyes...so strange that at first they were all I
saw...[he] had a way of looking at you which drew you to
him...you felt a sort of dizziness...."[9] At the Nuremberg Trials,
Marshal von Blomberg testified:

It was almost impossible to contradict Hitler...he swept you
along with him....

His personal magnetism was tremendous. He had an enormous power of suggestion.[10]

"Magnetism...an enormous power of suggestion." We have
heard that before. Surely Mesmer and Coue' would have stood
in jealous awe of this master manipulator of men and nations,
who took the hypnotic powers they had uncovered and used
them to mold millions to his evil will. Pointing out that *Mein
Kampf* "is a succession of rambling, banal, and intensely
wearisome monologues by a thoroughly third-rate mind,"
Gerald Suster says: "...whatever powers Hitler did acquire were
wholly independent of the intellect."[11] Then Suster adds: "One
does not acquire such power by accident! Someone who
believes that will believe anything. One acquires it by patient
training."[12] The obvious question follows immediately: training
by whom, and for what?

Though most historians have shied away from mentioning
it, there is overwhelming evidence that Hitler was adept at
various forms of Eastern mysticism. Suster points out that he
was involved in a wide range of esoteric practices: "the wisdom
of Gurdjieff, derived from Sufi mystics and Tibetan lamas,

and the Zen mysticism of the Japanese....These teachings stressed the existence of certain centers of power, or *chakras*, in the human body...[to be] activated by dint of yogic or magical exercises [which] bring to the practitioner some rather unusual powers, most notably that of being able to impose one's will upon others....The most important of these centres...[is] between and behind the eyebrows...known by some as the Ajna Chakra, by some as the Third Eye...."[13]

It all sounds alarmingly familiar, so very much like the beliefs and practices that have become extremely popular in the Human Potential Movement of the 1980's. In his day, only Hitler and a relatively few others took these things seriously. And those who did were involved in the numerous secret occult societies that were experiencing a revival in the 1920's and 1930's across Europe. This was not for the general public—at least not to be acknowledged openly. Today, however, the very beliefs and practices that the evidence so clearly indicates formed the power base for Nazism are the everyday fare of tens of millions of people. Indeed, the entire New Age Movement is based upon the Yoga, chakras, astrology, reincarnation, vegetarianism, Zen, and other forms of a syncretistic mysticism that was practiced by the Nazi elite. We are much more susceptible to the deadly deception of the Antichrist than was the world of Hitler's day.

The Occult Connection

One of Hitler's earliest and most important mentors was the master occultist Dietrich Eckart, who seems to have recognized in Hitler from the moment he saw him the Messiah he had so long awaited. An indication of Hitler's great respect for Eckart and the central role that his "spiritual leadership" played in the rise of Nazism is found in the last sentence of *Mein Kampf*. There Hitler lauds black magician Eckart as one "who devoted his life to the awakening of our people...." Awakening them to what? That becomes very clear.

The high priest of the Thule Society, a secret occult group which Hitler joined when he was still unknown, Dietrich Eckart has often been called "the spiritual founder of National Socialism."[14] The Thule Geselschaft took its name from the mythical Nordic Garden of Eden in the far north that had supposedly been peopled by E.T.'s, or gods. Goethe's *Faust* and Wagner's *Parsifal* expressed the Germanic preoccupation with the legend of Thule, also known as Hyperborea. Nietzsche, whose writings heavily influenced Hitler, began his key work, *Anti-Christ*, with the sentence, "Let us see ourselves for what we are. We are Hyperboreans."

Among the fabled descendants of the Hyperboreans were initiates who had allegedly received from the gods themselves the occult Gnosis, or Primordial Knowledge (fruit of the Tree of Knowledge), giving them power to unlock the secrets of the universe. To recapture this mystical force for himself and Germany became Hitler's passion and that of his close associates. Hitler would later send expeditions to Tibet in search of the Masters of Wisdom from Atlantis and Hyperborea, who, according to occult traditions, were living high in the Himalayas. In his May 1982 news conference in Los Angeles, Benjamin Creme declared that "The Christ" mentioned in those full-page ads of a month earlier came to London in 1977 from the Himalayas, where he had been living "at the 17,500 foot level for the past 2,000 years."[15] Apparently Creme's "Christ" has the same backing as did Hitler.

The occult was Hitler's absorbing interest from his youth. Among his favorite books were those involving Germanic mythology and Eastern mysticism, especially Tibetan occultism. He greatly admired the mystical poet Gerhart Hauptmann, whose esoteric works carried the message of a revived paganism, often portrayed in Buddhist terms, opposing and conquering traditional Christianity. Another of Hitler's favorite authors was the poet Stefan George, to whom Hitler offered the presidency of the German Academy in 1933. Like Erwin Guido Kolbenheyer, another producer of what Hitler called great National Socialist literature, George conveyed Hinduism's view that the physical world is *maya*, an illusion. His writings were a condemnation of traditional Christianity and a promotion of Eastern mysticism, including the merging of the individual with the universe itself. This same "Unity Consciousness" would be experienced under LSD and TM a generation later by millions of the followers of Timothy Leary,

Maharishi Mahesh Yogi, and other gurus in the "consciousness revolution." Memories are short, however, and few people would see the significant connection between Nazism and the New Age Movement/Aquarian Conspiracy. There is no denying it, however, for those whose eyes see.

Under the leadership of the Thule Geselschaft, a merger of most of the rising mystical-occult groups in Europe was to take place. On this ecumenical-mystic base a pagan Germany, purged of all non-Aryan blood, would be rebuilt by the Nazis. At the head of the New Order would be Hitler, the Supreme Initiate of an occult tradition with roots going back through Tibet and India to Thule. The Aryan Messiah would establish the millennium promised by prophets. Hitler loved to call the Third Reich "The Thousand Year Reich." The Aryan ambitions of the occultists in the Thule Society became much of the platform of the Nazi Party under the leadership of its New Age Messiah. That this occult connection was a very real one can easily be seen by noting some of the Nazi leaders who were active in the Thule Geselschaft:

> Max Amann, later editor-in-chief of Nazi publications;
> Rudolph Hess and Alfred Rosenberg, among Hitler's closest advisors;
> Anton Drexler, founder of the German Workers' Party, which became the Nazi Party;
> Dietrich Eckart, spiritual high priest of the Nazi Party;
> Gottfried Feder, deputy of the Reichstag in 1924 and co-founder of the Nazi Party;
> Karl Fiehler, Obergrueppenfuehrer SS and Reichsleiter of the Nazi Party;
> Hans Frank, legal advisor to the Nazi Party and later Governor-general of Occupied Poland;
> Baron Rudolf von Sebottendorf, chief astrologer to Hitler;
> Hitler himself.

The Hierarchical Masters of Shamballah

The Vril Society, still in existence in India today with swastika-engraved temples and millions of members, had numerous branches in pre-Nazi Germany. Hitler belonged to the Vril Society as did Alfred Rosenberg, Dr. Theodor

Morrell (who later became the Fuehrer's personal physician), Hermann Goering, and Heinrich Himmler, who became the second-most-powerful man in Germany as head of the infamous SS, whose "inner core...took irreversible vows in service of Lucifer."[16] The Vril's leader in Berlin was Karl Haushofer, brilliant ex-general and university professor, who kept his occult activities so secret that he fooled many a historian. "Taught by Gurdjieff in Tibet and by the Green Dragon Society in Japan,"[17] Haushofer took over the spiritual education of Hitler after the death of their mutual friend, Dietrich Eckart, and initiated him into Theosophist Blavatsky's *Secret Doctrine*.[18] Today these beliefs lie behind much of the New Age Movement; they were enlarged upon by Alice Bailey and are at the heart of Benjamin Creme's pronouncements concerning "Lord Maitreya," who he claims is "The Christ" now present upon earth. Ravenscroft's comments are instructive:

> By divulging *The Secret Doctrine*, Haushofer expanded Hitler's time consciousness...[and] awakened Hitler to the real motives of the Luciferic Principality which possessed him so that he could become the conscious vehicle of its evil intent in the twentieth century.
> And finally, Haushofer himself took on the role of Mephistopheles, when he initiated Adolf Hitler into the occult significance of the blood and the part which occult blood rites would play in creating a magical mutation in the Aryan Race...which would bring about a new stage in human evolution, the birth of the "Superman."[19]

The compelling obsession of the Vril Society was the belief that Germans were related to a Master Race of Aryans (the early Hindus), who were descended from the gods that once inhabited Hyperborea and Atlantis. Some of these Supermen were alleged to be still alive in Tibet, high in the Himalayas or in the Gobi Desert, in a mysterious place called Shamballah. In Blavatsky's *The Secret Doctrine* and in the Lucis Trust (originally Lucifer Publishing) books of Alice Bailey and other occultists, Shamballah was also connected with a Force that held the key to rejuvenation of the human race. According to Blavatsky, Bailey, et al, humanity is guided by a Hierarchy of Masters of Wisdom toward its rightful destiny of godhood. Similar teachings come from Elizabeth Clare Prophet (Guru Ma of the Church Universal and Triumphant, who stumps for the New Age "Revolution in Higher Consciousness") and a host of other occultists today, including Benjamin Creme. His "Lord Maitreya, the Christ" is alleged to be the leader of this Hierarchy of Masters from Shamballah. There is little question that Hitler not only believed in them devoutly, but thought he was in contact with these "Masters of Wisdom," who Creme says are at last ushering in the New Age.

In altered states of consciousness achieved through Yoga and other occult practices of the Vrilists that Hitler engaged in, one could supposedly communicate with these Masters of Wisdom, thereby gaining initiation into the secret Tibetan Gnosis. By this means psychic powers could be developed and the restoration of the Master Race begun. The Nazi initiates endeavored to maintain telepathic communication with the Unknown Master, who was the alleged leader of the Tibetan Supermen. Systematic *visualization* was the key to contact with the Masters. We have already seen that this same occult practice has been revived and popularized in today's New Age under a variety of names and techniques: as "guided imagery" used by psychiatrists and psychologists, in Christian "healing of the memories," in Silva Mind Control, in success and management seminars, and as part of Confluent Education and other New Age learning methods in public schools and self-help groups. The list is endless and so is the danger.

Hitler's involvement in these occult practices produced startling results. He seems to have gone beyond telepathic contact to visions of (or even actual visitations from) the Unknown Master himself. Herman Rauschning, Governor of Danzig, who knew Hitler intimately, tells of Hitler "trembling in a kind of ecstasy" while making the following announcement:

> The new man is living amongst us now! He is here! Isn't that enough for you?
>
> I will tell you a secret. I have seen the new man. He is intrepid and cruel. I was afraid of him![20]

The Terrorized Messiah

Some of those closest to Hitler came to believe that he was "manipulated by invisible forces, those 'Unknown Superiors,' " as the Nazi elite sometimes called them. In a 1934 speech, Rudolph Hess declared: "We believe that the Fuehrer is obeying a higher call to fashion German history."[21] The "higher call" was not from God by any means, but from these "Unknown Masters" that Hitler both served and feared. Although Hitler believed they were highly evolved humanoid creatures possessed of supernatural powers (much as Uri Geller believes his E.T.'s are today), their effect upon Hitler and other Nazi leaders was too much like demon possession for coincidence. Historian Alan Bullock has written: "Until the last days of his life, he retained an uncanny gift of personal magnetism, which defies analysis....His power to bewitch an audience has been likened to the occult arts of the African Medicine-man or the Asiatic Shaman."[22]

Those who can "bewitch" others must first of all have been bewitched themselves. A careful study of the Nazi Messiah offers strong evidence that something more than the human mind must be involved in autosuggestion and hypnosis. Could there indeed be, as Uri Geller and so many believe, *other minds not of this world* exerting their influence from behind the scenes? No other explanation of Hitler's powers seems feasible. Like Uri Geller, Hitler confided in those closest to him that he was under "orders" from "higher beings," whom he often implied would not allow him to tell all that he knew of his unique mission. "I will tell you a secret," Hitler told Rauschning: "I am founding an Order...the Man-God, that splendid Being, will be an object of worship....But there are other stages about which I am not permitted to speak...."[23] Reflecting upon his experiences with Hitler, Rauschning declared with awe:

> One cannot help thinking of him as a medium...the medium is possessed...beyond any doubt, Hitler was possessed by forces outside himself...of which the individual named Hitler was only the temporary vehicle."[24]

Even more than his public tirades, Hitler's conduct in private with those who knew him best bore all the marks of classic demon possession. The mysterious Masters of Shamballah not only gave Hitler his orders and his hypnotic powers; they also terrorized him. From inside sources, Rauschning learned that Hitler often "woke up nights shouting convulsively." The account continues:

> He yells for help...seized with a power which makes him tremble so violently that his bed shakes.
>
> Hitler was standing there in his bedroom, stumbling about, looking around him...distraught....
>
> He was muttering, "It's he! It's he! He's here!"
>
> His lips had turned blue. He was dripping with sweat.
>
> He was given a massage and something to drink. Then, all of a sudden, he screamed: "There! Over there! In the corner!"[25]

Possessed by the Unknown Master?

Was this invisible being that periodically terrorized Hitler the one he sometimes called the "Unknown Master"? Henri Bergson's brother-in-law, Samuel Mathers, founder of the secret order of the Golden Dawn (made up of high level Freemasons and Rosicrucians) had similar experiences. "As to the Secret Chiefs," Mathers wrote, "...I have very seldom seen them in their physical bodies....I believe they are human beings living on this Earth, but possessed of terrible and superhuman powers....I felt I was in contact with a Force so terrifying...[I had] great difficulty in breathing...cold sweats, bleeding from the nose, mouth and sometimes from the ears."[26] Though smaller, the Golden Dawn, was comparable to the Vril Society; and here again we have the classic symptoms of demon possession, similar to the terror that seized Hitler at times, and which today affects alleged UFO "contactees," who may in fact be the victims of hypnosis.

The demons are very versatile, passing themselves off under a variety of labels and outward forms to suit the temperament and beliefs of those they are manipulating. The message they preach, however, remains monotonously the same as that which Blavatsky, Besant, Bailey, Wells, Creme, and a host of others, including Hitler, embraced: "higher" states of consciousness, reincarnation, Yoga, expanded self-awareness, self-realization, the deification of man, and a coming world government, all under the benevolent guardianship of the Unknown Masters, of course. The seducers and the seduction remain the same; only the seduced, the human puppets being manipulated on stage, change. When will the curtain open for the final act?

Jesus Christ came 1900 years ago to establish the kingdom of God in men's hearts. He was rejected and crucified. The instigator of that foul deed, in which we have all joined, is clearly involved in an all-out effort to establish his own kingdom. There can be little doubt that this is the world government which New Agers imagine will finally bring lasting peace and prosperity based upon inherent human goodness. As for that, here are Hitler's own words:

> I had to encourage "national" feelings for reasons of expediency; but I was already aware that the "nation" idea could only have a temporary value.
> The day will come when even here in Germany what is known as "nationalism" will practically have ceased to exist. What will take its place in the world will be a universal society of masters and overlords.[27]

Clearly the conspiracy to install a world government does not originate with the Trilateralists or Club of Rome. They are mere pawns in a game with much higher stakes than they imagine. When they meet the world ruler, they will be like Goebbels, awed and worshipful. The Antichrist will probably not be possessed by mere demons, but by Satan, the "Unknown Master" himself. Though he failed in his mission, Hitler's "possession" seems to have been of that order. Some Bible scholars feel that the Antichrist will be Satan incarnate, more than a man. Goebbels confided one day to Prince Schaumburg-Lippe, his aide-de-camp:

> I see him almost every day, and still there are times when he loses me completely. Who can claim to know him as he really is?...
> Is he really human? I would not want to swear on it. There are times when he gives me the chills.

Hitler seems to have been chosen for his mission from

childhood. Raised in the village of Braunau-am-Inn, in an area described as a hotbed of mediums, Hitler was undoubtedly involved in spirit seances as a boy. That probably is how and when he first became demonized. This explains his unusual receptivity to the occult initiations and instructions he later received in the Thule and Vril societies under those dedicated occultists Deitrich Eckart and Karl Haushofer. Eckart, who used drugs (probably including peyote) and prayed to a black meteorite which he called his "Mecca Stone,"[28] wrote these amazing prophetic words ten years before Hitler would come to power:

> Follow Hitler! He will dance, but it is I who have called the tune. We have given him the means of communication with Them.
>
> Do not mourn for me: I shall have influenced history more than any other German.[29]

For plotting against Hitler, Karl Haushofer's son, Albrecht, was machine-gunned to death by the infamous SS beside Klaus Bonhoeffer, brother of the noted pastor, Deitrich Bonhoeffer. He seems to have understood and feared what his father had done in initiating Hitler into black magic. Rudolph Hess has credited Karl Haushofer with being the secret Master who unleashed the forces of evil through Germany's occult messiah. Taken from a pocket of the jacket he wore when he was executed was a poem in Albrecht's handwriting. It ended with these lines:

> My father broke the seal—
> He sensed not the breath of the Evil one,
> But set him free to roam the world.

The Myth of Blood

Years later, Hitler reportedly told an aide that "as he lay wounded" during World War One, "he received a supernatural vision which ordered him to save Germany."[30] The fact that he was 30 years old at the time, the same age at which Jesus Christ began His messianic mission, was of great significance to Hitler. Perhaps unaware that according to the Bible he was thereby bringing the wrath and judgment of Israel's God upon his nation, Hitler ordered the murder of 6 million Jews. This could be the principal reason why, instead of "saving Germany," he destroyed it and most of Europe.

The Fuehrer's obsessive hatred of the Jewish race and his determination to wipe them from the face of the earth was more than the fanatical prejudice of a madman. It can only be understood in its occult origins and Eastern mystical roots. The Hindu-Aryan mysticism that Hitler adopted was a carefully calculated, point-by-point rebuttal of the Biblical gospel: that redemption comes through the shedding of the Messiah's blood in a death that would pay the penalty for man's sin. In contrast, the occult Messiah of the "Thousand Year Reich" determined to sacrifice the Jewish people in a vain attempt to "purify" German blood and thereby restore their lost godhood.

In spite of modern attempts to do away with it, the abhorrent caste system remains in India, for it is central to Hinduism. One cannot buy or work one's way into any caste, for it comes only by birth: i.e., by *blood*, which can only be purified by spiritual evolution over many reincarnations. Nazi mysticism, however, had a plan for shortening the process. Alfred Rosenberg, a Thulist and one of the highest Nazi officials, wrote in his book *Myth of the Twentieth Century*, "Today there awakens a new faith, the myth of blood, the faith, too, for defending the blood, the divine essence of man." Referring to *Myth of the Twentieth Century*, Hitler declared, "When you read Rosenberg's new book, you will understand...!" Voicing a lie that is as old as the Garden of Eden, yet is at the heart of today's New Age Movement, Hitler declared: "Creation is not yet at an end...Man is becoming God...Man is God in the making."[31] The "Man" that Hitler had in mind was the blond, blue-eyed *German*—and the stepping-stone to his godhood was the sacrifice of the *Jews*.

Hitler's Aryan dream of pure blood had another side: the *Lebensborn*, which sprang up across Germany and were operated almost like human stud farms as part of Hitler's plan to breed a Master Race of Superman. "It was a great honor to be an unwed mother in Germany, if one were carrying a future blond, blue-eyed 'child for the Fuehrer.' Children born at a Lebensborn were graded—the most desirable were adopted, the others were either sterilized or eliminated." There were alleged "wholesale kidnappings of...'desirable' non-German children from other countries for the purpose of adding to Germany's breeding stock."[32]

Black Magicians of the Order SS

In charge of the extermination camps—and the Lebensborn—was Heinrich Himmler, "the most sinister figure in the Third Reich after Hitler himself."[33] Headed by Himmler, the infamous SS was the secret elite corps of Nazi occultism, a religious order that practiced with fanatical dedication Hitler's Aryan mysticism. Known as the Black Order, the SS was undoubtedly the most powerful society of black magicians the world has ever seen. Yoga exercises, Eastern meditation, and visualization, as well as belief in karma, reincarnation, cosmic evolution to godhood, and the unity of all life as part of one living organism, the Cosmos, were central beliefs and practices of the SS. This was a Hindu religious order that spent more money on occult investigations and genealogical research, tracing the mystical origins of Aryan Supermen back to India and Tibet, than the Americans spent to develop the first atomic bomb! The systematic and efficient extermination of Jews and other "undesirables" was carried out as a ritual sacrifice to the gods. It was all part of an ongoing evolutionary process. The death of individuals along the way was incidental; what mattered was the eventual development of a new species, the Aryan God-man. "At a speech made in Dachau in 1936, Himmler informed high-ranking SS officers that they had all met before, in previous lives, and that after their present lives had ended, they would meet again."[34]

Suster calls the SS "the high priesthood of the New Age, the standard bearers of the coming Superman...magicians who had formed alliances with the mystic Tibetan cities of Agarthi and Shamballah...."[35] Their "glorious mission" was to create "a New Age, a New World, a New Man."[36] In their dedicated fulfillment of this mission given to Hitler by invisible "higher" beings, "the SS murdered 14,000,000 men, women and children....For the sake of the magical vision of Adolf Hitler and his associates, the Second World War claimed the lives of almost 50,000,000 human beings.''[37] Yet they saw themselves as decent, sensitive men who didn't like to see animals suffer. How can this glaring contradiction be explained? They had believed what Krishna taught Arjuna in the Bhagavad-Gita: that there really is no death, so killing isn't murder because the souls come back again in another form. Like Arjuna, the SS were only performing their sacred duty.

Himmler believed in communication with the spirit world. "To his masseur, Felix Kersten, he boasted of his ability to call up spirits and converse with them.''[38] The Bible forbids necromancy on the ground that it is a deception; it is not the spirits of the dead one converses with, but demons impersonating them. The same deception was involved in the communication with the "Unknown Masters"; but Hitler, Himmler, and their associates were convinced by their initiation into Tibetan-Buddhist occultism that they were in touch with real Supermen who inhabited the Himalayas. A colony of Tibetans was even brought to Berlin—and when the Russians took that city, they were amazed to find about 1000 Tibetan corpses.

Hindu-Buddhist philosophy was at the heart of Nazism. It is therefore extremely disturbing to note that this is also at the heart of the New Age Movement today. There is every reason to believe that this ominous connection is not by chance. As Jean-Michel Angebert has said:

> Those who induced Germany to embrace the swastika are not dead. They are still among us, just as they have been in every era, and doubtless will continue to be until the Apocalypse.
>
> National Socialism was for them but a means and Hitler was but an instrument.
>
> The undertaking failed. What they are now trying to do is to revive the myth using other means.[39]

12

The Aryan Connection

We have seen that the "messianic myth" refuses to die because it is perpetuated in one version (the true one) by the Spirit of God working in men's hearts, and in a counterversion by Satan, who is called in the Bible "the god of this world."[1] If he is to win the battle for planet Earth, then Satan must install his counterfeit Messiah. Moreover, through the Antichrist Satan must bring peace, prosperity, and goodwill among men—not through their believing the gospel that Jesus Christ died for our sins and was resurrected, proving that the penalty had been paid in full, but through their rejecting this gospel and claiming their own inherent perfection and godhood. Commenting upon this continuing conspiracy, the French philosopher René Guénon wrote insightful and instructive words in 1921:

> The false Messiahs we have seen so far have only performed very inferior miracles, and their disciples were probably not very difficult to convert. But who knows what the future has in store?...
>
> When one thinks...of the series of attempts made in succession by the theosophists, one is forced to the conclusion that these were only trials, experiments as it were, which will be renewed in various forms until success is achieved....
>
> Not that we believe that the theosophists, any more than the occultists and the spiritualists, are strong enough by themselves to carry out successfully an enterprise of this nature.
>
> But might there not be, behind all these movements, something far more dangerous which their leaders perhaps know nothing about, being themselves in turn the unconscious tools of a higher power?[2]

The "higher powers" push Hinduism, whether it be through Blavatsky's Theosophy, H.G. Wells's Open Conspiracy, Donald Keys's Planetary Initiative for the World We Choose, or Benjamin Creme's Lord Maitreya. This was true in Hitler's case also: Aryanism is Hinduism, and this is the Antichrist's universal religion. It is quite well known that Hinduism with its "embrace that smothers" ultimately absorbs all religions except Biblical Christianity. Syncretism is the attempt to swallow Christianity also by turning Jesus into just another Hindu avatar, a temporary manifestation "for his time" of the "Christ consciousness" that is attainable by all of us. The lie of the Aquarian Gospel—that Jesus studied in India under the gurus—is central to that attempt to turn Jesus into a "Hindu Christ."

As early as 1961, theologian Nels Ferre' said: "The main fight, make no mistake, is between the Christian faith in its inner, classical meaning and the new Orientalized versions....The winds are blowing gale-strong out of the Orient."[3] Those gale-strong winds converted Hitler to the Aryan (Hindu) "myth of blood" and blew with hurricane force out of Germany across Europe and the world at the horrible cost of untold millions of lives.

In the last two decades, those winds from the East have blown into Europe and America a steady stream of Eastern mysticism and assorted "holy men." This is not by chance. It is part of The Plan. The long battle may be reaching a climax. The holocaust will be far greater this time.

Invasion from the East

Most people naively presume that the recent invasion of the Western world by Buddhist monks, Zen Masters, Yogis, swamis, babas, and other assorted Buddhist and Hindu gurus has been a natural development of a growing mutual interest between East and West. On the contrary, it is a deliberate and final stage in the creation of a new world order. Those behind it have enlarged and accelerated their efforts since Krishnamurti failed his lone mission. Not surprisingly, The Plan is still closely linked with the swastika and Hitler's shattered dream of a New Age for Aryan man. That The Plan involves conversion of the world to Hinduism is very well known. What is almost unknown, however, is the fact that much of the credit for establishing today's New Age Movement belongs to a secret but very large worldwide *missionary network* of Hindu and Buddhist leaders known as the Vishva Hindu Parishad (VHP).

The average Hindu in India or elsewhere will protest, often sincerely, that Hinduism "respects all religions and does not proseletize." This false idea is persistently promoted by Hindu leaders in order to justify the strong position taken against Hindus being converted to other faiths. This attitude was publicly proclaimed once again in uncompromising terms at the World Hindu Conference (WHC) held in Katmandu, Nepal, during June 11-14, 1982. "In a strongly-worded statement, the WHC condemned the activities of Muslim and Christian missionaries among Indian people...[and] called for Hindu countries to pass laws banning such conversions."[4] Yet the WHC is backed by the VHP, whose main goal is to convert the entire world to Hinduism!

Such bald hypocrisy can only be understood in the context of Hinduism itself. Because of their belief that all is illusion, Hindus have no conscience about changing meanings of words and denying objective facts when it serves their purpose. Maharishi Mahesh Yogi, for example, was specifically commissioned by his guru Dev to develop a method for converting the world to Hinduism. Transcendental Meditation is that method. It is pure Vedic Hinduism packaged for deceptive sale in the West. Originally Maharishi called it the Spiritual Regeneration Movement. Few Westerners bought it because they were not interested in Hindu religion. So without changing the contents or even the wrapping of the package, Maharishi simply gave it a new label: the Science of Creative Intelligence. Thereafter, Maharishi and his growing organization denied that TM was related at all to religion and insisted, even under oath in court, that it was strictly a science.[5]

Similar deliberate lies are used with apparent good conscience by almost all of the gurus. Paramahansa Yogananda, founder of the Self-Realization Fellowship, was specifically sent to the West by his guru to teach Kriya Yoga, which, like TM, is pure Hinduism right out of the Hindu scriptures. "Self-realization" is the goal of all Yoga, and it means to "realize" that one is God. Nothing could be more religious than that; yet with straight faces all of the Yogis insist that practicing Yoga will not change anyone's religious beliefs. On the other hand, Yogananda claimed that during the 32 years he spent fulfilling his mission in the United States, he had personally initiated (converted) over 100,000 Westerners into Kriya Yoga (Hinduism). Every Yoga teacher is a Hindu or Buddhist missionary, though like Yogananda he or she may wear a cross, insist that Jesus was a great Yogi, and protest that Yoga is not religion but science. This is the most blatant of lies. Yet it has been so widely proclaimed and believed that in America's public schools, beginning in kindergarten—and in almost every other area of society today—Yoga and other forms of Hindu-Buddhist occultism are taught and accepted as science. In contrast, Christianity has been thrown out of the schools and is being crowded out of every other area of life in the "broad-minded" move to replace religion with New Age "science"!

The Vishva Hindu Parishad

Professor Johannes Aagaard of Arhus University in Denmark tells of traveling in India in January 1979 and reading in the newspapers of a World Hindu Conference being held in Allahabad, India. "I immediately began to investigate what it was," related Dr. Aagaard, "but nobody could give me any information." There were 60,000 participants, with many thousands of these coming as delegates to this huge conference from other countries. Dr. Aagaard continues:

> It seemed very strange that so large a conference could take place without even the indigenous theologians and students of religion knowing anything about it....
>
> Only in June, 1980...did I discover that the Vishva Hindu Parishad (VHP) was behind the huge conference of 1979.
>
> Even the Hindus knew nothing more about the organization, or at least they were unwilling to tell me anything.[6]

Professor Aagaard relates how he finally succeeded, only after much persistent investigation, in locating and visiting the headquarters of the VHP in Delhi, India. He also managed to buy the 1979 Conference Report and similar reports from other conferences held around the world. Eventually he located and purchased copies of all of the back issues of VHP publications. Materials printed by the VHP make "a stack a meter high" and are strictly for its own members. The organization operates under such complete secrecy that Aagaard's investigations discovered:

> No European libraries have those publications. It was even more surprising that the public research libraries in Delhi did not know of them, nor are they registered in the common listings.[7]

By poring over the material he had uncovered, Dr. Aagaard was able to confirm that "the VHP is, in fact, Hinduism's international *missionary* council." One of the primary goals listed in its constitution is: "To establish an order of missionaries, both lay and initiate, [for] the purpose of propagating dynamic Hinduism representing the fundamental values of life comprehended by various faiths and denominations, including Buddhists, Jains, Sikhs, Lingayats, etc. and to open, manage or assist seminaries or centers for spiritual principles and practices of Hinduism...in all parts of the world...."[8] And this is the organization that denounces Christians and Muslims for converting Hindus!

Hindu-Buddhist Tolerance and Ecumenism

The close cooperation and relationship between Hinduism and Buddhism in this plan of creating a new world order is revealed by the fact that the president of the 1979 VHP-backed, missionary-minded World Hindu Conference was none other than the Dalai Lama, spiritual leader of Tibetan Buddhism.[9] Yet whenever he tours the West, the Dalai Lama is widely received by church and political leaders as a spokesman for religious tolerance and ecumenism—which simply means converting everyone to the Hindu-Buddhist world view. This kind of "tolerance" has been called "the embrace that smothers." For example, Hinduism, in the name of tolerance for all religions, generously receives Jesus Christ into its all-encompassing embrace. This, however, turns him into a Hindu Jesus, another avatar like Rama or Krishna, the very antithesis of the Biblical Jesus, who has been destroyed in the name of tolerance and ecumenism.

Included under the VHP umbrella organization are such groups as Aurobindo's Integral Yoga, the Practical Yoga of Vivekananda's Vedanta Society, the Theosophical Society of Blavatsky, Rudolph Steiner's Anthroposophy, and virtually every other Buddhist and Hindu sect operating in the West.[10] These are all missionary organizations, and they have converted millions of people to the Hindu-Buddhist world view. Such activity by Christians would not be tolerated for a moment in a Hindu country. India has excluded foreign missionaries from entering its borders since shortly after it gained independence—yet she sends her missionaries to the world protesting their tolerance for all religions and claiming to teach only science. Strangely enough, this lie has been believed and it has become the very foundation of the New Age.

The VHP shares a common leadership with the Rashtriya Swayam Sevak Sangh (RSS), which is the "strongest religious-political factor in India...and knowledgeable sources believe that the RSS will take control [of India] within the next decade."[11] When that happens, it will be forbidden by law in India for a Hindu to "convert" to another faith. Of course, this law will be passed in the name of Hinduism's broad-minded tolerance for all religions. Few people will notice the glaring, hypocritical contradiction, because so many have accepted Hinduism's teaching that all is illusion and we can create with our minds anything we wish. Such is the teaching of the Unity School of Christianity, Religious Science, Mind Science, Christian Science, est (Erhard Seminars Training), and scores of other "positive thinking" and assorted New Age self-help groups.

Hitler's Nazism represented exactly the same brand of tolerance and ecumenism, which may be why it is still so widely respected in India today. He espoused a "Positive Christianity" that embraced every religion within the New Reich Church. The ecumenical slogan was "One People, One Reich, One Faith." Dr. Hans Kerrl, Nazi Minister of Church Affairs, declared: "True Christianity is represented by the Party...the Fuehrer is the herald of a new revelation...."[12] Like the New Age today, Hitler's "new revelation" was a rejection of the Bible and a return to Hindu-Buddhist occultism. Its Jesus

Christ was anything but what the Bible taught. New Age leaders echo this same Hindu-Buddhist perversion of Jesus Christ. Swami Rama, founder of the Himalayan International Institute of Yoga Science and Philosophy in Chicago, explains New Age pseudo-Christianity like this:

> In order to become true members of the Church of Christ, a person must know not who Jesus was, but what Christ is.
>
> Christ, Ishvara, is the very personal force pervading this universe that guides and illuminates every aspirant....
>
> It is not an embodied person, but rather the force in which all individual beings are divine sparks....
>
> Jesus Christ was perhaps the greatest of all Yogis.[13]

In making that statement, Swami Rama has identified himself with the spirit of antichrist by the classical Biblical test given in 1 John 4:1-3. Hitler not only identified himself with this spirit from hell, but he came the closest to being the actual Antichrist of anyone who has ever lived on this earth. He may have been the final test run engineered by the "higher beings" before the real Antichrist appears. The close relationship between Hinduism, Tibetan Buddhism, and Hitler's Nazism, therefore, tells us something important about the coming world religion of the Antichrist. It also tells us something significant about the New Age Movement, which is very closely related to Hindu-Buddhist philosophy. Though it professedly rejects Hitler's Nazism, the New Age Movement is in fact a revival of most of what Hitler believed, under new labels; and often new labels are not even bothered with, and no one seems to notice or care.

Swami Hitler

In India today, even among the well-educated, many Hindus continue to regard Hitler as an avatar who punished the British for their earlier enslavement of India. Many Indian intellectuals still believe that the phenomenal success of the Germans during the early stages of World War Two was due to the fact that "the Germans somehow got hold of [ancient Hindu religious] texts, which had not even been completely published in India...and built their tremendous weapons from the 'recipes' provided by those texts.''[14] The attitude toward Hitler still held widely in influential circles in India today is summarized in the following remarks made by Swami Svatantrananda to a learned Hindu audience:

> Whatever you may say against him, Hitler was a mahatma, almost like an avatar.
>
> He did not eat meat, he did not have intercourse with women, he never even married, and he was the visual incarnation of Aryan polity.[15]

When the Nazi extermination camps, gassings, and ovens are mentioned, many devout Hindu leaders refuse to believe the reports, no matter how well-documented. Those who are more honest fall back upon the "ancient wisdom" in the Vedas, and especially the teaching of Krishna in the Bhagavad-Gita, that there is no death—no one can kill the soul—so what is done to the body does not really count. An avatar, such as Hitler, is not really killing and torturing even when that seems to be what is happening. Anything can be justified by simply 1) remembering that our limited understanding is obscured by *maya* (illusion), and 2) shifting to a "higher" state of consciousness, where the godhood at the end of the evolutionary process is seen as full justification for any intermediate stages.

Hitler's Aryan link with Hinduism was so strong, yet so few people are willing to admit it, because Hinduism has become the prevailing world view in the West. There were deep spiritual bonds between Nazism and Hinduism that Hindu religious leaders recognize and admire. Now and then it slips out, as when Swami Hari Giri Maharaj, an active member of the Congress Party, publicly declared in front of a large assembly: "Sir, you have no right to abuse Sri Hitler and the pandits of Germany!"[16]

The Sacred Swastika—and Initiation

Most of all, it was Hitler's use of the swastika as the symbol of the Third Reich that won the admiration and loyalty of so many Hindus. There is no symbol more sacred in Hinduism. The following words are engraved on a large stone monument honoring the swastika near Delhi, India: "This symbol is most sacred and ancient. At least for more than [the] last 8,000 years, it has been the mark of Aryan civilization and culture. This symbol signifies an implied prayer for success, accomplishment and perfection in every walk of life, under the guidance of the Almighty. It is found not only in India, but in the Buddhist and other foreign countries. All the Aryan scripts (Sanskrit, Pali, Tibetan, Chinese, Japanese, Burmese, Siamese, Sinhalese, Roman, Greek, Latin, etc.) are believed to have originated from this very symbol."[17]

What could possibly be wrong with a symbol that signifies a prayer to God? Clearly everything depends upon who this "God" is. Part of the religious catechism that each SS member had to learn and swear went like this: "We believe in God, we believe in Germany which He created in His world and in the Fuehrer, Adolf Hitler, whom He has sent us!"[18] What "God" sent Hitler to the Germans? There can be no doubt that it was Brahman, the "God" of Hinduism, for in their catechism the Death's Head SS also learned that "the only living being that exists is the cosmos or universe...all other beings...are only the various forms...of the living universe."[19] Again, that is Hinduism, which is Aryanism.

So it was the Aryan God of Hinduism who willed Hitler upon the world. Heinrich Himmler made this clear when he declared: "It has been ordained by the Karma of the Germanic world that he [Hitler] should wage war against the East and save the Germanic peoples—a figure of greatest brilliance has become incarnate in his person."[20] Karma and reincarnation are primary Hindu beliefs that follow directly from the teaching that God is the universe and that we are all God in various manifest forms. This is also the "God" of Benjamin Creme; and it is belief in this "God" that turns Creme's "Christ" into a Hindu avatar—the same Aryan "Christ" in which Hitler believed. As Creme has said:

> ...the Gospel Story holds before humanity the promise of Divinity, a Divinity realised not alone by one extraordinary man—the Son of God—but a Divinity attainable by all who make the necessary effort to expand their consciousness to include the spiritual levels; a Divinity achieved, too, by a

scientific process of which the Christ and His Masters are the custodians—the process of Initiation.[21]

This is Hinduism again, and this is Hitler's Aryanism. The *initiation* is also common ground. Is it mere coincidence that the newspaper of The Planetary Initiative for the World We Choose is called the *Initiator*? Hitler was an initiate and so were all of the Nazi leaders and members of the dreaded SS. Benjamin Creme and other New Agers and/or followers of Lord Maitreya would deny any link with Hitler or Nazism. Nevertheless, the idea of realizing one's own godhood through an initiation process involving "higher" states of consciousness is common to all Hindu-Buddhist occult systems, Hitler's as well as Creme's. There are many in the New Age Movement who would deny that they are part of any movement at all; and they would also deny that they believe anything even remotely related to Hitler's Aryan occultism. They are allowing themselves to be deceived by labels. As Suster so well said:

> As long as our terms are sufficiently "modern," we are on safe ground: yoga we can label *Psychocybernetics*, and magic, *Applied Mind Dynamics*, and this makes them respectable.
>
> Unfortunately, in considering Adolf Hitler, we are also forced to consider the possibility that the world of spirits and demons may have some objective existence....[22]

Today's New Age swamis and gurus expect the same surrender of mind and will as did Hitler, and their "new" or "higher" revelations (reached on drugs, in Yoga, etc.) are usually just a rephrasing of Hitler's Aryan mysticism. We can see with clarity the horror of Nazism; yet millions of sincere Germans failed to recognize it until it was too late. Is it possible that today's world is being deceived by the same lie on an even grander scale? If so, then the coming holocaust will be indescribable by present language or concepts.

If prophecies in the Bible are to be believed (and they have proved 100 percent accurate to date), then Hitler and National Socialism gave us a preview of something far bigger and more evil yet to come. Those who fail to recognize this will become the next victims. We must seriously ask ourselves which is the greater blindness—the inability of those living at that time to face up to what was really happening in the 1930's in Germany, or our refusal today, with all the facts laid out before us, to acknowledge the real truth about Hitler.

The Hindu-Buddhist-occult connection is clearly there for all to see who are willing to face the facts, and so is the equally obvious link to the present New Age Movement. There is, however, another force in the world today that poses as the enemy of Hitler's Fascism, yet is its twin—and the world honors it. This force claims to work for peace and prosperity, when in fact it will play a key role in the coming holocaust.

13
Marxism—
Pattern of the Future

Western leaders seemed genuinely shocked when Soviet forces invaded and seized control of Afghanistan at the end of 1979. Far from surprising, however, the takeover was only a continuation of a carefully calculated plan that the Kremlin has consistently followed for 60 years and repeatedly reminds us by word and deed that it intends to follow until it controls the entire world. This undeviating goal of global conquest is reaffirmed in almost every major policy statement by Soviet leaders. For example, in his important November 2, 1977, speech (on the occasion of the sixtieth anniversary of the Russian Revolution), Leonid Brezhnev declared:

> ...[having] opened the road along which...the whole of mankind is destined to travel...we are advancing towards the epoch when socialism...will be the prevailing social system on earth....
>
> This prospect...is daily brought nearer by our work and struggles, comrades...[in] the continuation of the cause begun by the October Revolution.
>
> May the light of the immortal Marxist-Leninist ideas shine ever more brightly over the world!...Onward, to the victory of communism![1]

The undeniable fact that Soviet-led international Communism is working day and night to conquer the world could not be stated more clearly. Every seeming concession or agreement that Communists make is but a further step in the direction of their unchanging goal. Soviet exile and Nobel prize-winner Aleksandr Solzhenitsyn reminds us that "Waves of immigrants [from Communist countries] have warned you of what is happening."[2] Yet influential liberal leaders still manage

155

156 • *Peace, Prosperity, & The Coming Holocaust*

to steer Western governments along a path of appeasement that assumes the Communist world conquest can be stopped by reasonable discussion. Solzhenitsyn warns again: "...we hear [of]...'dialogue with Christianity.'...In the Soviet Union this dialogue was a simple matter: they used machine guns!"[3] Based upon his years of personal experience and insight, this celebrated author and victim of Soviet oppression declares:

> ...the fight for our planet, physical and spiritual, a fight of cosmic proportions, is not a vague matter of the future; it has already started.
> The forces of Evil have begun their decisive offensive, you can feel their pressure, and yet your [TV and movie] screens and publications are full of prescribed smiles and raised glasses.
> What is the joy about?[4]

Oblivious to the obvious, many church leaders delude themselves and others with continued "Christian-Communist dialogue," as though all we need to do is to "understand" each other. How is it that Westerners refuse to understand what the Communists have been telling us in the plainest terms for years? The *Lexicon of Atheism* (Moscow, 1959) bluntly declares: "Communism is based upon the granite foundation of...materialism [dedicated to]...the liquidation of religion. Communism leaves no room for religion!" Then how would the Soviet Union and other Communist countries join in worshiping the Antichrist?

The Worship of Man

Marxism, like its twin in the West, secular humanism, is the worship of Man in place of God. This is exactly what the Antichrist will demand for himself; and those who have already deified Self will welcome worship of the Antichrist as the next logical step down the path they have chosen. Moreover, like Hitler's fascism, Marxism is also a religion with the same Hindu-Buddhist roots as the Antichrist's coming world religion.

Buddhism, like Marxism and Nazism, is atheism. Buddha rejected both Hinduism's *atman* (soul) and Hinduism's gods. Of course this was only a cosmetic change, for *atman* (individual soul) is a mere illusion (*maya*) to be dissolved at last through union (*yoga*) with Brahman (universal soul). Furthermore, Hinduism itself is atheism, for its millions of gods are mere fictions representing Brahman, the All—i.e., the universe, which itself is *maya*. Hinduism (pantheism) merely puts into mystical terminology Communism's scientific materialism, which is identical to capitalism's secular humanism. Carl Sagan's worship of the Cosmos as "all there is or ever will be" is merely a sophisticated scientific paganism.

The goal of Soviet and Western scientists is the same: by technological conquest of space, time, matter, and disease, to enthrone Man as Master of the Cosmos. Hitler's black magicians of the Order SS hoped to do the same by mystical Hindu-Buddhist initiation into psychic control over universal occult forces. The Yogi's goal of Self-realization—to "realize" that Man is God—was also the goal of Nazism and is the goal both of Marxism and Western secular humanism. Thus the logical person to unite East and West, Communist and capitalist, mystic and materialist in one world government and religion is the Antichrist. Through mastery over the secret cosmic forces, he will demonstrate the most frightening display of psychic powers imaginable. All the world will worship him.

Hitler's astrologers warned him not to attack Russia. That was when his own ego took over in rebellion against his "Unknown Masters." The insanely suicidal orders that Hitler's egomania imposed upon his generals on the Russian front doomed the previously invincible German forces and hastened the Allied victory. One of those Allies, however, carried the satanic legacy of Marxism, and that cancer has now spread worldwide. The billions of dollars in arms and food that America poured into Russia during Hitler's attack are never mentioned in Soviet history books. World War Two is described as a battle between "world socialism and imperialism," and every Communist knows that the leader of world imperialism is that archvillain, the United States, which ultimately must be destroyed. It is self-deception to imagine otherwise. In that same November 2, 1977, speech Brezhnev gave the Marxist view of World War Two:

> We won in the grim, fiery years of the Great Patriotic War, when the country's existence depended on whether socialism

would withstand the onslaught of world imperialism's shock forces and save mankind from fascist enslavement.[5]

To the Marxist, World War Two was merely a continuation of the October Revolution that must lead ultimately to Communist control of planet Earth. The fact that some Western "imperialist" nations helped to rescue the very socialist country that will one day "bury" them is just one more proof of their naivete' and lack of moral courage. As the twin of Hitler's Nazism that was defeated, Communism still advances across the earth.

Whether it is called the subconscious or higher consciousness, Self is being deified today. We have already referred to the Human Potential Movement, which claims that infinite power dwells within man. Public-school children are taught to hold a mental image of themselves as *perfect*. This is also a common PMA visualization technique, taught in success and salesmanship seminars and used by self-help groups throughout the Western world. The same deification of man is at the root of Marxism-Leninism, which controls the Communist world. As Arthur M. Schlesinger, Jr., has said, Communism's similarities to fascism "are vastly more overpowering and significant than the differences."[6] Were Marx and Lenin also controlled by Hitler's "Unknown Masters"?

Marxist Religion and "The Plan"

Clearly Marxism has an important part to play in "The Plan" to establish the New World Order that H.G. Wells, Alice Bailey, and others wrote about. Marxism and the New Age Movement share the common goal of a socialistic world government. Socialist leaders declare, "The ultimate object of...the Socialist International is nothing less than world government."[7] George Bernard Shaw left no doubt about what this would mean: "We, as socialists, have nothing to do with liberty."[8]

Marxism is not just any kind of atheism, but the same apostasy predicted in the Bible that Darwin, Blavatsky, Besant, Freud, Wells, Bailey, Creme, and the New Age Movement represent. In his personal letters, Marx blasphemes and raves against the God he once believed in as a young Christian but now hates with a passion. In a poem he writes, "I wish to avenge myself against the One who rules above"; and in another, "My soul once true to God is chosen for hell!" A friend, Georg Jung, remarked, "Marx will surely chase God from his heaven!"[9] That obsessive ambition—not freeing the masses from capitalist tyranny—is expressed in the following verse that Marx wrote. It sounds too much like Satan's declaration to be mere coincidence:

> I shall build my throne high overhead.
> Cold, tremendous shall its summit be.
> For its bulwark—superstitious dread.
> For its Marshal—blackest agony.[10]

God is treated with scorn and hatred in the many museums of atheism throughout the Soviet Union, but Satan is given a certain honor. As many as 2000 visitors a day pass through the "Devils' Museum" in Kaunas, Lithuania, where about 4000 "devils" are displayed. Compared with the way God is portrayed, the devil seems like a folk hero. The standard speech at the "Devils' Museum" gives one the feeling that the guides have a certain affection for Satan.[11] After all, he hates God too. Lenin wrote:

> Marxism is materialism. As such it is without mercy for religion.
> Every religious idea, every idea of God, even flirting with the idea of God, is unutterable vileness.[12]

What Lenin meant was that the very idea of God and every rival religion must be destroyed in order to establish Marxism as the official state religion in the Soviet Union. In a country where the word for Sunday means "resurrection day," the new religion of Marxism could never hope to compete with Christianity unless its Messiah had also conquered death. In a mystical sense, Lenin lives on to guide the dedicated Communist today. Schoolchildren in the U.S.S.R. are told to ask themselves what Lenin would do in any situation, and are promised that he will "light the way" for them. An elderly delegate told the 1961 Party Congress, "Yesterday I asked Ilyich [Lenin] for advice and it was as if he stood before me, alive, and said, 'I do not like being next to Stalin.' " Her remarks brought prolonged applause, and Stalin's body was removed from the mausoleum.

The veneration of Lenin has gone beyond Hitler worship. With religious reverence, he is spoken of as "this name *sacred* to us." Anything less is *blasphemous*. The untold millions of busts, pictures, pins (such as Lenin's baby picture inside a small red star), postcards, statues, banners, and other memorabilia support a booming Lenin-worship industry that has outdone by far the Orthodox Church's production of religious trinkets and icons. The sacred work of renewing Lenin's corpse in its glass sarcophagus is faithfully performed by the State Laboratory for the Preservation of Lenin's Body.

Guarded by the uniformed KGB troops, the body of Communism's God in its *sanctum sanctorum* on Red Square has been visited by nearly 90 million worshipers to date. With the innumerable larger-than-life murals and statues of Lenin, all across Russia one is accosted again and again by the tiresome Communist *mantras*, like a Soviet version of Coue''s repetitive autosuggestion: "Lenin lived...Lenin lives...Lenin will always live...Lenin is more alive than the living!" As Lenin lives on, so does his declared policy: "The energy and mass nature of terror must be encouraged." This is still the method of today's Lenin-worshiping Kremlin leaders, now headed by former KGB Chief Yuri V. Andropov. As Francis A. Schaeffer recently stated:

> Lenin wrote before he ever came to power that...one of the early attempts at revolution in France was not successful [because]...they had not killed enough people.
>
> We must understand that oppression is not an incidental thing in the Soviet bloc, but an integral part of their system.[13]

Terror and Mass Murder

Marx's ambition has been magnificently fulfilled. The movement he bequeathed to the world has used treachery, violence, murder, and revolution to enslave country after country. Azerbaijan was Sovietized in April of 1920; Armenia in December of the same year; the Ukraine was absorbed in 1923; Estonia, Latvia, and Lithuania became Soviet "republics" in 1940; East

Germany, Poland, Czechoslovakia, Bulgaria, Romania, North Korea, North Vietnam, South Vietnam, Cambodia, Laos, Cuba, Mozambique, Angola, Ethiopia, and Afghanistan comprise only a partial hint of the spreading terror and mass murder that accompanies Marxism wherever it gains power. And as the New Age Movement hides its true face behind a mask of euphemisms, so does Marxism. Enslavement is called *liberation*, ruthless totalitarianism is called *democracy*, and the ironfisted rule by a tiny group of Communist elite goes by the name of *people's republic*.

The new Marxist Ethiopia, once a nominally Christian nation, now bows to new gods under its state religion of atheism. Could Marx but see the transformation, he would be very proud. Beginning in kindergarten, children are taught to play "Red Terror" games, a name given by the Communist leaders to their "campaign to wipe out class enemies by death or rehabilitation." Young adults who have thoroughly absorbed Marxist indoctrination are privileged to join the armed "Red Terror" squads, which roam the countryside arresting and often executing on the spot all people not in full sympathy with the "liberation" of Ethiopia. In one period of two months, an estimated 1000 persons were killed and 10,000 arrested by such squads in Addis Ababa alone.[14] Marxist-Leninist theory *prescribes* terror and violence as *necessary* to purge all reactionaries from society. Hitler used similar methods, as will the Antichrist, but even more vicious.

Why do those who loudly condemn racial discrimination in America or South Africa shrug their shoulders at a terror so great that millions of people risk their lives to escape it in spite of Iron Curtains? Why are there no escapees from the West trying to get into Russia or China or North Korea or Cambodia? The answer is so obvious that it makes the continued popularity of Marxism among intellectuals in the West all the more inexplicable. The 1978 graduating class of Harvard University sat in grim silence as Solzhenitsyn warned them:

> ...the most cruel mistake [was] the failure to understand the Vietnam war...members of the U.S. anti-war movement wound up being involved in the betrayal of Far Eastern nations, in a

genocide, and in the suffering today imposed on 30 million people there.

Do those convinced pacifists hear the moans...? Or do they prefer not to hear?...

Your shortsighted politicians who signed the hasty Vietnam capitulation seemingly gave America a carefree breathing pause; however, a hundredfold Vietnam now looms over you![15]

How often it has been said that if the world had only known Hitler's intention to murder 6 million Jews there would have been a great outcry. It has also been said that such atrocity would never be allowed again. Yet the world leaders *did* know what Hitler was doing; and we have all known for years of far worse crimes on an even larger scale being repeated again and again in Communist countries. Yet there is no outcry in the West as there was against America during the Vietnam War, and no protest marches, not even when the evidence is presented that the Soviet Union and its allies have used deadly chemical and biological weapons in Southeast Asia and Afghanistan in violation of international agreements.[16] In recent testimony before the U.S. Senate, today's Soviet slave-labor camp population was estimated at up to 17 million, with an estimated 500,000 prisoners dying annually from "exposure, disease, inadequate food and hazardous working conditions" on such projects as the Trans-Siberian natural gas pipeline.[17]

An Intriguing Question

As though gripped by some strange, self-imposed delusion, Westerners watch country after country fall victim to ruthless force and brazen deceit, yet somehow manage to convince themselves that the vow of world domination is mere rhetoric. In spite of the murder by Communist regimes of about 130 million people, many Western intellectuals continue to praise Marxism. Arnold Beichman reported in the *Wall Street Journal*: "One of the biggest growth industries on U.S. campuses today is...Marxist studies. [Marxism] is being taught as a moral code, a form of secular salvation, an incontrovertible analysis of failing democracy, and cruel and collapsing capitalism."[18] As one of the approximately 10,000 Marxist professors on American campuses, Bertell Ollman has said:

A Marxist cultural revolution is taking place today in American universities. More and more students and faculty are being introduced to Marx's interpretation of how capitalism works.[19]

Martin F. Herz, former U.S. Ambassador to Bulgaria, made a study of six popular history textbooks used in American high schools. He found that they all presented a view of the U.S. as "basically an imperialist country bent upon killing a lot of innocent people...in the service of something known as the military-industrial complex," whereas Communism was presented as "essentially benevolent, the Russians [as]...more sinned against than sinning, and the U.S. as up to no good in world affairs." America's attempted defense of the South Vietnamese was a crime to be protested; yet the calculated torture and murder of the same people by the North Vietnamese is called "liberation." Though it has retreated on every front for decades, the West still represents "imperialism," while the Communists, who have subjugated nations and enslaved hundreds of millions of people during the same period are seen as "anti-imperialist" friends of the people. How can this distorted view be so widely accepted, particularly on American campuses?

In Cambodia, a very small pacifist country of only 7 million population before the Communists took over, a minimum of 3 million and perhaps as many as 5 million people have been brutally murdered, because it was easier to kill them than to reeducate them into Marxists. The enraged, self-righteous voices that so loudly and sincerely protested the American bombing of North Vietnam are strangely silent concerning the premeditated murder of women and children and the calculated destruction of this gentle land, once a Buddhist showplace, where every temple is now closed and where both priests and worshipers are slaughtered and scattered. Why the silence now? That is an intriguing question and an important one. It demands an answer.

Solzhenitsyn has said that Communist regimes have prospered only because of "the enthusiastic support from an enormous number of Western intellectuals who...refused to see communism's crimes....In our Eastern countries, communism has suffered a complete ideological defeat...but Western intellectuals still look at it with interest and with empathy....''[20] Thousands of professors on American campuses are Marxist sympathizers who extol the virtues of Communism in their classes, put down free enterprise, and ridicule belief in God as unscientific and bourgeois. In a New York speech, Aleksandr Solzhenitsyn cried out in anguished unbelief at the seeming blindness in this country:

> Isn't it possible to assess the menace that threatens to swallow the whole world? I was swallowed myself....I come to you as a witness....
>
> The tanks have rumbled through Budapest and into Czechoslovakia [and since then into Afghanistan]. Communists have erected the Berlin Wall. For 14 years people have been machine-gunned there. Has the wall convinced anyone? No....
>
> The communist ideology is to destroy your society. This...aim...has never changed....[Communism] is a focus of hatred, a continued repetition of the oath to destroy the Western world....
>
> They trade with you, they sign agreements and treaties, but they still...curse you....They never call you anything but "American Imperialists."
>
> ...we are approaching a major turning point in history....A concentration of world evil, of hatred for humanity is taking place, and it is fully determined to destroy your society.
>
> Must you wait until it comes with a crowbar to break through your borders?[21]

Such Montrous Lies

One can sense in the passion of these words the frustration of this famous exile, who came out of Russia with facts and prestige yet his urgent warnings to the Western world have been largely ignored. Judged at Nuremberg and soundly condemned for its crimes against humanity, Hitler's Nazism has been thoroughly discredited all over the world. Yet Marxism-Leninism, which is responsible for the murder of 10 times as many victims, the enslavement of hundreds of millions of people, and the shameless violation of nearly every treaty (at least 50) it has ever signed is praised in our schools, legitimized by our businesses and institutions, and honored among nations. In New York, Communist flags fly in front of the headquarters of the United Nations, which has largely been a vehicle for Communist influence supported by the West. It is therefore not difficult to believe that the coming Antichrist will be honored among nations and worshiped even more fanatically than Hitler and Lenin.

Secretary-General Kurt Waldheim's January 8, 1976, message of condolence to China upon the death of Premier Chou En-lai was a classic example of the mad delusion that already grips world leaders. Together with Mao Tse-tung, Chou presided over what the *Guinness Book of World Records* describes as the greatest massacre in human history (between 34,300,000 and 63,784,000 victims, according to a Senate study); yet Waldheim lauded Chou as "His excellency...a most distinguished and esteemed leader who served his country and his people with great devotion...fostering better understanding among nations and international peace...." On April 7, 1970, Waldheim's predecessor as Secretary-General of the U.N., U Thant of Burma, "praised Vladimir I. Lenin, founder of the Soviet Union, as a political leader whose ideals were reflected in the U.N. charter."[22] U Thant's mentor, Burmese Prime Minister U Nu, earlier declared: "If we now look back to history, we find that Stalin followed the right path."[23]

America provides a large percentage of United Nations financial support; yet United Nations agencies continue to finance Communist takeovers around the world. Even funds given to such highly regarded bodies as UNICEF (United Nations Children's Fund) have been deliberately channeled to groups such as the Vietcong during the Vietnam War or to Communist revolutionaries in Central America and Africa.[24] No wonder Senator Barry Goldwater called for American withdrawal from the United Nations, to be followed by a request that the U.N. move to a new headquarters "more in keeping with the philosophy of the majority of voting members, someplace like Moscow or Peking."[25] More recently, William A. Rusher, publisher of the *National Review,* called for United

States withdrawal from the U.N., "upset because the...United Nations labored for a full year and came up with a list of 22 violations of...Human Rights, and 'not one of them in any country behind the Iron Curtain.' "[26] Typical of the U.N. projects that American dollars finance is the widely distributed UNESCO booklet praising Soviet enslavement of Lithuania, Latvia, and Estonia as "one of the major social triumphs of our day, a model of freedom and democracy." The booklet also declared:

> It was the Communist Party which showed the peoples of Russia the way to free themselves [and gave]...equal political rights to all the nationalities and all the races of the USSR....
>
> The Soviet Union is a brotherhood of free and equal peoples comprising 15...republics in voluntary association on a footing of complete equality....[27]

How can such montrous lies be believed by anyone? Yet they are! There is no logical explanation for the continued high regard with which a thoroughly discredited and murderous Marxism is held throughout the Western world. This gross deception exceeds the Fuehrer's mesmerization of Germany in the 1930's. We seem to be confronted with a diabolical influence similar to the hypnotic power that emanated from Hitler.

Freud's Contribution to Marxist Terror

Soviet leaders declare anyone *insane* who loves God or seeks Him, and they have developed special techniques for "curing" the "mentally ill." Their definition of "mental illness" is backed up by Freud, who called "those who believe in God sick."[28] Professor of psychiatry Thomas Szasz calls psychotherapy a religion and asserts that when it is "allied with the modern state" the result is "a force at once arrogant and arbitrary, despotic and destructive."[29]

This despotic force is destroying morals and lives in the West under the cloak of medical science. In the Soviet Union one sees more clearly the raw evil of psychotherapy as an instrument of the State unleashed against religion and dissent. More than anything else, Soviet citizens fear "treatment" in psychiatric hospitals. This special fear comes through in the following note written by Yevgeni Barabanov on September 8, 1975, and smuggled out to the West:

> Alas, the ink did not have time to dry on the Helsinki Agreement before the witch-hunt began once again....
> ...the threat of losing my freedom is hanging over me once more, this time by means of forcible internment in a psychiatric hospital....
> ...disagreement with bureaucratic ideology and religious conviction are entirely sufficient grounds for being called not simply a criminal, but...a madman....
> Our psychiatric hospitals are immeasurably more terrible than prisons and concentration camps...this cure for dissent is a monstrous moral distortion, a crime against the very nature of man, against the right to think, speak, believe and be free....
> ...it is spiritual murder....

In the West, psychiatrists increasingly usurp God-given conscience and Biblical authority by redefining, in the name of science, "normal" behavior in every area of society. In Communist countries, they extend their sphere by pronouncing what political views are sane as well. Viktor Fainberg, for example, was declared insane because he protested the invasion of Czechoslovakia. He was told, "Your ailment is your dissident way of thinking." Retired Red Army General and Soviet war hero Pyotr Grigorenko, whose tragic story was documented on American television, was twice committed to prison psychiatric wards for the criminally insane because he openly declared his belief in God—a sure mark of insanity for any high-ranking Soviet officer. Fortunately he survived the six years of "treatment" by the KGB and was granted political asylum in the United States in April 1978.

Referring to General Grigorenko's case, Dr. Andrei Snezhnevsky, of Moscow's Serbsky Institute, tried to justify Soviet psychiatry by saying, "You have to understand the Soviet culture to recognize this illness." It is far less complicated than that. Most psychoanalysts even in the West consider faith in God a form of mental illness. In close agreement with Marx, Freud called religion "the universal obsessional neurosis of

humanity."[30] Governments do whatever is necessary to stamp
out malaria or Asian flu. Should they not act in the same
authority to stamp out mental disease and quarantine (im-
prison) those who resist the "cure"? Concerned about the
direction that psychiatry is taking worldwide, internationally
respected research psychiatrist E. Fuller Torrey has pointed out:

> As religious influence has died...there has been a search for
> a new set of absolutes. Psychiatry has been willing to sanctify
> its values with the holy water of medicine and offer them up
> as the true faith of "Mental Health." It is a false Messiah.[31]

To be forewarned concerning the dangers of psychiatry in
the West, we ought to take seriously what it is doing in the
Soviet Union. In April 1979, Valeria Makeeva, an Orthodox
nun, was sentenced to indefinite confinement in a psychiatric
institution for the criminally insane, because of her religious
attitudes and activities. Two people sentenced more recently
for their faith are the Baptists Vladimir Khailo (psychiatric
hospital in Dnepropetrovsk, Ukraine) and Anatoly F. Runov
(special psychiatric facility in Leningrad), where the KGB is
trying to get them to deny their faith in God. Many other examples could be cited. Who could read the following appeal
smuggled out of a Soviet psychiatric "treatment" center by
mathematician and poet V.I. Chernyshov without weeping?
This is not something out of the distant past that can be blamed
upon Stalin. It is happening today.

> In America, Angela Davis was arrested. The whole world
> knew...she has lawyers, people protest in her favor.
> But I...not once did I meet a lawyer, I wasn't present at the
> trial, I have no right to complain....
> ...they tie protesting political prisoners who refuse to take
> food or "medicine," give them a shot, after which they can-
> not move, and forcibly feed and "treat" them...with aminazin,
> which results in a loss of individuality, the intellect gets blunt,
> the emotions are destroyed, the memory disappears.
> Even though I am afraid of death, let them rather shoot me.
> How vile, how repulsive is the thought that they will defile,
> crush my soul!
> I appeal to believers. N.I. Broslavsky, a Christian, has
> languished here for over 25 years. And Timonin...they jeer at

[his] religious feelings, they demand that he repudiate his faith, otherwise they won't let him out.

Christians! Your brothers in Christ are suffering. Stand up for their souls! Christians!

I'm...terribly afraid of torture. But there is a worse torture...the introduction of chemicals into my mind. The vivisectors of the 20th century will not hesitate to seize my soul; maybe I will remain alive, but after this, I won't be able to write even one poem. I won't be able to think.

I have already been informed of the decision for my "treatment."

Farewell![32]

The Soviets are only carrying the basic tenets of psychotherapies to their logical conclusion. It is easy to see how the Antichrist could justify his totalitarian control as the means of "curing" the world once and for all of humanity's "universal obsessional neurosis" with the blessings of psychiatrists everywhere. We may be farther down this path than we realize. It would seem so, judging by the following statement from G. Brock Chisholm, former Director-General of the United Nations World Health Organization and President of the World Federation for Mental Health:

If the race is to be freed from its crippling burden of good and evil, it must be psychiatrists who take the original responsibility....

With the other human sciences, psychiatry must now decide what is to be the immediate future of the human race. No one else can. And this is the prime responsibility of psychiatry.[33]

14

Capitalism—
Over the Cliff

The real battle for human freedom and destiny is not between capitalists and Communists; and by imagining that it is, the West has doomed itself to eventual and certain defeat. Marxism is a religion that is determined to destroy every rival faith. In spite of its worldwide destruction of lives and freedom, Marxism retains its mystical hold upon Western intellectuals because it embodies a rebellion against the God of the Bible that has a peculiar power to seduce human imagination. New Age psychospiritual technologies that seem to demonstrate that Self is God only reinforce this endemic rebellion and hasten the eventual destruction of Western civilization.

Anyone disputing the proven economic superiority of free enterprise over Marxism is denying the evidence of the past 65 years, during which Soviet-led international Communism has failed completely to prove Marxist-Leninist theories. Nevertheless, capitalism will never defeat Communism, because the battle is a moral and spiritual one, which the West is ill-prepared to fight. "In God we trust," once the genuine motto of America, has become for the majority of Americans an embarrassing carry-over of superstition from our forebears. We have doomed ourselves and our children to the fate that William Penn prophesied: "If men will not be governed by God, then they must be governed by tyrants."[1] General Douglas MacArthur warned:

> History fails to record a single precedent in which nations subject to moral decay have not passed into political and economic decline.
>
> There has been either a spiritual awakening to overcome the moral lapse, or a progressive deterioration leading to ultimate national disaster.[2]

170

The Fatal Disadvantage of Western Democracies

Capitalism will eventually lose its battle with Communism, because moral degradation is undermining capitalist democracies much more rapidly than it is Communist countries. Rejecting moral absolutes, Marxism blatantly proclaims its determination to drag God from His throne and destroy all religion. In the West, we hide our rebellion against God behind a facade of broad-minded respect for all religions; we sanctify our practical atheism with Christmas carols and observances of Yom Kippur and Easter. Justifying our hedonistic love of pleasure and selfish lust for money, possessions, and power as the legitimate capitalist pursuit of business or personal success, we salve our consciences with the specious slogan, "Success is not a sin." We are only too eager to believe psychology's lie, preached from modern pulpits, that guilt is a neurosis, a loss of self-esteem, to be cured by positive thinking, rather than what it really is: the universal indictment of conscience that all have sinned against God and desperately need forgiveness. Solzhenitsyn puts it well:

> We have placed too much hope in political and social reforms, only to find out that we were being deprived of our most precious possession—our spiritual life.
> This is the real crisis.
> ...only moral criteria can help the West against communism's well-planned world strategy.[3]

In the name of sophisticated liberalism, Westerners have rejected moral absolutes—exactly what Communists have done in the name of militant atheism. The Communist Manifesto clearly states, "We reject every...moral dogma whatsoever...." However, the Marxist state does not allow immorality to run wild, as we do in the West. On the contrary, it imposes harsh laws and enforces them ruthlessly. Lenin explained it this way: "Our morality is wholly subordinate to the interests of the class struggle." In other words, the Marxist state invents a "Communist morality" that has nothing to do with good and evil but has everything to do with the destruction of whatever stands in the way of Communism's strategy for global conquest.

This places Western democracies at a fatal disadvantage. They tolerate rebellion, anarchy, and a moral deterioration of society that totalitarian Communist regimes—not for moral reasons, but for self-preservation—would not allow for a moment. That will be our downfall, unless some miracle intervenes. Solzhenitsyn has commented: "Strangely enough, though the best social conditions have been achieved in the West, there still is criminality...considerably more of it than in the pauper and lawless Soviet society."[4] Though Marxism has destroyed individual freedom, it has also kept criminals under control. One can walk the streets of Moscow or Peking at any time of day or night without fear of being mugged, raped, or robbed. The same cannot be said of New York (a mugging every five minutes!), Chicago, or Los Angeles. Unless the deepening moral sickness in the West is cured very soon by turning back to God, Western civilization is doomed to go the way of Rome, with the Communists taking over. Unfortunately, as Abraham Lincoln remarked of his contemporaries:

> Intoxicated with unbroken success, we have become too self-sufficient to feel the necessity of redeeming and preserving grace, too proud to pray to the God that made us![5]

Today the Vaccum—Tomorrow the Holocaust

The Western world is plagued by the disintegration of the home, escalating crime, and the rampant use of drugs (not only by teenagers and dropouts but by successful businessmen, screen stars, and athletic heroes). The demoralizing influence of nude bars and openly flaunted homosexuality and pornography, as well as the filth that is dumped on us from TV and movie screens—all under the banner of "liberation" from moral absolutes and protected by our courts in the name of "freedom of expression"—have unquestionably eroded the Judeo-Christian ethic that is so essential to a free society. New Age placebos of "higher states of consciousness," guided imagery, positive affirmations, and Self-deification may seem for a time to have the answer, but the promise of "infinite potential" will prove to be a delusion in the end simply because it trusts Self instead of God and confuses the two.

Once Americans sang sincerely, "Our fathers' God, to Thee,

Author of liberty, to Thee we sing. Long may our land be bright with freedom's *holy light*; protect us by *Thy might*, great God *our King*." More recently, however, psychologists and sociologists have persuaded us that freedom comes not from obeying God but from rebelling against Him and "doing our own thing." Having no "totalitarian ethic" to put in place of the Judeo-Christian one we have abandoned, we are left with a false "freedom" that produces emptiness, restlessness, alienation, disillusionment, and cynicism—the existential malaise that leads only to self-destruction and hastens the Communist victory.

Into this moral and spiritual vacuum, as we have already explained, the Eastern gurus came. They have persuaded us to believe an ancient lie (called by some the "ancient wisdom"): the lie of our own inherent goodness, greatness, and godhood that has enshrouded the Hindu-Buddhist world in untold misery and darkness. Having become the vehicle of this lie in the West, the New Age Movement sincerely believes, in spite of abundant evidence to the contrary, that a new world can be created on the foundation of inherent human goodness and infinite potential. We simply need to begin to love one another. One hears again the haunting echo of the Flower Children's catchy slogan, "Make love, not war," that ended in the disillusionment of Big Sur and Haight-Ashbury. But this time around it is not a few counterculture dropouts waving the naive banner—it is top scientists, university professors, wealthy business leaders, and high-level politicians. Consequently, the destruction that will follow in the wake of this movement will not be confined to Jonestown and hippie communes, but will be a worldwide holocaust beyond imagination.

Love "Rediscovered"

Darwin turned man into an animal. Marx turned him into an evil beast. Freud decided that man was a sexually oriented bundle of neuroses programmed by Oedipal conflicts in early childhood that could be cured by psychotherapy. In a vain attempt to achieve the status of "science," psychology and sociology became very professional and very impersonal. Human beings were studied like so many experimental animals in a laboratory. Whatever rats did became the standard for humans. Leo Buscaglia, who teaches "Love" at the University of Southern California in Los Angeles, writes: "My students and I did a study. We went through books in psychology. We went through books in sociology. We went through books in anthropology, and we were hardpressed to find even a reference to the word 'love.' This is shocking...."[6]

Since then, Professor Buscaglia has brought "love" into psychology and made it famous. Wherever he speaks, lecture halls are crowded to overflowing with admirers, who stand in line for 30 minutes or more afterward just to get a hug from the man who rediscovered "love" and has sold it for a considerable profit. This is not to cast any doubt upon Buscaglia's sincere motivation. His audiences grooving on "love" seem hauntingly reminiscent of those that crowded lecture halls in the 1920's to hear Coue' repeat his famous formula, "Every day and in every way I am getting better and better." Buscaglia's message is even more appealing: we do not have to get better, for we are already perfect just the way we are. We have, however, good cause to question the validity of Buscaglia's brand of "love." Indeed for all his brave words, it seems that he is after all not so sure himself, for he says:

> Therein lies the only certitude, that we can only be certain about uncertainty.[7]

Unfortunately, while love is as beautiful as Professor Buscaglia paints it, the human heart is just as capable of hatred. This raises some serious problems that he does not face. The Bible declares, "Let us love one another, for love is from God...for God is love."[8] It goes on to explain that the supreme act of love was God becoming a man to die for our sins, and that those who believe this good news and receive God's forgiveness in Jesus Christ are "born of God and know God," and because of this are able to love one another. Buscaglia's brand of "love," however, comes from self, which he confuses with God. "Love and self are one,"[9] he asserts, and "self-love and love for others are identical."[10] Whether or not Buscaglia's New Age love is really God's love will become clear to everyone as earth approaches its holocaust.

With uncritical approval, Buscaglia quotes from Anne Frank's diary: "No matter. I still believe that at heart man is good." In typical New Age fashion, he calls this naive statement "Perhaps the greatest tribute to the good in man...."[11] But of course it is not a tribute at all. Far from being a mature judgment based upon experience and facts, it was the wishful dream, the vain hope of a young girl desperate to deny the evil that was about to swallow her family as it already had so many millions. Her idealistic illusion was tragically trampled under the heavy, blood-stained boots of fascist monsters who actually took pleasure in torture and murder. The same fate awaits those who imagine that if we will only lay down our weapons, then the Soviets will do likewise and the whole world will suddenly recognize our oneness with each other and the cosmos, and live happily ever after making love instead of war. Can we really explain away Hitler's holocaust by blindly affirming "that at heart man is good," or escape the far greater nuclear holocaust hanging over our heads by New Age "creative visualization"? As part of their continuing plan for world conquest, the Soviets are preparing for nuclear war. We will not charm them out of it by chanting the appealing mantra, "Love! Love! Love!"

The major weakness in Buscaglia's New Age brand of "love" is that it is self-oriented and therefore has no principles and no commitment except to one's Self. When asked what the first commandment was, Jesus replied, "Thou shalt love the Lord thy God with all thine heart...." In contrast, Buscaglia says: "[One's] first responsibility in love is, and always will be, to himself."[12] "Love given out of a sense of duty or obligation is the greatest insult and therefore not love at all."[13] So Buscaglia's "love" can make no promise to be faithful and true. What kind of "love" is that? Jesus said, "A new commandment I give to you, that you love one another, even as I have loved you."[14]

In the New Age, there simply is no unfaithfulness, no sin, no guilt. Buscaglia says, "No one is guilty. We are all innocents."[15] Presumably this includes mass murderers such as Hitler, Stalin, and Mao. Everything has to be positive in the New Age. Positive affirmation of our infinite potential and inherent perfection is offered as the solution for the evil that Hinduism, like Christian Science, tries to pass off as an illusion. As W. Brugh Joy says, "There [are]...no rights or wrongs...only the infinite interaction of forces...."[16] Buscaglia adds. "We become the powerful force ourselves."[17] There are no absolutes in the New Age, because we are each God, one with the universe and each other, so there is no one to pass judgment upon us. This rediscovered "love" is the same old rebellion dressed in a new suit of the emperor's clothes.

Why Communism Is the Oddsmakers' Favorite

Buscaglia knows how to make us "feel good about ourselves." He declares that man's "main function is to help unfold his true Self[18]...he is still the creator of his own destiny...by listening to himself."[19] This leads to such absurdities as his statement: "If you feel like smearing ink on a wall, you do it. Say, 'That came out of me, it's my creation, I did it, and it is good.' "[20] Hitler, Stalin, Mao, Jim Jones, Charles Manson, et al, could say the same thing: "I felt like murder and destruction, it came out of me, it's my creation, I did it, and it is good."

This blanket sanctification of self-will with its accompanying fear of inhibiting self-expression has made teaching in America's high schools one of the most dangerous professions and has turned the streets of our major cities into jungles and our criminal courts into wrist-slapping mockeries more concerned for criminals than for their victims. Buscaglia's New Age faith in self as perfect in whatever it does only proves G.K. Chesterton right once again:

> When a man ceases to believe in God, he doesn't believe in nothing, he believes in anything.

Nature is ruthless and evolution is utterly without sympathy for weakness. If evolution is true, then Hitler, Stalin, and Mao were right and the rest of us are wrong. Denying our Darwinian faith, we build hospitals, promote charities, and spend billions in research to assist the survival of the diseased and handicapped, thus working against the very evolutionary process that we jealously guard as the one and only "scientific" theory of the origin of life that can be taught in our public schools. With a citizenry that demands the right to do its own thing, Western governments cannot win the battle for this planet in competition with totalitarian regimes that force their enslaved subjects to sacrifice pleasure, possessions, and life itself for the "victory of Communism." It should be no surprise that we have been losing this battle; and the eventual outcome, barring a miracle, is plain to be seen for those who refuse to delude themselves any longer. If we sincerely turned back to the true God, there would be hope. Unfortunately, however, the New Age has enthroned Self in His place.

Selfism and Occultism

Martin L. Gross has called Americans "the most anxious, emotionally insecure and analyzed population in the history of man."[21] Marilyn Ferguson writes, "The search for self becomes a search for health, for wholeness...."[22] Americans spend 100 billion dollars annually on health care, which is about one month's salary for every worker in America! No other nation even comes close to this. Psychology and the New Age Movement have obsessed us with self. Within three pages, Ferguson mentions a new understanding of self, multiple dimensions of self, the merger with a Self yet more universal, self-knowledge, redefining the self, the self released, an unapologetic self, an even larger Self, when the self joins the Self there is power, beyond the collective Self, and a transcendent, universal Self.[23] Buscaglia speaks of loving yourself, the pursuit of self, the discovery of self, a growing Self, self-discovery, and self-realization.[24] Gross goes on to say:

> We live in a civilization in which, as never before, man is preoccupied with *Self*....
> ...as the Protestant ethic has weakened in Western society, the confused citizen has turned to the only alternative he knows: the psychological expert who claims there is a *new scientific standard of behavior* to replace fading traditions....
> Mouthing the holy name of *science*, the psychological expert claims to know all.
> This new truth is fed to us continuously from birth to the grave....The schoolhouse has become a vibrant psychological

center....The need for psychological expertise follows us doggedly through life.[25]

Western psychologists and psychiatrists are the gurus of the 1980's, leading us into New Age mysticism. Under their direction, we have believed the serpent's lie and have mistaken ourselves for God. Carl Jung wrote, "I have called this centre the *self*. It might equally well be called the 'God within us.' "[26] Abraham Maslow's "Self-actualization" is Hinduism's "Self-realization" thinly veiled in the jargon of humanistic psychology. Maslow said, "Therefore, if the individual can touch these depths within himself...he discovers not only himself, but also the whole human spirit. The nonacademic psychologists [witch doctors] of the East have always known this; we in the West must learn it too."[27]

New Age Thinking for Capitalist Businessmen

Within the past two decades, the "down-with-the-establishment" and "up-with-me" attitude in the West has taken a mystical leap to the East that can only hasten the Communist victory. Selfism has now become the new panacea of medicine, psychiatry, sociology, politics, once-materialistic science, and even of business. When the pragmatic, profit-oriented businessman has embraced selfism as the most up-to-date, scientific method of achieving his goals, then we are very far down the road indeed. Training in New Age thinking has taken the Bell Telephone System (AT&T) by storm, beginning with top executives and working its way down through all levels and finally to families and retirees. The 1983 Planning Calendars for Pacific Telephone managers are all in New Age motif. Marilyn Ferguson writes:

> One Aquarian Conspirator who works with top management people around the country refers to the new "businessmen-philosophers" who talk to each other until three in the morning about their own changing values and their discoveries of human potential....
> Big business...is becoming aware of the networks of the Aquarian Conspiracy....
> ...one such underground network [is described]...whose main orientation is radical science and transpersonal psy-

chology and whose photo-copying is furnished by the vice-chairman of American Telephone and Telegraph.[28]

The New Age Movement is gaining followers and influence in the business world. Professor Russ Ackoff, of the famous Wharton Graduate School of Business, University of Pennsylvania, is one of the most brilliant and entertaining speakers at high-level management seminars of America's leading corporations, where he spreads his Eastern world view. Through his best-selling book *Think and Grow Rich*, Napoleon Hill promotes a subtle and dangerous form of spiritism. Hill tells of regularly "visualizing" Edison, Paine, Emerson, Darwin, and five other men he admired from the past as his "Invisible Counselors." In time, these "imaginary figures became apparently *real*," according to Hill, and their advice proved invaluable. In *Grow Rich! With Peace of Mind!* Hill explains that his philosophies and principles were learned from a "disembodied voice" belonging to one of "The Great Masters," who came to him by astral travel.

Like millions of people in every other area of society, businessmen are finding the secret to greater happiness and success, at least temporarily, through scores of different self-help and success seminars. Typical would be Lifespring, which is very similar to est (Erhard Seminars Training). Most of these courses are a blend of humanistic psychology with Eastern mysticism, making them part of the New Age Movement. Lifespring's philosophy is basically the same as that of Leo Buscaglia or W. Brugh Joy: "At the essence, or core, of each of us is a perfect, loving, and caring being...each of us already has everything necessary to achieve and be all we want in our lives...we literally create our experience of life based upon our beliefs about ourselves and how we expect the universe to react to us."[29] Those who take Lifespring and other mind dynamics courses often develop psychic powers such as astral travel and clairvoyance.

The revival of occultism that began in drugs and moved on into Eastern mysticism has become so pervasive throughout our society that it has almost become the norm. Experiences that would have been frightening to almost anyone ten years ago are taken for granted today. One top nuclear physicist confessed at a cocktail party that he receives some of his most brilliant ideas out in space, where he sometimes finds himself "out-of-body" and in the company of other scientists being taught advanced concepts by spirit beings. Of course, in the New Age, very few really believe in spirit beings. Although they may be called that for convenience, they are considered to be like the "imaginary guides" introduced to kindergarteners by Confluent Education or the Inner Teacher that Brugh Joy consults: i.e., just some mysterious manifestation of our own infinite Self.

New Age Occult Technology

Western technology has invented, designed, manufactured, and marketed commercial devices for automatically producing the so-called "higher" states of consciousness that open the door to occult experiences and psychic powers. What used to take a powerful dose of LSD or months of Yoga meditation and vegetarianism can now be accomplished in a few minutes through new devices that are multiplying at an alarming rate. Biofeedback was one of the first such mechanisms. That those who developed it realized what they were doing is indicated by the fact that biofeedback is called "electronic yoga." The Menninger Clinic of Topeka, Kansas, has a promotional film titled "Biofeedback, the Yoga of the West." In other words, biofeedback puts you into the same state of consciousness and develops the same control over involuntary bodily functions—and the same occult experiences and psychic powers—that have been the stock in trade of great Yogis since the Garden of Eden. Elmer and Alyce Green, of the Menninger Clinic, leading authorities on biofeedback, reflect this Hindu-Buddhist occult world view:

> In working with patients we do not often point out that the "detachment" to which we refer is a basic feature of yogic training....There are other similarities between biofeedback training and yoga.
> I guided myself through the development of these ideas [in the book] by the intentional use of hypnogogic imagery. Whenever I was "stuck" I made my mind a blank and asked

the unconscious to get the information I needed from wherever it was, from...the collective mind, or from the "future"....

I believe that this technique, which I developed over a period of years, is not unique to me, but can be learned by anyone who takes time and makes the effort.[30]

The film "Altered States" was about a scientist who experienced an incredible metamorphosis in a "sensory isolation tank" that he had invented. Like so much of the science fiction being presented to us on the screen, it is not as fictitious as many people think. Another ingenious product to take advantage of the boom in selfism looks exactly like the tank in the movie. In order to find relief from the stress in our modern world, "participants...spend up to $17 an hour to float in an isolated, weightless and soundproof environment."[31] One of the producers is a Beverly Hills firm called Samadhi, Inc., with a plant capacity of about 600 of these tanks per month, which sell for about 3500 dollars each. Inside the tank one is entirely isolated from sight and sound, floating alone in an Epsom salt solution. Heartbeat and breathing cause the body to move eratically, which, together with the sense of weightlessness, creates an altered state of consciousness that can produce out-of-body experiences and develop psychic powers. "Psychologist Eleanor Portner, of Pacific Palisades, uses the tank for patient therapy and said, 'Taking away the external stimuli enables someone to move toward the core, their self.'"[32] The Dallas Cowboys plan to install video screens in their tanks and expect to use the unique tanks as part of a future "learning center." One psychologist cautioned that "it can be dangerous for some people to come in touch with themselves."[33] One wonders why that should be, if it is really only oneself one is coming in contact with. Could it be something else? *Samadhi* is a Hindu mystical experience of union with Brahman. The Buddhists call it *satori*. The Fall 1982 issue of *Self Discovery* magazine featured an attractive model on the front cover sitting in yoga position. The caption read, "*Samadhi* is Loose in America."

The "Astral Sounds Cassettes" offer "a natural high!" Distributed by Effective Learning Systems, Inc., the sounds on the tapes were developed by the most modern computer technology and are guaranteed to do much more than simply relax the listener. Users report a wide range of experiences spontaneously produced by the tapes, all the way from "physical sensations of a highly sensual and sexual nature, such intense pleasure [words] can't describe the feeling...erotic sensations" to "explosions of light and color inside my head...visions, images, a kaleidoscopic visual imagery...out-of-body and psychic experiences."[34] The tapes were reportedly "examined by two agencies of the United States Government, the U.S. Bio-Accoustic Scientific Laboratory and the U.S. Army Research Institute for the Behavioral Social Sciences" and were "awarded an official GSA [General Services Administration] catalogue number [as]...approved for U.S. Government and Military purchase."[35] The Soviets have also purchased some of the tapes, reportedly for their mind-control experiments.[36] This should be brought to the attention of the United States Senate as a cheaper and quicker way to *samadhi* than TM, in view of the very favorable Senate "Resolution to Increase Public Awareness of [the benefits of] Transcendental Meditation."[37]

Science over the Cliff

Swami Rama, star performer at the Menninger Clinic and founder of the Himalayan Institute of Yoga Science, has been sponsoring an annual "International Congress of Yoga, Meditation and Holistic Health" in Chicago since 1976. In 1978, the inaugural speaker was New Age leader Dr. Buckminster Fuller, world-renowned innovator and architect and a leading spokesman for the cosmic gospel. The speakers presented to the large audience a blend of Hinduism and Western science that will form the basis for the new world religion of the Antichrist. President Carter sent a message wishing the participants of the congress well. In part it read:

> The constructive melding of Eastern and Western philosophies and the practice in the medical and health field can be of considerable importance to society and to the well-being of all mankind.

In fact the invasion of the West by Hindu-Buddhist philosophies is destroying mankind here just as it has in the East. Participants in the 1977 Congress explained the "ancient wisdom" of Eastern mysticism and what it would do in developing our full potential. Kabbalist Rabbi J. Gelberman said, "God can't do anything without me." "Our nature is identical with that of God," added Yogiraj Roy E. Davis. Chitrabhanu declared, "The belief that you are a sinner hinders your growth"; and Jagdish Dave affirmed, "My consciousness is God." The following words from Jonathan Stone were prophetic:

> I feel that there is coming a world order in which science will merge with monistic philosophy and all the world will be swept up in a new consciousness.
> The one distinguishing feature in that world order will be the credo: "All is one."[38]

That is exactly where science is heading at breakneck speed. A few years ago, Fritjof Capra wrote *The Tao of Physics* to explain "The striking parallels between ancient mystical traditions and the discoveries of 20th century physics."[39] Capra's latest book, *The Turning Point*, purports to show "how the revolution in modern physics foreshadows an imminent revolution in all the sciences and a transformation of our world view and values."[40] Taoism is a syncretistic blend of Hinduism, Buddhism, Confucianism, and spiritism; and this, says Dr. Capra, is where modern science is going. He is exactly right.

As we have already mentioned, following his trip to the moon on Apollo 14, Edgar Mitchell abandoned the exploration of outer space to join the exploration of inner space, the pursuit of the Self or the "God" within. This is the new frontier of science. Increasing numbers of scientists today are deciding that the universe is a living organism, a universal mind, rather than a mechanism. They reason that we can explore the universe by going deep within ourselves, journeying through "inner space" to contact this Universal Self. This is the old occultism, which is fast becoming new science. For example, Brian Josephson, winner of the 1973 Nobel Prize in physics, "has staked his enormous scientific reputation on the possibility that he can gain insights into objective reality by practicing traditional Eastern meditational techniques [i.e., looking within himself]...."[41]

Edgar Mitchell describes the mystical experience that changed his life as "an overwhelming sense of universal consciousness," which answered his questions about the future of planet Earth. As a result he founded the Institute of Noetic Sciences, whose goals can be described as an attempt to get in touch with man's inherent godhood and to tap into the psychic powers available to the human mind in "higher" states of consciousness. Like other leading scientists today, Mitchell refers often to what he calls the "ancient wisdom," which is simply the old occultism that can be traced back through the secret gnostic societies such as the Masons and Rosicrucians to Babylon, Babel, and the Garden of Eden. Dr. Mitchell promotes the idea that science needs to rediscover the psychic powers that the Yogis, witch doctors, and voodoo priests have always displayed.

The President of Mitchell's Institute of Noetic Sciences is Stanford University professor and Stanford Research Institute scientist Willis W. Harman. Like Dr. Ackoff, Dr. Harman is a brilliant and popular speaker before the top management of America's largest and most successful corporations, where he spreads his occult philosophy that is gaining increasing acceptance and application in business. Harman is a close friend of Marilyn Ferguson, who has written *The Aquarian Conspiracy* to document that the "transformation of consciousness" that Capra, Mitchell, Harman, and other top scientists advocate is indeed taking place throughout society.

Approaching the End

This New Age "transformation of consciousness," with its belief that "all is one" and that we only need to make positive affirmations to change the world, could be the final straw that breaks the capitalist camel's back. Buscaglia enthusiastically declares: "I fully believe that we now have sufficient knowledge and understanding of the potential of personhood to make hatred, fear, pain, hunger, war and hopelessness obsolete...we are enough. There is no 'others' [i.e., Communists] to blame—each of us *is* the other."[42] Beautiful words, if they were only true; but the entire history of humanity mocks them.

There is every reason to believe that Beverly Galyean's "imaginary guides," Brugh Joy's "Inner Teacher," Leo Buscaglia's "Self," creative visualization's "Higher Self," spiritualism's "spirit guides," and Hitler's "Unknown Masters" are only different names used by the same Mastermind in enticing humans to join his cosmic rebellion against the one true God by honoring in His place infinite human potential operating through an alleged Universal Consciousness. The Soviets, we may be sure, are in touch with the same "Unknown Masters" under some of the same and different names. They are, however, using the supposed "infinite potential" of their psyches to further the Communist victory, which they never cease to think about and work toward.

As Westerners' naive trust in their ability to use the "light side" of this dark Force for "good" grows, the Communists cheer us on, encouraging our visualizations and positive affirmations of "love" and "peace." There are about 4000 Soviet agents in the United States promoting the nuclear freeze and disarmament rallies. Such demonstrations, however, are not allowed behind the Iron Curtain. The closing words of John Barron in the October 1982 *Reader's Digest* condensation of his new book, *The KGB's Magical War for Peace*, tell the story:

> On August 8, 1982...a cofounder of Moscow's only independent disarmament group is being administered drugs against his will in the psychiatric hospital where he is being held....
>
> And at Harvard, students and faculty reserved some of their loudest applause for a [disarmament] spokesman from the KGB, a man from the Lubyanka Center [KGB headquarters].

Capitalism, the archenemy of Communism (forget detente, that is a fiction) is over the cliff, barely hanging on. The freedom it boasts has been abused and now works against it. The profit motive, once the secret of its success, has become capitalism's downfall. American citizens have turned traitor-spy, betraying their country for the 30 pieces of silver which the Soviets offered for military secrets. Greedy salesmen and businessmen, motivated by lust for profit and power, have sold the Soviets the very advanced technology with which they now threaten us. The vultures are circling, watching their next meal grow more vulnerable, exercising patience, knowing that it is only a matter of time.

This is not to say that Reaganomics will not work. The prophesied unprecedented peace and prosperity will assuredly come, and probably lies just ahead. The financial collapse of the Western world will be postponed. Bit by bit, however, worldwide socialism inevitably spreads and grows daily stronger. Even now there is a distribution of wealth underway as Western democracies, directly or through the International Monetary Fund and World Bank, continue to funnel billions of dollars to Communist and Third World countries in the form of "loans" that will probably never be repaid. As poverty, disease, and famine increase in the underdeveloped areas of the world, the mounting pressure upon Western nations will cause an increasing redistribution of their wealth to the world's poor.

However, there is not enough time left for that lengthy scenario to take place. We will not gradually fall into the Soviet's lap, nor will they destroy us in a nuclear barrage. The new world government will come about through a surprising chain of events—yet they are all logical.

This chain reaction will be triggered by an incredible happening, frightening beyond imagination, that will leave the world in a state of shocked paralysis. In one staggering moment, the United States will have been reduced to chaos and collapse. This event, however, will have rescued the world from a Communist takeover, for the Soviets and Chinese will be in a state of shocked immobility also. It will be "out of the frying pan into the fire," however, for the new world government that will emerge from this vacuum will be far worse than if the Kremlin itself had assumed control.

15

Disappearance And Collapse

The time has now come for us to consider the mysterious event that will cause the sudden elimination of the United States as a world power. *When* it occurs is of the utmost importance to our *contrary scenario*. Based upon Bible prophecies and referred to by evangelical Christians as the *rapture*, this event is the expected sudden removal by Christ of all true Christians from the earth. Numerous books and sermons have thoroughly examined the many Bible prophecies foretelling this long-awaited catching up of the church to heaven. We will not go over that ground again, except to quote two of the principal New Testament Scriptures supporting this belief:

...flesh and blood cannot inherit the kindgom of God; nor does the perishable inherit the imperishable.

Behold, I tell you a mystery; we shall not all sleep [i.e., our bodies lie in death], but we shall all be changed [i.e., our bodies transformed from perishable to imperishable]—

in a moment, in the twinkling of an eye, at the last trumpet; for the trumpet will sound, and the dead will be raised imperishable [i.e., their bodies resurrected and made no longer subject to death], and we [the living at that time] shall be changed [i.e., our bodies transformed to immortality also].[1]

...we do not want you to be uninformed, brethren, about those who are asleep [i.e., whose bodies lie in death], that you may not grieve, as do the rest who have no hope.

For if we believe that Jesus died and rose again, even so God will bring with Him those [i.e., their souls and spirits that have been with him in heaven] who have fallen asleep in Jesus [i.e., who died trusting in Jesus].

For this we say to you by the word of the Lord, that we who are alive, and remain until the coming of the Lord, shall not precede [i.e., be transformed and caught up ahead of] those who have fallen asleep.

For the Lord Himself will descend from heaven with a shout, with the voice of the archangel, and with the trumpet of God; and the dead in Christ shall rise [i.e., their bodies resurrected, transformed to immortality and caught up to be reunited with their souls and spirits coming from heaven with Christ] first [i.e., before the living are transformed and caught up].

Then we who are alive and remain shall be caught up together with them in the clouds to meet the Lord in the air, and thus we shall always be with the Lord.

Therefore comfort one another with these words.[2]

It seems fairly clear from these two Scriptures that: 1) the souls and spirits of those who died believing in Jesus Christ will come with Him from heaven to be reunited above the earth with their bodies when the Lord resurrects them from graves all over the world; 2) immediately thereafter, the true followers of Jesus Christ still alive on planet Earth will experience the instantaneous transformation of their bodies into immortal bodies similar to Jesus Christ's own resurrected body; 3) they will instantly be caught up from earth to join Christ and those just resurrected; 4) this new species of immortal humans will thereafter always be with Christ; and 5) taking place somewhere "in the air" above planet Earth, this reunion will probably not be witnessed or understood by other humans, who will only know that millions of living people and dead bodies have suddenly disappeared from this planet.

It is true that there are other Scriptures which declare that "every eye will see" Christ at His second coming, and that He will descend visibly to the Mount of Olives outside Jerusalem and miraculously rescue Israel from the Soviets and other armies intent upon destroying her at that time. However, many evangelical Christians find the many prophecies of the second coming to be coherent only if there are two distinct phases to this event: 1) the *rapture*, when Jesus catches away His bride (the church) from the earth; and 2) the *second coming proper*, when He visibly returns to the earth, accompanied by His resurrected followers (now called "the armies which are in heaven")[3] to rescue Israel and judge the nations.

For sake of discussion, we will assume this interpretation to be correct. If it is not, that will became apparent in our analysis.

The Importance of Timing

For our purposes, it is not necessary to examine the many Scriptures prophesying the second coming in order to verify or reject the "two-phase" interpretation. That study has been admirably undertaken by many others (though differences of opinion still remain). We propose, instead, to examine very carefully the *consequences* of the rapture.

It is necessary to examine the *timing* first of all. Significantly, it is this very question that divides evangelicals into several camps. We will consider only the two major positions: 1) those who believe the rapture will occur *before* the 3½- to 7-year period of incredible worldwide destruction known as the Great Tribulation (called the pretribulational position); and 2) those who believe it will take place *after* the Great Tribulation (called the posttribulational position). The timing of the rapture must significantly affect the occurrence and sequence of major events forming the framework of our contrary scenario. Those events are: 1) a time of unprecedented peace and prosperity; 2) the uniting of the entire human race together under a) a world government and b) a world religion; and 3) the coming holocaust, which we have identified both as Armageddon and World War Three.

Before we can intelligently consider the consequences of the rapture happening at either of these two times, we must first understand the event itself in detail. What reaction would it create on planet Earth if it actually happened as the Bible indicates?

The Awesome Initial Panic

To be confronted with an event that one knows is absolutely impossible, yet at the same time to see evidence that it has actually happened in violation of all known laws, would drive most persons insane. When it is not merely a personal event in one's private life, however, but worldwide—the disappearance of perhaps hundreds of millions of people from every part of the globe—then there exist all the ingredients for an epidemic of such mass hysteria as no one can imagine. Secular humanists dogmatically declare that they "trust in human intelligence rather than in divine guidance [and]...approach the human situation in realistic terms: human beings are responsible for their own destinies."[4] Brave words, but a very heavy burden to bear when confronted by this awesome and incomprehensible event!

To realize that an event which is *impossible* by all known experience and laws has actually happened would shatter one's confidence in everything from government institutions to one's own five senses. Moreover, the mysteriousness of this event would pose a continuing and frightening threat. Millions of people have actually *disappeared!* Many of them went in broad daylight and plain view, and all of them went instantly, inexplicably, and without a trace. Were they snatched by aliens in UFO's? Were they somehow sucked into a "black hole" or some alternate reality that exists in a dimension side by side with ours? Or is this some kind of cosmic joke, an aberration in the evolutionary process?

New Agers who have been seeking a "transformation of consciousness" will be staggered by a transformation of this proportion and suddenness. The followers of various esoteric or syncretistic philosophies, such as Science of Mind, Unity School of Christianity, or World Goodwill, who look upon man as "a unit of divine life within an ordered and purposive universe,"[5] will be thrown into a blind panic. What kind of "universal order" is this? What has the Universal Mind done? Was it an act of anger? Whatever the explanation, might it not happen again? *When* and to *whom*? Is this good or evil? Can it be prevented by proper meditation or visualization?

Just the panic itself (aroused by fear of the unknown, and not a vague fear, but something very definite yet mysteriously inexplicable) would undoubtedly throw the entire world into a state of chaos if not collapse. Total terror would grip every rational human, obliterating for the moment everything else. Members of the United Nations Security Council, pale and shattered, would gather somehow in an emergency session, their sleep-deprived eyes swollen even larger by fear reflecting a mutual and horrifying recognition of a reality confronting them far beyond their capacity to cope. Computers would hum, tabulating the frightening statistics coming in from around the world, trying to analyze *who* is missing, categorizing in every conceivable way, searching for some pattern that would provide a clue to an explanation, and finding none. Worldwide pandemonium beyond description!

One Unacceptable Explanation

What about the obvious? Wouldn't anyone remember having read books like this and Bible verses that predicted this very event? No doubt many people would; but the same Bible that predicts the rapture also warns that those who are left behind will be given by God a "deluding influence so that they might believe what is false."[6] This implies that those who have read or heard the gospel and rejected it ("who did not believe the truth")[7] will be thoroughly convinced that this event has nothing to do with anything the Bible has to say. There will be plenty of explanations when once the panic subsides. The Lucis Trust has been saying for years that "The Plan is concerned with rebuilding mankind."[8] Such predictions will suddenly be seen in a new light. Prophecies like the following will bring comfort for those who refused to receive the comfort that was offered to them in Jesus Christ:

> Humanity needs to realise that there IS a Plan and to recognise its influence in unfolding world events, even when these appear as hindering factors, operating by means of destruction.[9]

New Age philosophies will gradually evolve an answer that the whole world will accept: a new kind of evolutionary event, a quantum leap by the entire species to a higher order of Being—not a literal "second coming" of a historic Jesus. Humanists would not be able to deny the event, but would staunchly stick to their philosophy of denying "that such experiences have anything to do with the supernatural" but are purely a result of "dynamic natural forces" at work in the universe.[10]

There will be millions of church members left behind—entire congregations, Protestant and Catholic, including many people who claim to be born-again Christians. They will be Exhibit A in evidence that this disappearance had nothing to do with Christianity, religion, Bible prophecies, or an alleged rapture. Those were mythological ideas; the glorious event itself must be explained in New Age terms. For those left behind, the sudden disappearance of family, friends, and acquaintances will give birth to a worldwide religion, which we will deal with later.

Would the timing of the rapture make any real difference? Definitely. The initial panic, for example, would have little effect or significance at the end of the Great Tribulation. The world at that time would already be in a state of chaos and destruction, overcome with fear. The sudden disappearance of millions of people would add little to the situation then. Coming before the tribulation, however, the rapture would create specific consequences absolutely vital to our contrary scenario. As we shall see, this event itself would be the key to bringing the Antichrist to power, establishing his world government and world religion. To those left behind, words such as the following by well-known science writer John White in the *1979 Directory for A New World* would seem prophetic and take on a very special significance:

> The human race is quickly coming to one of history's great divides....Survival demands a change of consciousness...[and] also evolution...which is always at work....
>
> Teilhard de Chardin spoke of noogenesis and a movement toward the Omega point...a mighty leap forward...a vast sorting-out process among people.
>
> ...Higher Intelligence is working....We can become in a sense co-creators with the cosmos...as a new and higher form of humanity takes control of the planet...*homo noeticus*....
>
> The name of the game is survivolution...no one is guaranteed a place in the New Age.[11]

Modern civilization's witch doctors, the psychologists and psychiatrists, will attempt to calm the world. Their brave assurances will rationally build upon present theories, such as the following statement by Carl Rogers: "...the paranormal may change us...perhaps opening up vast new fields of knowledge and power—a quantum leap. And every time new forces or energies have been discovered in our universe, they have changed our perception of reality and have opened new doors and new opportunities for the human being."[12] When the panic subsides, those "left behind" will eventually refer to themselves as the survivors, the lucky ones, chosen by Hierarchy or the Universal Mind or Unknown Masters or the Force to enter the New Age.

Collapse of the United States

Regardless of varying personal beliefs or skepticism, for the sake of argument we are examining the consequences should the rapture happen as those who believe in it expect it to. Since this is a doctrine of fundamentalist evangelicals, it can only be fairly examined in the context of their belief that only "born-again" Christians will be caught up from earth by Jesus Christ at this time.

It is obvious that there may be as many real Christians in the Soviet Union as in the United States; and China, with its estimated 80 million believers, may very well have more than either of these other two countries. It seems likely that Africa also has more real Christians today than the United States. When we consider *who* the Christians are in various countries, however, mere numbers lose much of their significance. In the U.S.S.R. and China, for example, Christians are denied a higher education and decent jobs; it would be a rare Christian who has a position of any importance.

The sudden disappearance of 100 million Christians from Africa might even be considered beneficial by certain parties. It would certainly ease the food shortage, with that many less mouths to feed; and the millions of unemployed who fell heir to the jobs once held by the missing would perhaps consider this a lucky break, never mind how it happened. In the Soviet Union, China, and other Communist countries, the disappearance of agricultural workers, laborers, housewives, children, and a considerable number of prisoners from slave-labor camps would be a hard blow. On the other hand, those troublesome Christians would be out of the way.

In the United States, however, the consequence of the rapture would be devastating. From the president, who claims to be an evangelical Christian, on down through the White House staff, the Cabinet, important advisors, Senate, Congress, and the Pentagon, the missing would come from every strata of society: business leaders, scientists, doctors, lawyers, airline and fighter pilots, soldiers and sailors, key men and women in computer centers. There is no question that if there are only half as many born-again Christians in the United States as the latest polls indicate, then the rapture would put this country into a state of total chaos and collapse.

In the Arab countries, almost no one would be missing; this would also be the case in the Hindu-Buddhist countries. The effect upon Israel would be greater, for there is a strong underground movement of those who believe that Jesus is the Messiah, and it reaches even into the upper levels of government and military circles. However, the effect would not be so great that the country would not recover quickly. Europe would be scarcely affected. It has few evangelical Christians. The state churches throughout Western Europe are poorly attended except for Christmas, Easter, christenings, confirmations, marriages, and funerals. Whether Protestant or Catholic, religion in Europe is more a matter of culture, formality, and habit than of real faith. The situation is different in Norway, which would be hard hit by the rapture; and the consequences in Australia and New Zealand would be greater than in Europe. It is the United States alone, however, that would suffer total collapse.

Dominoes and Desperation

The so-called "domino effect" has been referred to by many writers, but no one has ever imagined such a domino effect as this one. Wall Street is closed, and may not be opened for weeks. This is not only to prevent the panic selling that would make 1929 seem like a bull market, but it will take weeks to unravel the confusion. Brokers, floor traders, members of the New York Stock Exchange and other major exchanges for stocks and commodities, clerks, computer experts, and clients who had placed large orders both to buy and sell have all disappeared. Financial advisors, attorneys, and presidents of banks and other financial institutions have vanished. Owners of large blocks of stocks cannot be located. Stock exchanges in Tokyo, London, and other major financial centers are closed. They do not have the problems that New York has, but they cannot possibly function without Wall Street in operation.

America's entire computer network for credit and banking is in almost-complete chaos. This is not so much because of the disappearance of many of the key people who operate the computers, because that can be solved in a matter of days. The real chaos comes from the fact that as the initial panic has subsided a second wave of fear takes over. People by the millions begin to use credit cards and identification belonging to those who have vanished, as an epidemic of hoarding sweeps across America created by fear of the unknown. It is impossible to conceive the full consequences, in a modern society where everything has depended upon credit and identification, of suddenly not knowing who is missing and who is still here. Planes have fallen out of the sky as pilots have disappeared. The once-facetious saying, "Drive or fly with me at your own risk, I'm leaving in the rapture," has become a horrifying and boggling reality. It is impossible to sift through the scattered wreckage of the numerous downed jetliners to identify burned and torn bits of corpses to ascertain for certain who on the flights vanished and who came down with the plane. As quickly as possible, a new census must be taken; everyone must appear personally at designated centers to be photographed and fingerprinted for new identification. Eventually, out of the chaos, a completely new society, new structures, new standards, a new world order will painfully emerge, as the inconceivable consequences of the rapture are faced up to by a stunned world.

The American military is in a shambles. So many officers and enlisted men and women with key roles to play are missing that the United States is impotent to defend itself. The Mexican Army could march across the Rio Grande and take back Texas and California if it acted swiftly. However, no one is acting, much less swiftly. NATO headquarters in Europe is in a panic. Though it has few missing personnel, its electronic network, defense plans, and day-to-day operations are so closely linked with the United States forces that everything is in chaos.

In desperation, NATO, now under European leadership, moves decisively to provide the United States with replacements for its missing key military personnel. At a slower pace, bankers, auditors, financial experts, and thousands of specialists in manufacturing and management as well as tens of thousands of secretaries and factory workers will be brought to America. The process will extend over weeks; and when the shift in power is complete, the United States and Canada will be satellites of Western Europe, dependent upon though not members of the European Economic Community.

Why Wouldn't the Soviets Take Over?

The collapse of the United States would provide the ideal opportunity for the Soviets to fulfill their long-standing ambition of world conquest. They could take over the United States, dictating the terms of surrender, and Western Europe and the rest of the world would fall along with America like a house of cards. Two factors, however, make this unlikely.

Though all else was in chaos, America's nuclear strike force would remain operational. Regardless of the generals, colonels, computer experts, or whoever else might be missing, such emergencies are what this elite defense group is trained to handle. At least with regard to their professional duties, they would not succumb to the panic sweeping the world. In spite of the collapse of everything else in America, our nuclear strike force would remain intact, ready for instant retaliation; and this would be deterrent enough, particularly since the Soviets would have their own chaos to deal with.

It is not at all unlikely that 50 million people would vanish from the Soviet Union, and even more from China. Of these, several million would probably be agriculture workers, and that is where Russia has one of its most serious and chronic problems. This will be a devastating blow. China will have the manpower to fill in for the millions of missing persons, but the Soviet Union will be very hard pressed. Its bureaucrats will be in a panic, fearing for their quotas and loss of personal power. Even though the missing will almost all be from the lowest levels of society, the chaos in the Soviet Union will be nearly as great, at least initially, as in the United States, but for a different reason: their paranoia for keeping track of their citizens.

Except for a favored few high-level party members, athletes, and other celebrities, almost no citizen of a Communist country is allowed to exit the Iron Curtain to visit the West. True to a lesser and varying extent in the satellites, this is harshly enforced in the Soviet Union, where, for example, right now there are thousands of Jews who have been begging for immigration for years; not only have they been refused, but they have been fired from jobs, harassed, and imprisoned for complaining about the lack of freedom. There are almost always several people on hunger strikes in Russia trying to obtain permission to leave the country to join husband or wife in the West, and those requests are nearly all denied.

As with other Communist countries, the Soviet Union has been plagued by defections: fighter pilots, top spies, athletes, chess players, and opera stars. The borders are guarded, mined, and patrolled by dogs and helicopters to keep the number of escapees down to a trickle. Along the U.S.S.R.'s 41,595 miles of border, the KGB captured more than 2000 people trying to flee in 1965 alone. The Western press reported nothing of these attempted escapes, for it knew of almost none of them. That is the atmosphere: then suddenly 50 million people are missing all at once from the Soviet Union! It is impossible to imagine the wild and mounting consternation that would grip the Kremlin! Waves of suspicion and fear would sweep across the country in the wake of investigations and threatened purges. It might be days, even weeks, before Kremlin leaders could be persuaded that there was not some huge security failure, a reactionary-hatched plot somewhere along their borders allowing for mass escape.

By that time the United Nations Security Council, meeting in emergency session almost around the clock for days, would have the data in hand to convince everyone that the human race has been confronted with a worldwide phenomenon without precedent and beyond comprehension. For the moment, at least, narrow national interests would be set aside. Sharing in a common disaster of staggering proportions and faced by a continuing mysterious threat that is so frightening as to be mind-shattering, the nations and peoples of the world will experience a new sense of oneness, of belonging to and needing one another, such as they have never known in human history. It will be recognized intuitively by almost everyone as the transformation to "global consciousness" that the New Age Movement has been working toward for so long.

Without doubt, for those left behind, the rapture would be a turning point that would change the entire course of world affairs. This would not be true, of course, were it to happen at the end of the Great Tribulation. The rapture loses its significance and effect for those remaining on planet Earth unless it happens *before* the 3½- to 7-year period of prophesied worldwide destruction that culminates in the visible return of Jesus Christ to earth with "the armies of heaven."

When Will the Rapture Take Place?

No one can set a date for the rapture. Jesus said, "But of that day and hour no one knows...but the Father alone."[13] He explained the deception that would seduce humanity just prior to His return, preparing the world for the Antichrist. We have noted that the New Age Movement embraces the very deception that Jesus warned against. If this is not coincidence, then we would expect the New Age Movement to play an important role in recognizing and endorsing the Antichrist.

In spite of the fact that no one would know the "day and the hour," it seems that the Lord wanted His followers to be prepared for His return. The fact that we do not know *exactly* when He will come was intended to keep us in readiness for this event at all times. Jesus said, "Therefore be on the alert, for you do not know which day your Lord is coming."[14] In addition to this general warning, He listed several characteristics of the "last days" so that we would recognize the conditions upon earth that would tell us that His return was drawing near. We have already referred to statements by Jesus that caused us to adopt our contrary scenario:

> For the coming of the Son of Man will be just like the days of Noah.
>
> For as in those days which were before the flood they were

eating and drinking, they were marrying and giving in marriage, until the day that Noah entered the ark, and they did not understand until the flood came and took them all away, so shall the coming of the Son of Man be.

Then there shall be two men in the field; one will be taken, and one will be left. Two women will be grinding at the mill; one will be taken, and one will be left.[15]

Certainly the world before the flood, according to the words of Jesus, enjoyed peace, prosperity, and plenty of pleasure; the last thing they were expecting was destruction. That did come, but Noah was lifted above it in the ark. Yet almost everyone today is predicting gloom and doom, the death of the dollar, worldwide financial collapse, and the imminent outbreak of World War Three through a Soviet attack upon Israel. This has become a popular position among evangelicals as the condition of the world *prior* to the rapture. However, there is considerable evidence for a contrary scenario that ought to be carefully considered.

Those who are convinced that the church will go through the Great Tribulation warn that Christians who expect to be raptured beforehand will not be prepared to endure the persecution under the Antichrist if they have to face it. To find oneself in the tribulation after expecting to be in heaven would definitely, as some suggest, be a shattering experience. However, the argument is even stronger the other way around. Persecution has been less effective than prosperity in destroying faith. "The blood of the martyrs is the seed of the church." Persecution tends to drive one closer to God, whereas peace, prosperity, and pleasure are a temptation to turn away from Him.

Jesus does not warn us to be ready for persecution, but for His coming. In the parable of the ten virgins, *all* sleep peacefully, the wise as well as the foolish, while waiting for the bridegroom. That is not a common symptom of those who are being persecuted, hunted, tortured, and killed for their faith. This parable, and others, certainly fit the contrary scenario of peace and prosperity before the Great Tribulation, but hardly seems the likely attitude of Christians or anyone else in the midst not only of persecution but the greatest destruction the world has ever known.

The Laodicean Church, mentioned in an earlier chapter, and which most Bible scholars equate with the church at the very end, says of itself, "I am rich, and have become wealthy, and have need of nothing." Christ, however, calls it "wretched and miserable and poor and blind and naked."[16] Clearly it is exceptionally wealthy materially, but poverty-striken spiritually. Again, this hardly would be descriptive of a church that has undergone great persecution and exists at the end of worldwide destruction, but it fits perfectly a period of peace and prosperity and plenty *prior* to the Great Tribulation. And it will be during a time of peace and prosperity—"just as in the days of Noah"—that Jesus will return for His bride. Perhaps this is why Jesus warned: "Therefore, be on the alert ...lest he come suddenly and find you asleep!"[17]

It would indeed be a shock to find oneself persecuted to the death under the Antichrist, having expected to be raptured beforehand. However, many people who are expecting everything to get worse and worse as the world sinks ever deeper into ruin could have their faith shattered if instead the world seems to have its problems solved and enters a time of unprecedented peace and prosperity. That could prove to be particularly seductive for Christians who have emphasized "healing and prosperity" as the birthright of all believers. They could even imagine that they had made themselves "rich and increased with goods" by their positive confession. That could be deadly!

Our contrary scenario seems to be reinforced by a very strange warning that Jesus gave: "For this reason you be ready...for the Son of Man is coming at an hour *when you do not think He will*!"[18] Surely someone who had survived the Great Tribulation would not need a warning like that, for there would be nothing else left to expect but the return of the Lord. Yet Jesus seems to be warning that He is coming back for His bride at a time when, if she sat down and thought about it carefully and looked around at conditions in the world, she would say to herself, "Jesus certainly wouldn't come now!" Again this seems to fit our contrary scenario perfectly. The

Scriptures indicate that Christ will return at a time of peace and prosperity, a time of partying and pleasure, "just as in the days of Noah," when the last thing anyone expected was judgment. Indeed, it sounds strikingly similar to the very world which the New Age Movement hopes to build!

Entering the New Age Together

The international network of thousands of New Age groups will survive the rapture intact, with very few of its members missing. Leaders of the movement will quickly see the "Great Disappearance" as positive evidence for New Age beliefs. They have been expecting something to trigger a global consciousness, and now it has happened! Haven't they been talking of a "quantum leap" for years? Did anyone imagine it could happen without some very spectacular phenomenon?

New Agers would see in the Great Disappearance exciting proof that the universe is indeed a living organism, a Universal Mind, of which humans are but single cells. No one is concerned when his body rids itself of cells. This happens constantly. Then why should anyone be concerned that the Universe has somehow in its wisdom marshaled natural forces to rid itself of cells that apparently stood in the way of the great evolutionary leap forward? This event may well be taken as exciting confirmation of the latest theory that evolution happens in leaps. This has been offered as a tentative explanation for the wide gaps in what Darwin thought was a continuous process and the sudden disappearance of old life forms and appearance of new forms seemingly out of nowhere. Now the human race has been privileged to witness and participate in a similar occurrence related to its own species—a quantum leap to a higher consciousness!

It is easy to see how reasoning such as the above not only would develop to calm the panic, but would eventually create a new sense of excited anticipation. Great and good things must lie ahead, incredibly positive developments for the human species! It could also provide convenient justification for the Antichrist when he rids the universe of more cells—those who refuse to receive the mark and worship him. That would also fit right in with New Age thinking: the belief that humans have matured to the point where we can now take an active role in our own evolution.

Out of what appeared to be overwhelming tragedy will come a seeming triumph, with a euphoric feeling of togetherness. There will be a sense of destiny—that the peoples and nations of the world, united at last by this act of Universal Mind, are entering a New Age together. Words such as the following from a Planetary Initiative for the World We Choose flyer would seem so prophetic, so remarkably wise in the context of the Great Disappearance and the panic that followed:

> The Planetary Initiative for the World We Choose is a positive and concerted program being conducted on a global scale. It is designed to offset the widespread sense of pessimism and anxiety being felt by many and to give people a role in choosing their future. It is a program in which every person can have a part, and in which you are needed....
>
> People need to know, first of all, that the shape of the world is of their own choosing, and that they can change it to something better for all of us. The Planetary Initiative is a means for people in many different countries to overcome their sense of helplessness and become part of the process of change.[19]

It will all seem remarkably part of "The Plan" that there were New Age networks and leaders ready with the insight, explanation, and organization just when needed. This will increase everyone's confidence. Surely this must be "The Plan," and it must be working right on schedule under the guidance of Hierarchy or E.T.'s or whatever one prefers to call "them" or "it." Nor will the world be surprised that one man has been chosen by "them" to lead the human race at this crucial point in history. No one will suspect that he is the Antichrist, for no one will believe in those myths anymore.

16

When Antichrist Takes Control

Interpreting Bible prophecies and analyzing trends in current world events is a precarious business that we have tried to approach cautiously and without dogmatism. We have deliberately avoided heavy theological arguments and detailed analyses of Bible passages. Instead, we have analyzed the New Age Movement within the context of the messianic myth and have carefuly considered the likely effects of the rapture, should it occur as evangelicals believe. On that basis, we have found that the scale tips heavily in favor of the pretribulational interpretation, and that the New Age Movement seems to be a major factor in preparing the world for this event and the acceptance of the Antichrist that will follow.

Many evangelicals seem to expect World War Three as the next major event in God's prophetic timetable. A popular view is that the death of the dollar, worldwide financial collapse, and the world's greatest war to date (with its accompanying horrible destruction) are necessary crises to pave the way for the Antichrist's ascension to power as world ruler. However, there are several serious problems with this view. No great world leader emerged from the ruins of World War Two, and there is no more reason to expect one from World War Three. Moreover, it is difficult to imagine that World War Three could be fought without the use of nuclear weapons or come to an end without the defeat of either the Soviets or the West.[1] How the ashes of nuclear war could metamorphose into worldwide prosperity and the sense of ultimate security that characterized Noah's day would take a lot of explaining.[2] Certainly chaos, unrest, unhappiness, and worldwide poverty—not prosperity—would result if the Soviets won. And if they were defeated (as turns out in General Sir John Hackett's intriguing and highly authentic scenario of *The Third World War, the Untold Story*), then how could the Soviet Union and her satellites attack Israel a scant 3½ to 7 years later to precipitate Armageddon? And what of China? This scenario just does not fit the pieces of the puzzle together.

As an alternate view, our contrary scenario suggests that the next great prophetic event will not be World War Three (that will come later), but the *rapture*, coming in the midst of a period of booming prosperity and great optimism over the prospects of peace. This seems to be tailor-made for the Antichrist—far more so than World War Three. Both would produce a worldwide crisis, but the peculiar nature of the crisis created by the rapture seems to be the ideal catalyst.

Skeptics ridicule the possibility of hundreds of millions of people disappearing instantly from planet Earth. Yet New Age ideas are accepted instead, which are equally preposterous if not more so: that human potential is infinite, that we can create our own universe with our thoughts and bend metal with our minds, and that by getting in touch with our "higher self" we can solve all problems, cure all disease, and abolish poverty and war. The Great Disappearance may well be explained as a macrocosmic occurrence related to subatomic materializations and dematerializations, which are commonplace. Eventually, this seemingly impossible event will be accepted as a natural occurrence that substantiates modern evolutionary theory and has nothing to do with the supernatural. That will make it all the more frightening: what might Nature do next?

The New World Order

The masses of humanity will be so shaken by the Great Disappearance that they will be eager to accept stringent controls over their lives. Antichrist's suggestion, then command, that everyone have a number on forehead and/or hand will be accepted gratefully not only to eliminate chaos from extra credit cards floating around that belonged to now-missing persons, but because it will restore to the masses a feeling of personal security: someone cares and is keeping track. People will be grateful to the new world government for putting a number on them and watching over them. Those left behind will want to stick together, for who knows what bizarre development might be next? It is best to trust oneself to the experts, keep in touch, be informed, cooperate with the system.

The Soviets will not have to be forced, for like everyone else they will want to be part of the New Order. They lack the technology and equipment necessary to accomplish this themselves, and will be only too pleased to receive it from the West and to tie into this international network that now controls every person and every transaction. It will usher in worldwide socialism, a long-standing goal of Communists. No one will be able to buy or sell without this mark. Rather than being resented, it will give the entire world a sense of belonging to each other and of pulling together to rebuild after this great crisis. Anyone refusing to cooperate would be looked upon not only as antisocial, but as unworthy of being a part of the New Age. Death will be the penalty, just as the Bible predicts. Nor would that be considered harsh in view of what "evolutionary forces" have just done in disposing of several hundred million people. The stakes are too high, the risks too great—anyone who is not willing to play the game by the rules will have to be eliminated.

With Western Europe, the United States, China, and the Soviet bloc all involved, there is no way the Arabs and Far Eastern nations could survive without joining. It will not merely be economic and military pressure. The "transformation of consciousness" experienced by humanity as a result of the rapture will have left everyone susceptible to the Antichrist's hypnotic control. The incredible psychic powers he suddenly manifests will not only make it nearly impossible to resist him, as the Bible predicts, but will identify him as the logical one to lead the race into the full benefits of this "quantum leap in evolution." After the rapture, numerous New Age prophecies will seem to have been clear references in advance to this incredible transformation in the species. They will even confirm the identity of the Antichrist.

Boggling But Inescapable

As we have already seen, the rapture will be beyond belief.

People will not pinch themselves once, but dozens of times. A similar situation, though not as dramatic, confronts us in the form of overwhelming evidence that this world is in the final stages of preparation for this event and the Antichrist's takeover that follows immediately. We also pinch ourselves many times and ask, "Is it really possible?" There is a natural reluctance to accept even the clearest evidence when it points to something so far beyond our experience that we find it incredible. It is too much to believe that this supernatural event so long foretold and longed for by suffering saints down through the centuries could actually happen in *our* day, and *soon*. So we shrug off as coincidence anything that otherwise would force us to face an event as boggling as the rapture. Later, perhaps; yes, sometime in the future before we die, but not now. That could not be.

Is it only coincidence that so many of today's New Age leaders fancy themselves to be in touch with the same Shamballah force and Hierarchy of Masters as did Hitler and his dreaded SS? Benjamin Creme's Lord Maitreya is alleged to be the leader of these Masters of Shamballah. The intriguing part that we feel compelled to dismiss as coincidence, but the mounting evidence will not allow us to, is the fact that Creme did not dream this up on his own. There definitely has been a Plan, and it represents the other side of the messianic myth. We have already explained why it could not have originated with humans; and we know full well why it did not come from God. Creme is only following The Plan as he understands it and the part he thinks he is supposed to play in it. Exactly who he and Maitreya are and where they fit into the puzzle we cannot say. The significant thing is that so many other people have received the same message, obviously from the same source. It is very much like the diverse characters in the movie "Close Encounters of the Third Kind," who kept getting those strange impressions that eventually led them all to the point of contact. In the New Age Movement, however, psychic guidance is called "transmissions," dictations from the Masters with considerable detail that ties in too closely with Bible prophecy—but from the opposite viewpoint—to be coincidence, no matter how reluctant we are to jump to conclusions about it.

Representative of the many "transmissions" that have been received from the Hierarchy of Ascended Masters and prophecies that have been presented by New Age leaders within the past few years was a very interesting address given by Mary Bailey at the Arcane School Conference in Geneva, Switzerland, in May 1975. The same Shamballah force that Hitler contacted was mentioned several times, as it is frequently throughout occult literature. From the following excerpt it is easy to see how such prophecies could be taken as precognitive warnings and explanations of the rapture:

> Humanity itself must be in a condition of "prepared readiness"...capable of conscious, intelligent cooperation in the manifestation of the kingdom....
>
> The decision to release the Shamballa force during this century into direct contact with the human kingdom is one of the final and most compelling acts of preparation for the New Age.
>
> The Shamballa force is destructive and ejective...inspiring new understanding of The Plan....The energy of Shamballa is [a new and potent]...demonstration of the will of God...[producing] radical and momentous changes in the consciousness of the race, which will completely alter man's attitude to life and his grasp of the spiritual esoteric and subjective essentials of living.
>
> It is this [Shamballa] force...which will bring about that tremendous crisis, the initiation of the race into the mysteries of the Ages.[3]

Turning the Bible Inside Out

A thorough study of the New Age Movement leaves one mentally gasping. In backward euphemisms and often-cryptic language, movement leaders seem to be speaking of the same events as the Bible, but from the opposite perspective. Will the "ejective" power of the "Shamballa force" become an explanation for the sudden disappearance of millions of people? Writing in a Lucis Trust publication a year after Mary Bailey's above speech, Alice Bostock declared: "When the Shamballa force meets a barrier...it proceeds to...destroy all forms that hinder the emergence of a new and better world."[4] So the rapture has been anticipated and explained in advance;

208 • *Peace, Prosperity, & The Coming Holocaust*

but it is not the Christians who are taken out of the world to preserve them from the Great Tribulation—it is the laggards of the species who stand in the way of the great evolutionary leap forward who have to be eliminated for the good of all by the Masters of Shamballa.

Not God, but the Shamballa force is credited with causing a "tremendous crisis" that will transform consciousness. Is this the Master of Shamballa's diabolically clever way of making it seem that the Great Disappearance is just part of The Plan after all, and is tremendously beneficial to human evolution? We have mentioned the Biblical warning that those left behind will be given a "deluding influence to believe what is false."[5] Is the Bible describing what the surviving New Agers will hail as a beautiful transformation to "global consciousness"?

It seems inescapable that what Bailey and others call "the initiation...into the Mysteries of the Ages" the Bible calls receiving a deluding influence to believe the ancient lie. This is where the two opposing messianic explanations clash most sharply. Clearly two nonhuman intelligences of incredible genius and power have been communicating supernaturally with the human race. They speak of the same future events, but in contradictory language. It is therefore obvious that one tells the truth while the other lies. Each individual has the freedom of choice to decide which one he or she will believe. That decision will determine everything else.

In the "deluding influence" which the Bible warns so strongly against, we are dealing with something much more seductive and clever than classical atheism, which simply denies that God exists. The New Age Movement goes far beyond that. It not only rejects the God of the Bible but enthrones man in His place. Then it turns the Bible inside out as the basis for a new world religion. Satanic rituals often involve quoting the Bible backward. Similarly, New Age philosophies seem to be a deliberate attempt to take major Bible doctrines and turn them around to mean exactly the reverse.

The Luciferic Initiation

By this time it should come as no surprise that there is a

long and honored Luciferic tradition behind the New Age Movement. In fact, the "initiation" they refer to is understood by insiders to be a "Luciferic" one. Initiation has always been the only means of entrance into witchcraft covens or other occult groups. Members are called "initiates." Is this why the Planetary Initiative for the World We Choose, with its relationship to the United Nations and involvement by many of the world's top political, scientific, and business leaders within its ranks, chose to call the periodical it publishes *The Initiator*?

One of the most obvious examples that New Age philosophies are Bible doctrines deliberately turned around to mean exactly the opposite is seen in the New Age treatment of Lucifer. In the Bible he is Satan, the deceiver and destroyer, archenemy of God and man, the liar and father of lies, and a murderer. New Age teachings, however, honor him as the one who initiates participants into the New Age. We have already noted that Lucis Trust was originally called Lucifer Publishing. David Spangler, Planetary Initiative Board of Directors member, and a New Age leader, writes:

> Christ is the same force as Lucifer...[who] is an agent of God's love acting through evolution...to make us aware of the power of creative manifestation which we wield....The laws of manifestation...are in essence...a Luciferic principle....
>
> Lucifer prepares man...for the experience of Christhood.... The light that reveals to us the path to Christ comes from Lucifer...the great initiator....
>
> Lucifer works within each of us to bring us to wholeness as we move into the new age...each of us is brought to that point which I term the Luciferic initiation....
>
> Lucifer comes to give us the final...Luciferic initiation...that many people in the days ahead will be facing, for it is an initiation into the New Age.[6]

What of those who do not take this Luciferic Initiation? Spangler comments on that in *Revelation: Birth of a New Age* (pp. 163-64). At the same time he reveals another occult concept that could become an ingenious and accepted explanation of the rapture:

> However, there are a few words which can be said about

where the old world and those attuned to it will go....[they may] be withdrawn into the inner worlds...another level of earth's own consciousness where they can be contained and ministered to until such time as they can be released into physical embodiment again.

An understanding of occult tradition reveals why the New Age initiation is a Luciferic one. Secret societies such as the Rosicrucians and Mormons became the preservers of the Luciferic knowledge that Satan imparted to Eve through the fruit of the Tree of Knowledge, and in turn was passed from Master to initiate: "After being admitted, the initiates were instructed in the secret wisdom which had been preserved for ages."[7] Robert Macoy, a Thirty-Third Degree Mason, credits the blessings of human culture to the occult societies that have preserved the "ancient wisdom" or Mysteries of the Ages.[8] Manly P. Hall of the Philosophical Research Society of Los Angeles explains that "much of the ritualism of Freemasonry is based upon the trials to which candidates were subjected by the ancient hierophants before the keys of wisdom were entrusted to them."[9] Freemasonry's initiation rites became the pattern for secret Mormon temple ceremonies, which participants swear never to reveal under penalty of death, and which hold the key to the Mormon quest for godhood.

This quest to "realize" man's alleged inherent divinity is at the heart of all occult traditions, and is practiced not only by Mormons but by literally thousands of other occult societies. The Tzaddi School of Metaphysics, for example, declares that its purpose is "to promote and present the ancient wisdom... [so] the aspirant can experience the transformation of consciousness proposed by all the great teachers...[called] Cosmic Consciousness...."[10] Benjamin Creme says that the human race will achieve its rightful divinity in the same way that Jesus achieved His: by a process of initiation into the mysteries of which Maitreya and the other Masters are the custodians.[11] The initiation rites for entering Himmler's SS involved an irreversible pledge of loyalty to Lucifer; and so it is in the New Age, though most of the people involved do not realize this as yet. The day is coming, however, when they will, and then it will be too late to turn back.

Lucifer's ambition to become equal with God turned him into the Devil. Following in the footsteps of the first two Luciferic Initiates, Adam and Eve, their descendants have sought their own godhood through initiation into the same occult knowledge via drugs (sorcery), communication with disembodied spirits (necromancy), Yoga (wizardry), and other forms of hypnosis (enchantment or charming)* leading to alleged "higher" states of consciousness, as well as through assorted religious rituals. The Bible seems to agree with David Spangler that this Luciferic Initiation will be obligatory for all people in the new world order under the Antichrist.

Robert Muller, Assistant Secretary-General of the United Nations and a board member of Planetary Initiative, as well as the U.N.'s "philosopher and prophet of hope," believes that Eve made the right choice for all of us. He says: "...in the story of the Tree of Knowledge, having decided to become like God through knowledge...we have also become masters in deciding between good and bad...."[12] Muller believes that we are about to experience a *New Genesis*, as he has titled his latest book. He believes the earth is soon to be transformed into a "showcase in the universe."[13] Aurelio Peccei, founder of and driving force behind the Club of Rome, agrees. One of the "First Endorsers" of the Planetary Initiative, Peccei has said: "I think mankind is building up something within itself whereby it will be able to make a jump"[14]—i.e., a quantum leap in evolution. Peccei believes that it will take "one disaster, one charismatic leader"[15] to trigger this transformation.

The "disaster" will be the rapture, the "charismatic leader" will be the Antichrist, and the "transformation" will be the Luciferic Initiation. For some months afterward, the New Age will be a satanic counterfeit of the millennium. This is the great delusion.

The "666" Messiah of Delusion

The Apostle Paul prophesied that a strong delusion would cause those left behind after the rapture to believe "what is

* See Deuteronomy 18:9-14 for specific prohibition of these and other occult practices, including astrology and divination.

212 • *Peace, Prosperity, & The Coming Holocaust*

false." In the Greek, this literally means "the lie." The Antichrist is not just a charismatic leader who pulls the world together after a big war. With compelling powers of persuasion far beyond those of Hitler, he convinces the entire world of a lie—not just any lie chosen at random, but *the lie* that destroyed Eve and is gaining increasing acceptance today as the "ancient wisdom."

This lie will reach its fullness and bear its awful humanistic fruit following the rapture. At first it will seem beautiful, a "new genesis," a new age of peace and plenty that expresses the universal brotherhood, inherent goodness and godhood, and infinite potential of all humanity—the "transformation to global consciousness" that Robert Muller and other New Age leaders sincerely believe in and promote. God will give man and Satan their chance to build their own utopia, but it will soon come apart at the seams, revealing the evil cancer in humans that only Jesus Christ can forgive and cure. The unrestrained wickedness produced by man's "higher Self" will become such a blight that God's judgment will fall.

The Antichrist's tremendous hypnotic powers will be aided by humanity's obsession with mind dynamics, TM, and other forms of Yoga and Eastern meditation, autosuggestion, self-hypnosis, occult visualization, and a variety of psychotherapeutic placebos, all of which have made humans vulnerable to deception. Humans will not, however, be mere robots or zombies, hypnotized into a trancelike obedience. Antichrist's control over them will be through their prior commitment to *the lie*. Their fate will be something that they have consigned themselves to by rejecting *the truth*.[16] As willing victims, this is what they wanted and what they chose. The extent to which this deception has already gained acceptance is illustrated by the following description of a college course. This curriculum was approved by the State of California, and the therapists it produces are licensed by the state.

> Transpersonal psychology is a blending of the ancient wisdom of the Eastern Schools of enlightenment, the great universal mystics and healers of all time, and the leading edge of Western psychotherapeutic techniques. Its approach leads

to an all-encompassing daily attitude and experience of that state called Liberation, Enlightenment or Actualization....

At the core of the program will be concentrations in Dream Therapy, Tantric Yoga, Shamanism, Music Therapy, Past Life Regression, Psychic Development and Meditation. This program will be an intensive experience of personal transformation and will facilitate a quantum leap in one's spiritual evolution.[17]

Jesus said, "My sheep hear my voice, and I know them, and they follow me."[18] Antichrist's disciples will follow him in the New Age because they know *his* voice and recognize *him*. He will have definite identifiable credentials, just as Jesus Christ had. There is a long tradition, a mythology behind the Antichrist, as there was behind Hitler. Antichrist is more than a political genius with great organizational and leadership abilities. The very same occult traditions that Hitler imagined he was destined to establish will be accomplished by the Antichrist. He will fulfill definite prophecies and thus identify himself as the one they have been looking for. For example, The Aquarian Gospel predicts:

But in the ages to come, man will attain to greater heights...and at last, a mighty master soul will come to earth to light the way up to the throne of perfect man.[19]

The lie is about *perfect man*: that we can perfect ourselves and our world by releasing the infinite potential within us through getting in touch with our "higher Self," which already is perfect. This perfection will be symbolized by the number 666, which the Bible identifies with the Antichrist. There are alleged to be 66 Masters of Shamballa; and in addition, Shamballa itself "is associated with the number 6...the number of idealism and of that driving force which makes mankind move forward upon the path...towards the light."[20] There has been much speculation about the number 666, which is already being used in conjunction with computers, especially in international commerce. Right now it is impossible to say exactly how this number will fit into the puzzle.

An interesting question would be why anyone, the Antichrist included, would be associated with 666 in any way whatsoever,

214 • *Peace, Prosperity, & The Coming Holocaust*

in view of the fact that the Bible identifies it with Satan and ultimate evil. That could be the very reason why those in the New Age would be most proud to wear this number. The use of 666 by the Antichrist would be a defiant declaration that Bible "myths" are rejected; and anyone afraid to take this mark would be considered guilty of harboring superstitious beliefs that would no longer be tolerated in the New Order. Taking this number would be a bold declaration of one's own inherent godhood and emancipation from narrow Christian dogmas of the past, and a commitment to a universal new religion under the New Age Messiah.

Antichrist, Master of the Shamballa Force

We are told that 666 is the number of a man who will be worshiped by the whole world. It reminds one of the "new man" whom Hitler claimed to have seen and whom he described as "intrepid and cruel," and of whom he said, "I was afraid of him." This may well have been an apparition of Satan in human form. Hitler also referred to him as the "God-man, that splendid being," and declared that "he will be an object of worship." Hitler's description sounds very much like the insight that God gave to Daniel concerning the Antichrist.

Daniel chapter 11 seems to come to a break and begins talking about a new king in verse 36: "Then the king will do as he pleases, and he will exalt and magnify himself above every god, and will speak monstrous things against the God of gods....And he will show no regard for the gods of his fathers ...nor for any other god: for he will magnify himself above them all. But instead he will honor a god of fortresses, a god whom his fathers did not know" (verses 36-38).

Several things are clear about this unique person: 1) in one sense, he is an atheist, denying every god there is or ever was; 2) he specifically proclaims his opposition against the God of the Bible, "the God of gods," one of the titles given to Jehovah in the Old Testament; 3) he is an apostate from the religion of his parents; and 4) he considers himself to be greater than any god or God. There seems little doubt that this is the same "lawless one" that Paul wrote of in 2 Thessalonians 2:4, who "opposes and exalts himself above every so-called god or object of worship, so that he takes his seat in the temple of God, displaying himself as being God."

Here Paul gives us just a bit more information, but it agrees with Daniel. This man plainly declares himself to be God by "taking his seat in the temple of God" and there displaying himself as God. No doubt this verse has its primary application in the Antichrist himself performing this act of blasphemy in the temple that will be rebuilt in Jerusalem. However, the human body is intended to be the temple of God the Holy Spirit. Therefore, the spirit of Antichrist would lead humans everywhere to look within themselves to realize their own godhood. This is not only rampant in our world today through the popularity of drugs, Yoga, TM, and other forms of Eastern mysticism, but as we have already pointed out, this is the spirit of the New Age and is characteristic of the entire Human Potential/Humanistic Psychology/Transpersonal Psychology/Self-help Movement.

Daniel tells us something else about this king that Paul does not mention specifically, yet is implied if our interpretation of Paul's remarks is correct. Daniel says that this man honors "the God of fortresses." This Hebrew word has a number of meanings, and the one chosen by the New American Standard Bible seems questionable. The Hebrew word comes from a primitive root that means "to be strong, or to strengthen oneself." This seems to agree with the character of the man. He is strong in himself, claiming to be God. The King James Version translates it "God of forces." Change that only slightly to "force God" and it begins to make particular sense within the context of today's world.

The movie "Star Wars" popularized the concept of a Force that permeates the universe, with its dark and light sides, that can be tapped into and used for good or evil. This modern concept of God has generally replaced all past ideas of God or gods. George Lucas is only one of millions of people who believe in this Force, including many of today's leading scientists; and his film series is an evangelistic tool for converting the world to this belief. This is basic Hindu-occult philosophy, similar to Hitler's beliefs, and it lies at the heart of the New Age Movement.

The Force is believed to be connected to human consciousness; hence the current obsession with "higher" states and "transformation" of consciousness. Devotees of the Force contact it by looking within the "temple of God," as the Bible describes the human heart or inner man, for there it allegedly dwells as the source of infinite wisdom and pure energy that can be manifest as psychic power. Could this be what is meant by "the god of forces"? The best way to determine that is to observe how this same word is used elsewhere in the Old Testament.

This particular Hebrew word occurs a number of other places in the Old Testament (2 Samuel 22:33; Nehemiah 8:10; Psalm 27:4; for example), where it clearly refers to a strengthening of the inner man by God. With this background, the usage of the word in Daniel 11 would seem to indicate that the Antichrist refuses to acknowledge the transcendent God as the source of his strength and life. Instead, he makes the inner force within himself into God, then claims it as his own and thus that he is God, because he can control this inner force himself. This interpretation seems to fit the usage of this word in the Old Testament, and it certainly fits the New Age Movement.

Paul goes on to say that this man of wickedness or rebelliousness is going to deceive the world with apparent miracles, which in fact he calls "false wonders." A miracle can only be done by the transcendent God, who reaches into this universe from outside and thus can transcend its laws. Anything done by human consciousness activating a force inherent in ourselves or nature is not a true miracle, because it is subject to natural laws; and when it seems to violate them, it is a deception. This is the difference between naturalism (which is the foundation of all occultism and which humanists and New Agers insist upon) and supernaturalism (intervention by the transcendent Creator). It is the difference between psychic phenomena and real miracles.

Paul also shows his agreement with Daniel when he says that this man operates "in accord with the activity of Satan, with all power...."(2 Thessalonians 2:9). The Greek word he chooses for "power" is *"dunamis,"* from which we get our word *dynamite*. In other words, a seemingly miraculous force is involved, but in fact it comes from Satan and its effect is to deceive those who are impressed by it. Satan seeks to initiate humans into the Force religion and to channel psychic power through them, persuading them that it is actually some power from within their own minds, in order to convince them that his promise of godhood to Eve and her descendants is true. This is *the lie*, and it can be found everywhere in today's society. One example is the following Rosicrucian ad that promises to reveal "little-known facts about man's *real self*" to those who write in for the free booklet *The Mastery of Life*:

> You and the universe are one. There is no division of supernatural and natural....
>
> The consciousness that directs the physical universe also pulsates in the cells of your being. Behind your thinking mind lies this reservoir of *Cosmic Conciousness*. It is your link with infinity to be drawn upon at will.
>
> The *psychic self* is a slumbering cosmic power that all humans possess but few understand and use....learn to attune to this psychic self, the *Cosmic Consciousness within*.
>
> Orthodoxy has ruled man's thinking too long. If you have an open mind and seek enlightenment, this message is for you.

The Antichrist is called the "lawless one" because he refuses to submit himself to the transcendent God. The ultimate rebellion against the Creator is to insist that the universe is explainable in terms of an evolutionary force that we can manipulate as we please to experience our "infinite potential" and to create our own universe with our minds. This is witchcraft, occultism, Hinduism, Aryanism, Nazism, Marxism, humanism. It is the foundation of the New Age Movement, and it is clearly the religion of the Antichrist.

World Religion for the New Age

The Peace Movement, Antinuclear Movement, and other huge grass-roots movements within the New Age Movement are not so much political as they are religious. Their religion is a universal one based upon the deification of man—the belief that our real self is perfect and therefore we can create a perfect world by working together. This philosophy seems to fit everywhere. It can be accepted by Communists, atheists, and agnostics alike. One of the recurring claims of New Age groups is that their systems will not conflict with any personal religious beliefs. These groups will be intact after the rapture and will welcome the Antichrist as the one who will now accomplish all they have worked toward. There are thousands of such groups that will welcome him ecstatically. Unity-in-Diversity (which brought the Dalai Lama to tour the United States for peace and brotherhood, successfully promoted the *Constitution for the Federation of Earth,* and publishes the annual *Directory for a New World,* which lists New Age network groups around the world) describes its purpose as follows:

> To establish a church based upon universal premises...for those who wish to follow a universal path (often called the "Maitreyan path," the Maitreya being the enlightened one yet to come), and to reach out to all other paths in openness....[21]

No matter how much talk there is of the Divine within and that each of us is God, humans feel a need to follow a leader. Bhagwan (which means God) Rajneesh, the Hindu guru building the New Age city on 100 square miles in Oregon, demands that his followers surrender their minds to him. The Antichrist will ask the same, and those who have been willing to do this for Rajneesh or the thousands of other gurus will find no difficulty in doing it for the Antichrist. They will have been prepared. Roy Masters, popular Los Angeles radio guru, teaches a method of meditation (as Eastern as TM, though he denies it) for putting people in touch with their True Self, which he says is perfect. Yet he does not leave them to follow this inner light; they are still dependent upon his guidance because he is 10 million years ahead of anyone else. The Antichrist will seem even farther ahead of everyone, but he will be the embodiment of Satan's promised godhood, the proof that we can all get there if we only follow him. The world is waiting for the great leader, and they will welcome him wildly after the trauma of the Great Disappearance. As the International Cooperative Council of Nigeria said, quoting a popular New Age affirmation: "...let the Light shine forth, may the expected One reappear to illumine the Shrine of human understanding in the fold of the Cosmology.'' This influential African group describes its purpose as:

> Contacting more and more people in Nigeria who have a consciousness of the New Age and gathering them together...to reach out by letter and bulletin worldwide and help strengthen the linkage of New Age people....[22]

The extent to which New Age ideas have permeated society and prepared the world for the Antichrist is staggering. "Imagine the following: you are sitting in the comfortable red velvet seats of San Francisco's plush Palace of Fine Arts. You are surrounded by over 1,000 successful people, influential in the fields of medicine, psychology, education, and related areas. The personal ease and confidence with which those people seem to move among each other is compelling.''[23] That's how Stanley Dokupil began his description of an important four-day conference in April 1982 sponsored by Marquette University and called "The Power of Imagination—Uses of Imagery in the Healing Arts.'' Dokupil found that much of what was being offered by leading physicians and educators was "an amorphous blend of secular scientific materialism and a disguised brand of occult philosophy.'' It appeared to him that "some of our best-educated professionals are actually practicing sorcery under the pretense of science and health care'' and that the practices they engage in serve "as a fairly wide-scale occult initiation.'' His description of the main content of the conference is as follows:

> The primary focus during the conference, however, was on the use of imaging in order to contact one's personal inner advisor or spirit guide....The technique is a simple one.
> After following the speaker's cue to enter a state of deep relaxation, the audience was told to "fix" on the first image that entered their imagination...[and] once the image was fixed in the mind it should be held and addressed as one would address an intimate friend.
> The inner advisor never lies, they said; it is *always* correct. At the end of the exercise, the audience was told to ask the advisor how and where future contact could be accomplished.[24]

It is not difficult to believe that one day millions of such "inner advisors" will confirm for those who have been following them that the Antichrist is the promised one who has come to lead the human race to ever-higher heights of self-realization. Not everyone will follow blindly, even at first. Those who have not known the gospel will begin to hear it and heed the voice of the Holy Spirit speaking to their consciences. They will refuse to take the mark and will be killed. It may become the greatest bloodbath in the history of the world.

Except for these few million (perhaps a few hundred million) rebels, everyone else will rejoice in the opportunity to cooperate together in building a paradise on earth. It will be one big Self trip. The humanists will love this golden opportunity under the leadership of this incredible man, the World Ruler, to prove the brave statement, "We are equal to immense challenges if we dare acknowledge and release our full humanity....Today we can experience ourselves as we really are, and discover the true authority of our Divine inner self."[25]

But deception and mind control, even under the Antichrist, can only go so far. The holistic vision of interconnectedness of all life, the universal brotherhood, will wear thin. The Prophet Jeremiah wrote: "The [human] heart is more deceitful than all else and is desperately sick; who can understand it?"[26] Jesus said, "For out of the heart come evil thoughts, murders, adulteries, fornications, thefts, false witness, slanders."[27] Infinite human potential sounds beautiful, and so does the Divine within. But what could possibly result from more than 4 billion little gods each expressing his independent right to rule his own life and create his own Utopia here on earth? After all, though brotherhood, cooperation, and universal love sound beautiful, a god is entitled to have things his own way.

The Soviets have tried for 65 years to control the thinking of the masses and failed. It will not work for the Antichrist either, in spite of his incredible powers. After the first euphoria of togetherness and as the trauma of the Great Disappearance falls further into the recesses of the past, the honeymoon will be over. The blooming rose of prosperity that looked so bright and smelled so sweet will fade and wither. Famine will sweep across continents. Riots will spread. With his absolute power, the Antichrist will slaughter millions to keep the world under control. But Moscow and Beijing (Peking) will begin to express some errant independence. Carefully at first. They will not push the World Ruler, but plans will be laid. Then one day all hell will break loose in the Antichrist's plastic paradise...the holocaust!

17
Russia and the Coming Holocaust

The Soviet Union will sooner or later launch a massive assault upon Israel. This is one of the most widely held convictions in the world today. Although they hope it will not happen, and try not to think of it, millions of persons around the world—from Soviet foot soldiers in Afghanistan to Jewish lawyers in New York, from Christian housewives in Los Angeles to Jewish schoolchildren in Tel Aviv, from Arab diplomats at the United Nations to Dutch Reformed ministers in South Africa—know with a strange certainty that this coming holocaust is inevitable. The Kremlin has been plotting this for decades, and the Israelis have been preparing for it. So have the Arabs.

Ever since the establishment in 1948 of the Jewish state of Israel, her Muslim neighbors have been determined to destroy her. For years this was declared openly by all of the Arab leaders. Lately, however, in an attempt to build a better world image, the repeated vows of annihilation have been disguised as public relations rhetoric about Middle East peace plans and equitable resettlement of displaced Palestinians in their own autonomous state. Today the PLO is the only group openly waving the old hate banner of nonrecognition of Israel and pathological determination to kill or remove all Jews from Palestine. However, she carries this banner at the head of a procession that still includes most if not all Arab states following behind, while pretending not to notice.

Most of us are only too happy to be deceived, if the lie is something we want to believe. In spite of the overwhelming evidence of continuing torture, murder, and suppression of human rights, Westerners grasp any propaganda straw to imagine that the Soviets and other Communist regimes have abandoned their goal of global conquest and are sincerely interested in mutual disarmament. This naiveté, as much as greed, necessitated the recent hiring of 300 new agents and investigators by the U.S. Customs Service "in an effort to staunch the flow of [American] high technology to the Soviet Union...a major source of both components for their own military systems and for manufacturing equipment with which to develop new systems."[1] What blindness to sell an enemy the weapons he intends to use against you! That same blindness is why we underestimated the Ayatollah Khomeini and cannot admit today that Islam, now in a worldwide revival, is as determined as the Soviets to destroy Israel and conquer the world. Islamic expert Lance Lambert has said:

> Islam has at its very heart a dogmatic belief that it must triumph....[Ultimately, those who] confess that Mohammed is not the Prophet and that the Koran is not the final word of God, they are only worthy of death....
>
> Westerners cannot conceive of nations that base their whole policy and program on Islamic theology. But that is precisely what is happening [in]...Iran, Libya and Saudi Arabia....
>
> It is the same thing that we witnessed in the rise of Fascism in Italy with Benito Mussolini, or the rise of National Socialism in Germany with Adolf Hitler...it is not just ideological, it is theological....[Muslims] actually believe that their God has given them the oil weapon in order to finally win....
>
> ...can you not see that Israel is an affront to Islam?...a Jewish nation, with a...Jewish leadership [and]...army is an obscenity in the eyes of Islam.
>
> That is why the Bible says there will be war after war—all centered upon those few square meters of land where the Temple once stood, where now the Mosques of Omar and El-Aqsa stand.
>
> Is it not interesting that Syrian President Assad disarmed every PLO man that's gone into Syria....They know they are producing terrorists for the subversion of the whole free world...in this little, beautiful land of Lebanon...the PLO established a worldwide base for terrorism.
>
> The KGB world center for terrorism has been in Beirut.[2]

The Soviet-Arab partnership is a strange and hypocritical one. Their mutual hatred of Israel has temporarily made friends of convenience out of hard-core Marxist atheists and fanatical followers of the one God Allah. The Kremlin hoped that with its backing the Arabs could destroy Israel. They could not. The wars of 1967 and 1973 made that clear. Now the Soviets know they must invade Israel themselves. It is only a matter of time until they do. A nuclear holocaust is coming. It will start with a coordinated Soviet-Arab attack upon Israel that will engulf the entire world. This invasion was foretold more than 2500 years ago by Hebrew prophets, who predicted the horrible consequences for Israel, the Soviets, and the whole earth.

A Long-Standing Prophetic Interpretation

Critics insist that the widely held belief among Christians concerning Russia's coming attack upon Israel is a recent interpretation of vague Bible prophecies that is derived mainly from observation of current world events. On the contrary, based solely upon the Bible, evangelical Christians have held the view for centuries that Israel would possess its land once again in the "last days" and there be attacked by a Russian-led confederacy of nations. The following excerpted analysis of Ezekiel 38 and 39, taken from a six-volume commentary written in England by an Anglican priest about 1815, reveals that the very same interpretation that is commonly accepted among evangelicals today had already, at that early date nearly 170 years ago, been established for some time.

> The prophecy without question relates to the latter ages of the world, when...Israel shall return into their own land.
>
> *Rosh* signifies those inhabitants of Scythia, from whence the *Russians* derive their name...this formidable invasion of the land of Israel...God will defeat it....
>
> The Persians [Iran and Afghanistan] from the east, the Ethiopians from the south, the Moors (Libyans) from the west...shall join with them in this onset...towards the end of the world...[after] the general restoration of the Jewish nation.[3]

In spite of the fact that Israel did not exist and Russia had no empire, Christians clung to this view simply because they knew that the Bible was true. Skeptics laughed. It was a joke to think of Russia attacking Israel, a nation that did not exist. And why would Russia be interested in a nothing place like Palestine? No one laughs about that today. After 1948, skeptics retreated behind the word "coincidence" to explain Israel's rebirth. It was another coincidence that since then the Soviet Union became the dominant world power that the prophets predicted it would. The Soviet-Arab alliance was called yet another coincidence. The excuse for unbelief was wearing thin.

"Son of man, set your face toward Gog of the land of Magog, the prince of Rosh, Meshech, and Tubal...Persia, Ethiopia, and Put [Libya]...Gomer [and] Beth-togarmah."[4] So begins Ezekiel's identification 2500 years ago of the vast army that would attack a restored Israel in the "last days" and be destroyed by God's direct intervention—but only after Israel has been severely punished. Magog, Meshech, Tubal, and Gomer were sons of Japheth, the third son of Noah.[5] Their descendants migrated to Southern Russia, and Togarmah's descendants to Soviet Armenia. Meshech has been associated with Moscow. Ezekiel's identification is unmistakably clear.

Hitler's Haunting Legacy

Ironically, Hitler's murder of 6 million Jews indirectly created modern Israel. Only the lingering horror of the Nazi extermination camps caused the United Nations to vote the partition of Palestine on November 29, 1947, in spite of war threats by Arab nations. Changing its mind at the last moment, the Soviet bloc unexpectedly cast the deciding vote. As a result, Great Britain, which had been preventing the Jews from immigrating to Palestine, terminated its mandate effective May 15, 1948. These unlikely events combined to fulfill the ancient Hebrew prophecies. Just another coincidence?

Hitler's "final solution to the Jewish problem" also lit a new flame in the hearts of the Jewish people everywhere. Traveling throughout Europe near the end of the nineteenth century and warning of coming persecution, Theodor Herzl was able to arouse little Jewish interest in a national homeland. The holocaust changed that. Of the 2 million Jewish survivors, about half were under the age of 12. Housed in some of the very extermination camps where their families had been murdered, these pitiful remnants of European Jewry were further traumatized by discovering that no nation on earth wanted them. Even the United States and Canada turned deaf ears to their cries. In 1946, for example, America allowed less than 5000 Jewish refugees to enter its borders.

No wonder the conviction grew that a Jewish state would be the only safe haven. Driven by that desperate hope, Holocaust survivors defied the might of Britain, whose Mediterranean blockade, ruthless internment of refugees on Cypress, and planned forcible return to their camps in Europe could not stem the tide that began to flow into Palestine. Hitler's cruelty had breathed life into the very spirit of Zion that he had been determined to snuff out. As the closing paragraphs in the booklet that one receives upon leaving *Yad Vashem*, Israeli memorial to the Holocaust victims, declare:

> Six million Jews...were murdered in the Holocaust....The very few who had survived...and who had returned to their native cities and villages in Eastern Europe, were received with anger and hostility.
>
> ...unwanted in their former homes and weary of a life of tribulation and adversity, [Jewish survivors] waged a stubborn struggle for the right to immigrate to the land of Israel. They formed the vanguard of the "illegal immigration" and constituted a powerful force in the political campaign waged for the establishment of an independent State of Israel.
>
> In fact, the majority of the survivors reached this country. Here they have made new lives for themselves and their children.

The irony goes even deeper. Hitler's invasion of Russia set in motion events that transformed the U.S.S.R. into a great world power capable of launching that attack predicted by the Hebrew prophets. In spite of her great losses, World War Two gave Russia everything she needed to pursue her global conquest: 1) the massive military and economic aid supplied by the "imperialist" United States, its source now conveniently forgotten; 2) the incredibly naive handing over of Eastern Europe by Roosevelt, Truman, Churchill, and Attlee to Stalin after the defeat of Germany (Roosevelt's trusted advisor was

Alger Hiss, accused Soviet spy, perjurer, and chief architect of the U.N.); and 3) a new unity among the Russian people and admiration in the eyes of would-be Communists everywhere, through the defeat of Hitler's *Wehrmacht*.

Upon this foundation, which Hitler helped to lay, Soviet Communism was able to build a worldwide empire that today threatens the very existence of the Western nations that helped it to survive. No idle threat, "We will bury you!" is just as much the goal of the present Soviet leaders as it was of Khrushchev. And they are no less determined to destroy Israel than Hitler was to exterminate the Jews. Anti-Semitism is official policy in Russia today. Meanwhile, in America, sympathy for Israel has declined sharply,[6] and anti-Semitism is rising again in Europe. Another holocaust is coming. This is not pessimism, but realism. The Hebrew prophets have predicted it, and they have never yet been wrong. Those who ignore or despise Bible prophesy will one day regret it.

Hatred with "A Certain Demonic Dimension"

Arkady Polishchuk* is a Russian Jew born in Moscow. Educated at Moscow University, where he majored in Marxist philosophy, Arkady became a leading Soviet journalist (managing editor of *Asia and Africa Today*, contributing editor for *Izvestia* and *Pravda*) and radio and TV commentator. Disillusioned, he became an active dissident and traveled all over the U.S.S.R. documenting Soviet violations of the Helsinki Agreements, particularly persecution of Jews and Christians. He eventually became a Christian himself, and is one of the fortunate few to have made it to the West. What he has to say is very instructive:

> Communism was my religion. [As a child] my first song was about Lenin, my first poem was about Stalin, and my dream was to become a Communist [Party] member. I was one for nearly 15 years.
> That's why it was so difficult for me to get rid of my Marxist

* He appears in the film "Russia and the Coming Holocaust."

ideology, because it was my religion. Isn't it a beautiful idea to build paradise on earth? Communism is the only ideology that promises that.

They have been fighting Christianity for 65 years, killing millions of Christians in Soviet camps and prisons. Communism can exist only where no other ideology exists. They have killed other ideologies, but Christianity continues to grow. That is why it's a danger.

Since coming to the West, I found out that you Westerners are also brainwashed. Being a liberal here is good, being a conservative is bad. If you want to put the strongest label on an enemy, you call him a Nazi Fascist, you never call him a Communist—yet Stalin killed far more people than Hitler. Every communist society today is based upon power and killing, fear and brainwashing.

Top church officials from the Soviet Union come to the West to tell about freedom of religion in Russia. The Soviets use these people as diplomats, as part of their propaganda machine, to make you believe there is freedom of conscience in the USSR.

As a boy in the streets of Moscow, I was beaten many times for being Jewish. There is real anti-Semitism there. I only got into Moscow University through unusual circumstances.

The Soviet Union is the most powerful empire in history. Like any other empire, it must keep growing. That's why they always try to expand, into Africa, the Middle East....

The Middle East is a very special place for the Soviets. Not just because of oil...and [military] strategy, but because of Soviet hatred of Jews. Soviet officials just hate Jews. They want to destroy the state of Israel.

There's a certain demonic dimension about this that's impossible to explain.[7]

Why should there be such hatred against Israel and anyone Jewish? The answer to that question unlocks the whole puzzle of Bible prophecy and the destiny of nations. All of God's promises are inextricably intertwined with Israel's destiny. Destroy Israel and you have discredited the God of Israel and the Bible. The Messiah had to be born of King David's family,[8] then rejected and crucified by the house of Israel.[9] It was to Jerusalem that the resurrected Savior would return to rescue the Israelis, now back in their homeland and beseiged by the armies of the world.[10] Had Satan been able to destroy Israel in time, there would have been no Messiah (He had to come before the temple in Jerusalem was destroyed).[11]

If Hitler, or anyone else before or since, could destroy world Jewry, there would be no Israel, no seed of Jacob to return to their land, as promised. Without Israel as a nation today, you could throw out the Bible and declare with Nietzsche that the God of Abraham, Isaac, and Jacob—the God of the Bible—was dead indeed. That is how important Israel is. Conversely, for those who are willing to face the facts, the very existence of Israel today proves the existence of her God. Moreover, He has greater proof yet to demonstrate in Israel, so that at last all the nations, the unbelieving Israelis included, will know for certain that the God of Israel is the God of history written in advance.

Hitler is dead, but his legacy remains to haunt us all. The "almost-Antichrist" was driven by a demoniacal hatred of anyone or anything Jewish. The real Antichrist will hate Israel even more passionately. That special hatred with a demonic quality already possesses the Soviet leaders. Soon it will lead them to make their greatest blunder: invade Israel. In the meantime, Soviet Jews suffer; and again, the world seems to look the other way. This madness betrays itself in strange ways, such as: "A few months ago, the Moscow Jewish kindergarten (the *Gan*) was raided by the KGB. Children were interrogated, left terrified."[12] Convicted on July 14, 1978, on a false charge of treason (his real "crime" was monitoring Soviet violations of the Helsinki accords) and sentenced to 13 years in prison, Anatoly Scharansky has become a symbol of Soviet oppression and anti-Semitism. Begging for help, his wife, Avital, writes:

> In December 1980, in a Soviet prison camp, Anatoly observed Hannukah. He dried bread from his daily ration, hardened it and carved out eight small indentations. For days, he scraped and collected oil from machinery and vehicles. He tore his own clothing to make wicks. Bread, crankcase oil, and cloth—these were his Hannukah lights. The guards were infuriated.
>
> He was sentenced to the special "punishment cell" for 15

days. His prayer book (a present I sent him) and his Jewish calendar were confiscated....

I will tell you what is in my heart:

My husband's life or death depends on the whim of the government. They—like all the morally bankrupt—constantly look over their shoulders to see if they are being watched as they commit their crimes.

Anatoly is but one of the Prisoners of Conscience in the Soviet Union—one of many whose only crime is a passion for freedom to live as a Jew. You must help them....

The Soviets want us to forget the Jews who are trapped, the Jews who suffer in prison camps and jails, the Jews who dream of leaving. You must let the Soviet government know that you are watching![13]

"The Jewish Problem"

For many centuries, unbelievers scoffed at the seemingly ridiculous predictions by Hebrew prophets that the climactic battle of world history would one day be fought over Israel—a nation that did not even exist for 2500 years. No one laughs about Israel now, certainly not the Arabs or Soviets. It is amazing but true that in today's world of 4.6 billion people the tiny (2.3 million population on a pitifully few square miles of reclaimed swamp and desert), newly reborn nation of Israel has become the great issue that entangles superpowers like a net and drags them ever closer to the brink of destruction—exactly as the Bible predicts.[14] Israel is an astonishing phenomenon. As Marv Rosenthal has said:

Since Israel's rebirth, she has fought five wars for national survival in her thirty-four years...at the same time, absorbing more than two and one-half million of her scattered sons and daughters from among more than one hundred nations of the world.

Military preparedness dictates that...almost 50% of her gross national product goes for defense. Experts acknowledge that she ranks fourth in the world in military capability, behind the United States, the Soviet Union and Red China. This is an absolutely astounding statistic....

Her pilots possess unique dedication, unsurpassed training and more combat experience than any pilots in the world. Their

achievements are unexcelled in the annals of aviation history.
During the past nineteen centuries...Jews went unresistingly and lamblike to their deaths. Those days are forever gone. Today the Jewish nation has become a lion committed to roar if necessary in the defense of her homeland.[15]

The Hebrew prophets were either egotistical fools blinded by Zionist nationalism or else they were inspired by God. The fact that their prophecies have been fulfilled one by one in meticulous detail down through the centuries and are still being fulfilled today argues strongly for divine inspiration. What audacity—or what prophetic insight—for Zechariah to declare more than 2000 years ago that in the "last days" Jerusalem would become "a cup of trembling...a burdensome stone" for the entire world that would eventually "cut in pieces...all the people of the earth...gathered together against it."[16] It still does not make sense. Why the destiny of the whole world should be so inextricably intertwined with tiny Israel seems as mysterious as the source of Hitler's irresistible power. Yet everyone knows this today by reading the newspapers. How did Israel's prophets know this more than 2000 years in advance? We had better pay close attention to what they said.

What diabolical insight caused Hitler to place such importance upon what he called "the Jewish problem"? Under that satanic inspiration, the "solution" he tried to effect was to eliminate the Jews entirely. Yet out of that very slaughter came the rebirth of Israel, thereby resurrecting "the Jewish problem" and eventually provoking Russia's future attack from the north to drag her into the very destruction of her armed forces that, strangely enough, will finally fulfill Hitler's mad design. The Antichrist's psychotic hatred of Israel will suck him into the same swirling maelstrom of annihilation.

It would take more faith to call this all coincidence or fate than to believe that the one true God inspired these prophecies. This does not mean that God's foreknowledge makes him the Author of the evils that His prophets predict. Humans have the power of free choice, so the evil they perpetrate, far from being God's fault, is the result of their rebellious abuse of the free will He has given them. That He does not interfere and prevent all evil is not proof of God's impotence or lack of love, but of His patience. He will not break our wills, turning us into robots, for that would destroy our capacity to love or be loved. He seeks to woo us to respond to His love. Nevertheless, He will have the last word. And that day, called "the day of the Lord"[17] and "the day of vengeance of our God,"[18] seems to be hastening upon us.

Inside Antichrist's New Age Paradise

How will Antichrist "solve" the "Jewish problem"? What kind of person will he be and how will he rule the world? Many evangelical books and films depict him as a monster who simply does evil for the sake of evil. On the contrary, there is every reason to believe that he will inspire his followers as the ultimate example of perfect humanity. At least at the first, they will not only worship him as their hero, but love and admire him. And his admirers—millions of New Agers in thousands of network groups around the world—will be sincerely implementing Antichrist's programs in the name of peace, brotherhood, and love.

The world will be deluded before it is terrorized, and many people, if not the majority, will never admit the horror and evil that will eventually engulf them all. Antichrist will be the embodiment of evil and terror only to those who recognize who he really is. To all the others, he will embody the perfect realization of New Age philosophies they have believed. He will not sprout horns, dress in red, nor carry a pitchfork. On the contrary, his government methods and personal tactics will be a logical extension and practical application of the very Hindu-Buddhist-occult New Age foundation that has been carefully laid over a period of years in preparing the world to recognize and receive the coming world ruler.

Many gurus and cult leaders have prepared the way, like John the Baptist did for Jesus, though in a different manner. Maharishi Mahesh Yogi has said in his commentary on the *Bhagavad-Gita* that there is a higher "state of consciousness which will justify any action...even to kill in love, in support of the purpose of evolution."[19] This state of consciousness is the goal of TM, as it is for all Yoga and other Eastern meditation techniques popular in the New Age Movement. It is not difficult at all to imagine that Antichrist's faithful followers would exterminate "in love, in support of the purpose of evolution" all those standing in the way of realizing the New Age dream. Long before Maharishi or Jim Jones came along, Brigham Young said basically the same thing from his pulpit in Salt Lake City: "This is loving our neighbor as ourselves...if it is necessary to spill his blood on earth in order that he may be saved, *spill it*!" Brigham taught that some sins could only be atoned for, not by Jesus Christ, but by the shedding of the sinner's own blood. Antichrist will have as good a justification for mass murder; and his explanations will probably be greeted no less enthusiastically than the Mormons greeted Prophet Young's doctrine of "blood atonement"—with cheers, applause, and shouts of "Hear! Hear!"

Krishna's beautiful advice to Arjuna that it was his duty to kill his relatives is justified in Maharishi's eyes by belief in reincarnation. Charlie Manson justified himself by the same Hindu doctrine, which is an integral part of the "ancient wisdom" that lies at the foundation of the New Age and will probably be the key tenet of Antichrist's worldwide religion. The bloodbath during the Great Tribulation will make Hitler and Mao seem small-time. To those in "higher" states of consciousness under Antichrist's hypnotic control, the slaughter of millions will not have happened. Christian Scientists and members of other Mind Science cults will see no evil at all during the entire Great Tribulation, for Antichrist will help them to see "only good."

To admit that a holocaust is taking place is to harbor negative thoughts, a heresy in the New Age. One must not allow his mind to be influenced by the delusion of disease or death, much less of murder or other illusions. That the horrors of the Antichrist's slaughter of millions of people could be ignored and that joy could be experienced amidst chaos and destruction by those grooving on "higher" states of consciousness is seen in this statement of Eckankar, which is only one of many Eastern mystical cults widely accepted in America today:

> The most distinguising facet of the ECKist's existence is a
> sense of joy, a joy which arises from his knowledge that death

234 • Peace, Prosperity, & The Coming Holocaust

is a myth, that the word "life" has a reality that encompasses states of consciousness beyond man's imagination; and the only thing which holds one from the realization of these states is his own self-limiting concepts.[20]

Strange Happenings in Jerusalem

Prophecy can be difficult to interpret in detail. We have not attempted to do that. Instead, we have concentrated upon what seems most clear. Even direct statements, however, present a peculiar picture. There are, for example, those strange street preachers troubling Jerusalem: God's "two witnesses [who]...prophesy for twelve hundred and sixty days, clothed in sackcloth."[21] The Antichrist is apparently forced to tolerate them during the first half of the seven-year period because their powers are even greater than his.[22]

During this time, Jerusalem is the scene of another paradox: Solomon's Temple is being rebuilt, in spite of its unforgivable offense to the Arabs and its total incompatibility with the new world religion. The Israelis feel compelled by "tradition" to get back to their roots. Oddly enough, the world ruler has given his approval[23]—the project could not proceed without that—and the nations can only watch and wonder. Unknown to the Israelis or anyone else, Antichrist has his own plans for this incredibly beautiful edifice that will settle the Israeli-Arab dispute over Jerusalem once and for all.

These first 42 months are a time of expanding prosperity and growing euphoria. And the wealth is being shared. Benjamin Creme says that Maitreya will establish both a world socialist order and a world religion.[24] Antichrist will no doubt follow this part of The Plan. The business boom that was in full swing at the time of the rapture will be only briefly interrupted by that shattering event, and will accelerate strongly thereafter. Truly it will seem like the start of a New Age that will see humanity solve all problems, conquer all disease, and develop godlike psychic powers.

But "in the middle of the week"—i.e., halfway through the seven-year period—Antichrist kills the two witnesses and leaves their bodies to lie in the street in Jerusalem for all the world to see. The startling evidence of a quantum increase in his psychic abilities is that he could finally overcome their incredible powers.[25] Having been tormented by these two "Jesus freaks" who for 3½ years preached an outdated fundamentalism that denied every New Age philosophy, the world is now ecstatic that their hero has finally demonstrated his superiority by killing them.[26] While the world is in the midst of this celebration, Antichrist enters the temple, declares that he is God, and demands that everyone in the world worship him. This is the final blasphemy. The gauntlet has been thrown down and the Creator will respond to the challenge. God's judgment will soon begin to fall.

It is probably at this time that Antichrist demands that everyone take his mark or die.[27] Until now, "his power and his throne and great authority" were given to him by "the dragon"[28]—i.e., Satan or Lucifer—who has been cast out of heaven[29] and probably personally takes possession of this evil man. Perhaps in his confrontation with the two witnesses, Antichrist suffered the "fatal wound"[30] that was miraculously healed. His authority "to make war with the saints and to overcome them,"[31] as he did the two witnesses, could come only from God, and apparently it is this extension of his power and kingdom that is limited to 42 months[32]—i.e., until the end of the seven-year period, when Christ returns visibly to earth in judgment. Now the real bloodbath begins, as those who have believed the two witnesses and refuse to take the mark and worship Antichrist are hunted down and killed by the millions.[33]

Problems in Paradise

Much of Israel feels honored with the unexpected use of the temple for Antichrist worship, now carried on through his image in the temple that speaks, answers questions, and even gives orders. Surely no nation would dare attack Jerusalem now. Many Jews are perplexed, however, unhappy that the traditional animal sacrifices have been halted. Remembering the warning that Jesus gave, thousands of Israelis flee to take refuge in nearby mountain strongholds.[34] A momentary wave of fear and confusion sweeps the earth as the two witnesses, after their bodies have lain dead on a Jerusalem street, suddenly return to life and are caught up to heaven. Now the Great Tribulation begins as God's judgment is poured out upon this earth. Although the Book of Revelation seems to depict supernatural acts of God from heaven, no doubt the "plagues" at least in part will result directly from specific evil being practiced upon earth. For example, genital herpes and its accompanying cervical cancer are related to sexual promiscuity;[35] a cancer-related pneumonia, amebiasis, Kaposi's sarcoma, and other deadly diseases seem to be related directly to homosexuality,[36] yet at the same time they are judgments from God for the violation of His moral laws.

Marxism's attempts to construct an atheistic Paradise out of inherent human goodness produce their own peculiar judgments: oppression, fear, deceit, slavery, slaughter, and poverty. These same "plagues" from God will bring an end to the booming prosperity. It is astonishing but true that "about one-third of Russia's meat, milk, eggs and vegetables comes from officially approved private plots that account for less than 2 percent of all farmland."[37] This unbelievable inefficiency factor, which is built into Communism, will have an eventual demoralizing effect under Antichrist, contributing to the growing famine and unrest.

Occult beliefs and practices also carry severe penalties from God. Man was created to be indwelt by the Holy Spirit, not by unholy demons. Numerous case histories prove the disastrous consequences of Yoga, Eastern meditation, spiritism, and other forms of occultism. Former followers of Maharishi Mahesh Yogi and other gurus have told of demonic possession, being thrown across the room by unknown forces, and moral, mental, and emotional deterioration culminating in self-destruction as a result of the practice of TM and other forms of Eastern meditation and occultism.* Nevertheless, under the Antichrist, parapsychology will become the most prestigious "science" as everyone enthusiastically pursues the Holy Grail of psychic powers. The accelerating mental, emotional, and

---

*   For further explanation, documentation, and references, see Dave Hunt, *The Cult Explosion* (Harvest House Publishers, 1980).

moral deterioration will contribute to the eventual disintegration of Antichrist's kingdom, which Revelation describes in terms of God's judgment poured out from heaven.

As a result of today's wide acceptance of Eastern mysticism, a worldwide "Spiritual Emergency Network, with its central registry at the Esalen Institute in Big Sur, California," involving "more than 4,500 psychologists, healers and ministers" has been formed to deal with "unexpected 'spiritual emergencies.' "[38] Marilyn Ferguson's *Brain/Mind Bulletin* explains:

> ...loss of body awareness, strange visions...uncontrollable tingling or shaking of the body, attributed to spontaneous release of "kundalini" energy from the base of the spine. Loss of personal boundaries, leaving one uncertain where the body ends and the rest of the world begins.
>
> Such experiences are common among people involved in yoga, meditation and other spiritual disciplines....
>
> The network's 24-hour answering service is available for immediate counseling [which]...begins with a "welcome-to-the-club talk," assurance that the caller's experience is not unique or crazy.
>
> In the future, Rohen said, most people may have such experiences.[39]

Network coordinator Rita Rohen's prediction will certainly come true following the universal Luciferic Initiation. Under Antichrist, an accelerating moral, mental, and emotional deterioration of mankind will unravel personalities and undermine the New Age, exposing the lie—for those able to see—upon which its seemingly perfect peace and prosperity have been built. Most of humanity, however, will be under such a strong delusion that they will continue to pursue their own godhood in hope of gaining powers like Antichrist's. The occult bondage will lead to deepening depravity, erratic behavior, fits of uncontrollable rage, murder, riots, all related to the plagues that Revelation describes as God's judgment being poured out upon the earth. Finally everyone will become suicidal, but will be unable to take their own lives to escape the awful consequences of their madness.[40]

Having undergone a Luciferic Initiation, which is tantamount to demon possession, the Antichrist's followers will openly worship not only him but Satan: "they worshiped the dragon, because he gave his authority to the beast."[41] Satan will give enough psychic power to the masses to lead them on; and the epidemic of deteriorating personalities, which will reach frightening proportions, will be shrugged off at first as the momentary side effects of great scientific advancement. Quantum leaps do not come easily. However, as spreading neuroses, famine, and disease dissolve the euphoria, Antichrist's total control over the world will begin to unravel at the edges. Disillusioned humanity will look for a scapegoat. As always, it will turn out to be the Jews.

"The Final Solution"

Today anti-Semitism is on the rise worldwide. It will accelerate rapidly during the second half of the seven-year period. The progressing demonization of the human race will produce its inevitable fruit: one final attempt to destroy the Jewish state. Although disarmament may have been agreed upon and may even be in process, the world's powers will still have the bulk of their weapons. Like Hitler, the world's demented leaders will be convinced that all of humanity's ills can be traced to the Jews. Plans will be carefully laid for a "final solution to the Jewish problem."

Led by the eager Soviet Union, the world's major powers invade Israel from all sides. Although the Israelis fight heroically and inflict heavy losses, they are overwhelmed. At that point the well-planned campaign becomes an unimaginable free-for-all. The mutual hatred which the Soviets, Arabs, Europeans, and Chinese have so long nourished for each other betrays itself as soon as it appears that the Israelis are going down in defeat. Abruptly the invading armies turn the full force of their arms upon each other in Israel's Valley of Jezreel. Armageddon has come at last!

The battle is not confined to Israel's soil. Nuclear missiles are unleashed by each of the four invading factions against the others' homelands. Charles Fillmore, cofounder of the Unity School of Christianity, said: "Whatever appears in your objective world is an image made by your own thoughts. You can change an appearance by changing your thoughts."[42]

Followers of Unity, the Mind Sciences, and other Hindu-Buddhist philosophies that have been accepted as the "new science" in the Antichrist's kingdom, will be hard pressed to affirm Unity's teaching of "the total unreality of evil"[43] in that day of unprecedented death and destruction.

The horror of this holocaust defies description. Jesus said, "Unless those days had been cut short, no life would have been saved."[44] To prevent the extermination of all life on earth, Jesus Christ suddenly returns to the Mount of Olives, accompanied by the armies of heaven. Neither psychic power from Satan nor the most sophisticated and fearsome weapons of war are a match for the real Messiah. This time He does not come meekly as a lamb to be crucified in our place, but as the Lion of the Tribe of Judah, taking vengeance.

It will not be rumored that He is hiding "high in the Himalayas" or has come down to a "Hindu-Pakistani community in southeast London," as Benjamin Creme has said of his "Christ Maitreya." Jesus said of His appearing: "For just as the lightning comes from the east, and flashes even to the west, so shall the coming of the Son of Man be."[45] John wrote: "Every eye will see Him, even those who pierced Him; and all the tribes of the earth will mourn over Him."[46] And Zechariah quotes Jehovah Himself making this astonishing statement: "They will look on Me whom they have pierced; and they will mourn for Him, as one mourns for an only son...."[47]

The devout Israeli, who waits today for the Messiah, must honestly ask himself when his Messiah was pierced. And the Jehovah's Witness must ask himself when *his* Jehovah was pierced. It is clear from Zechariah's statement above that Jehovah (Me) and the Messiah who was pierced (Him) are one and the same God: as Jesus said, "I and the Father are one,"[48] not merely in purpose, but in essence. The Hebrew word translated "pierced" carries a stronger meaning than the piercing of hands and feet with the nails of crucifixion. It means "piercing to death," and must therefore refer to the spear wound in Jesus' side. Wounds in hands and feet might be faked, so the prophet made it clear that the One who would come to rescue Israel was once dead and has been resurrected. This is obviously not Krishna, Buddha, Mohammed, or any other alleged "reincarnation of the Christ Spirit"; it can only be Jesus Himself.

The greatest mourning in its history will begin as Israel realizes that for all these centuries, just as the Prophet Isaiah warned they would,[49] Jews have rejected and despised the very One who is their Redeemer. The remnant of Israel that survives will repent and a nation will be born (again) in a day. Separating "the sheep from the goats," the Lord will judge those Gentiles who are left alive on earth for the way they have treated the Jewish people. Those who pass this test, plus all of Israel, will enter the millennium together. With Jesus reigning in Jerusalem, and resurrected believers governing under Him throughout the world, real peace will be established at last...but at what a cost!

Hitler was the "almost-Antichrist," but not because that devil-of-a-man was only a dress rehearsal. The powers of darkness tried desperately to fulfill The Plan through the Fuehrer, and almost succeeded. They were restrained from their full purpose because God's time had not yet come. Hitler was used, however, to restore Israel to her land and to turn Russia into a world power, setting the stage for the Antichrist's "final solution to the Jewish problem." The rapture will remove both the church and the restraining influence of the Holy Spirit that has worked through those millions of believers. Thereafter everything will move with precision and without further restraint from God to fulfill all that His prophets have spoken.

The prophets have warned us. They have also told us how to escape, and thereby made us responsible for rescuing not only ourselves but others. Francis Schaeffer has said: "The world quite properly looks back to the church in Germany during the early days of Hitler's rise and curses it for not doing something, when something could have been done."[50] The church in Germany was not just blind, but willfully blind. Are we? Will someone look back and properly curse us for not doing what we could and should have done?

A way of escape is offered to those who will take it. Time has not yet run out. Soon it will. How soon no one knows.

18

Escape from Delusion

We began in Chapter 1 by saying that predictions, both secular and Christian, of imminent worldwide financial collapse and global war just around the corner will probably turn out to be just so much gloom-and-doom hysteria. Instead, we suggested that the world could be about to enter a period of unprecedented peace and prosperity, notwithstanding the bulk of today's news that makes such a suggestion seem foolish. We warned, however, that Christians would become complacent and would fall asleep, reveling in their success and prosperity; non-Christians, living it up and enjoying the good times, would be convinced that a new age had dawned. At that point the rapture would take place. The peace and prosperity would become a trap, part of a great delusion that would be followed by a holocaust beyond the power of language to describe.

This contrary scenario raises a number of serious questions that we must deal with. Is there anything anyone can do to change the course of prophesied events, or must we helplessly watch it all happen on schedule? Hasn't this contrary scenario merely delayed the gloom and doom—and what is the benefit of that? Is there nothing *positive* that can be said?

A positive mental attitude is certainly preferable to a negative one. Solomon said, "A joyful heart is good medicine!"[1] A happy, positive attitude is good for one's digestion, glands, and nerves; it improves one's own performance and usually arouses a positive response from other people. But it does have limits that Positive Mental Attitude (PMA) enthusiasts often seem to deny. Unfortunately, many people emphasize positive or possibility *thinking* to such an extent that it balloons into a religious faith—a faith in *Self* instead of in God—that credits their minds with the power to cause whatever they are *thinking* about—good or bad—to happen. This is a basic belief

241

in Science of Mind, Unity, Religious Science, and other similar groups that have paraphrased Hindu occultism in Christian language. Called New Thought 50 years ago, this emphasis upon the power of the mind or belief was popularized by Harry Emerson Fosdick and later by Norman Vincent Peale. It has gained a large following within Protestant denominations through numerous people and organizations in recent years.

The Bible says: "With God all things are possible."[2] The New Age Movement, however, declares: "With man all things are possible," which means either that we do not need God or that we are God. Paul said, "I can do all things through Him [Christ] who strengthens me."[3] The New Age "Christ" is a state of consciousness rather than a historic Person. The Christian has a positive attitude not because he believes in the power of positive thinking, but because he is trusting in God. The PMA that is promoted in today's new age, however, is based upon humanistic psychology's first article of faith: "Human potential is infinite!" The real Christian is happy and positive in all circumstances because he believes that God, who alone is infinite, loves and cares for him. These two concepts— Christian and New Age—are mutually contradictory, in spite of the sincere people who believe they are the same thing expressed in different language.

Origin of a Most Seductive Lie

Though the idea is ridiculed by modern man, for sake of argument let's suppose for a moment that Satan exists and that what the Bible says about him is true. Next to God Himself, Satan was the most intelligent, beautiful, and powerful of God's creatures. Looking deep within himself to discover who he really was, Satan was seduced by the mystery of his own brilliant being and decided that he must somehow be an extension of God. He reasoned somewhat like this: God could not create something from nothing; therefore everything must be part of God; since God cannot be divided into parts, then everything is God and God is everything.

Deciding that the self-limiting concepts programmed into his mind were keeping him from experiencing his true Self, Satan made a daring positive affirmation: he declared himself equal to God. To convince both himself and others, he has been masquerading as God's equal ever since then. To prove his point, Satan began persuading other angels that they were divine, too. We do not know to what extent this rebellion swept through the universe, but it was apparently extensive. God could have locked away Satan and his deluded followers immediately and forever, but that would only have proved that His power was greater than theirs—it would not have proved who was right.

God created man in His image, without the powers that angels had, wholly dependent upon his Creator; for through man God would demonstrate the truth. Satan seduced Eve with the promise that she could also, like the other gods, become equal to God. However, Satan, like clever Napolean Pig in *Animal Farm*, considers himself to be "more equal than others," which is why he wants to be worshiped. This ambition will seem to have been achieved when he sits in the rebuilt temple of God in Jerusalem in full possession of Antichrist and declares himself to be God. Unlike the true God, who seeks to woo us with truth and love, Satan seduces by trickery and force—which will be the ultimate downfall of his false kingdom.

Human history has been an ongoing battle between God and Satan for the souls and destiny of mankind. God's weapon is truth. Satan's weapon is the Lie, which he embellishes with any deception that will best seduce the individual or culture at any given time. God's truth never changes; nor does Satan's Lie. However, Satan dresses it differently to make it seem flexible, broad-minded, liberal, generous—a mere lifestyle changing with the times (which is part of the delusion). It remains, however, the same barbed hook hidden by a variety of bait, and the end result for the poor creatures who swallow it never changes. Doesn't anyone ever see through the scam? Yes, everyone suspects the truth. However, the taste of the bait and the fear of losing Self eventually hook them. The mistaken belief that positive is always good and right, and that negative is always bad and wrong, prevents many people from being "negative" enough to admit the horror beneath the transparent facade.

The human race has been so thoroughly seduced that this Lie of lies permeates nearly every institution and has become the cornerstone of every human religion. The Judeo-Christian faith alone opposes it. Materialistic science has even succumbed. Atheism or secular humanism, with its declaration that there is no God and that man decides everything for himself, was always just a more devious way of deifying man, while pretending not to be religious.

Unveiling the Seduction Process

Humans are not just emotional beings but are also rational beings. Even in our love, joy, pleasure, ecstasy, and mystical experiences, whether on drugs or Yoga, science fiction or worship of idols, we cannot escape the reasoning process. Eastern mysticism is an attempt to do this, but it fails. Even the Yogi backs his experience of so-called pure consciousness with a philosophy. In all of his books recounting his fantastic seductions by Don Juan into the sorcerer's world, Carlos Castaneda continues to reason and build a surrealistic explanation of it all. We are not robots. If humans have been seduced with Satan's own lie, as the Bible indicates, then we should see the same steps toward the explanation of it being taken again and again in each generation. And we should also discover that we are like Alice in Wonderland, captivated by a delusion that does not really make sense, yet the garbled rationale supporting it is strangely seductive. It can hardly be chance that this is exactly what we discover by looking beneath the surface and behind the popular catch phrases.

If the ultimate truth behind the universe is God Himself, who is infinite and therefore beyond our proud but finite grasp, then every field of knowledge we explore must ultimately resolve itself into a faith system. Since the essence can never be proved, a step of faith must be taken. Einstein said that the more science discovers about the universe, the more we are driven to a conclusion concerning its origin that only faith can grasp. Everything ultimately becomes a religion, be it capitalism or Marxism, sociology or psychology. And every religion demands faith. Yet faith itself involves a choice between the truth and the Lie. If we choose to put our faith in anything except God, we are doomed. And it is right here, in its very concept and application of faith itself, that we see the human race following the same steps that Satan himself took, leading to full acceptance of the Lie. No stronger evidence could be given that this Lie has permeated the very soul of mankind.

The seduction is so powerful that it even takes key statements about faith from the lips of Jesus Himself as its starting point in arriving at the Lie. To a woman whom He healed, Jesus said, "Your faith has made you well."[4] And to His disciples He said, "If you have faith and do not doubt, you shall...say to this mountain, 'Be taken up and cast into the sea,' and it shall happen."[5] These statements become the basis for focusing upon faith instead of upon the One in whom we are to place our faith. Kenneth Hagin titled an article "Having Faith in Your Faith."[6] This is a far cry from what Jesus taught: "Have faith in God."[7]

Let's see how the seduction works if we assume that faith is the key to healing ourselves and transforming the universe about us. Since faith is believing, our assumption leads to the conclusion that if we really believe something will happen, then that makes it happen. If *believing* makes it happen, then it does not matter *what* or *in whom* we believe—we can make anything happen by *believing*. Since it is our minds that believe, and since we can decide whether and what to believe, then we can decide our own destiny and create our own universe with our minds. Consequently, we must each be God. Certainly we do not need to believe in any God or any reality external to ourselves. One's ultimate goal would then be to get in touch with his true Self. In finding his true Self, he would find God; for it is the mind, through positive thinking or negative thinking, that creates everything there is. It then follows that God, Buddha, Jesus, Krishna, tarot cards, crystal balls, and the zodiac are all the same thing called by different names: they are simply placebos that activate the Force in our minds.

Problems in Wonderland

It is reasonable and factual to acknowledge that what we believe affects us and our world in many ways. It is unreasonable and fanciful, however, to imagine that our minds create all reality—that if everyone would only think positive thoughts about health and good crops, then all disease and famine would go away. Yogis and various other brands of mystics have been saying for centuries that the universe has no reality but is only an illusion created by our minds. That this mystical view is not true should be evident. Otherwise, how would two scientists, one Chinese and the other American, separated by 10,000 miles and looking through microscopes independently of each other both see the same thing or discover the same virus?

Germs, disease, death, and the intricate universe within a single cell are not inventions of human minds, but do exist independently of our thinking. Obviously our thinking determines our perception of the universe; but our perception does not affect the object itself that we are perceiving. This is obvious from the fact that several observers may each simultaneously perceive the same object differently. We ought to be thankful that our minds do not create the world in which we live, in spite of the teaching of est and other mind control cults that we do create our own universe.

Children dream of a magical Alice-in-Wonderland world where the power of *thinking* creates whatever one wishes. However, such a wonderland would not be a dream, but a nightmare. Just imagine the chaos if there were no laws of physics or chemistry, for example, but everything was in a state of flux and took on shapes and qualities and functions that shifted and blurred in a surrealistic pandemonium of kaleidoscopic pseudoexistence with the changing moods and whims of humans creating it all with their positive or negative thinking!

If we all had Godlike powers, there would simply be too many Gods shuffling "reality" around to suit themselves and in the process conflicting with other Gods, whose minds were imposing a different form upon "reality" according to their taste. Not only is a Creator-God essential for the universe to exist, but any more than one God is too many and would result in a chaotic clash of billions of Darth Vaders and Lukes in constant conflict. Nevertheless, to exercise these dreamed-of mysterious powers has always been the secret ambition of the human race.

The fact that common sense and all experience tells us that it is impossible to rearrange the universe with our minds has not discouraged humans from trying to do it. As Brugh Joy implies, humans would pay any price to learn the secret of what could only be called "magic"—black magic or white magic, which are exactly the same, though those practicing them pretend there is a difference. All occultism, whether voodoo, sorcery, hexes, curses, witchcraft, or spiritism, has always been understood to involve a Luciferic Initiation of select humans—priests, shamans, mediums, Yogis—by the gods into magical powers that we could possess in exchange for giving "them" possession of our souls. Called "the magicians's bargain," it has been depicted since the beginning of time in myths, folklore, poetry, literature, and operas—such as Goethe's tale of Dr. Faust selling his soul to Mephistopheles. Though it denies the existence of gods or spirits, and claims to be scientific, the modern version of ancient occultism derives its power from the same source, and its names are legion: alpha training, self-hypnosis, mind dynamics, mind control, TM, PMA, autosuggestion, religious science, mind science, placebo effect.

The human claim to godhood has a huge obstacle in God's physical laws, which are too obvious and the consequences of violation too severe for people to be jumping out of airplanes claiming that a belief in the law of gravity is narrow-minded dogmatism. This is why the use of black or white magic to seemingly violate these laws is practiced in secret, which is the meaning of the world "occult." The Antichrist and his false prophet, however, will be able to make an open and public display of these powers of Satan before the entire world: "with all power and signs and false wonders, and with all the deception of wickedness for those who perish, because they did not receive the love of the truth so as to be saved."[8] As the verse indicates, occultism (the attempt to violate God's physical laws) is always associated not only with deception but with wickedness (violation of God's spiritual or moral laws).

In the moral realm, the consequences of breaking God's laws

248 • Peace, Prosperity, & The Coming Holocaust

(which eventually break us, since we cannot really break them) are not always obvious or immediate, because this involves the freedom of choice which God has given us, and He will not violate that freedom by force. It is in the moral area, then, that the seduction of the Lie bears its most horrible fruit, as we seem to be able to play God for a time, not only with our own lives but with the lives of others. Occultism ultimately involves trafficking in the souls of men, which is God's most solemn accusation against the Whore of Babylon, the false church under Antichrist.[9]

Secular psychology and psychiatry, being amoral attempts to explain human behavior and achieve fulfillment without God, through self-effort and self-deification, are uniquely designed as channels of the seduction process and embodiments of the Lie. This occult art can be expected to reach its peak capacity for destruction of human souls under the Antichrist.

Psychiatry and the Antichrist

Psychology is a largely pseudoscience riddled with confusion and contradiction and involving literally hundreds of different theories and schools of thought that conflict with each other. Regardless of their many differences, however, psychologists have been moving toward New Age thinking. This is clearly seen in the gropings after the real self and the steady progression toward today's humanistic and transpersonal psychologies that attribute infinite potential and Godlike powers to the mind. As New York University psychology professor Paul C. Vitz has characterized it, psychology has become a "cult of self-worship."[10] Largely under psychology's influence, an estimated 80 percent of adult Americans are actively engaged in finding life's answers and meaning within themselves,[11] many through regression under hypnosis into alleged prior lives. Carl Rogers has said, "Inner space may be even more important than outer space, and perhaps we can learn to live an important part of our lives in it."[12]

Psychology has turned heavily to the occult, with which it has always been closely associated. In his book *You Shall Be As Gods*, Erich Fromm explains his belief that man is God and the only sacred thing is the self. Est is a subcult of psychology that combines a variety of psychotherapies with Eastern mysticism. In his book *est: Playing the Game the New Way*, est graduate Carl Frederick says: "*You* are the Supreme being. Reality is a reflection of your notions. Totally. Perfectly...there isn't any right/wrong."[13] The reenactment in human experience of Satan's own self-delusion and fall— exactly what we would expect if our assumptions were correct— is too clear to be denied. It is everywhere in the New Age Movement. The vision of human godhood is spreading through New Age networks around the world, such as the International Transpersonal Association (ITA), which its president, Cecil Burney, describes as "a global networking model for groups that have been drawn together...by the glimpse of a common vision."[14] The pitiful wreckage of souls seduced by the Lie through psychology is strewn everywhere. As Jeffrey Klein wrote in reference to some of the therapy and encounter groups once the rage at Esalen:

> Although Fritz Perls' motto was "Take Responsibility [as God] for Yourself," he and the other leaders in the '60s rarely took responsibility for the atmosphere that was hallowing them as gurus.
>
> When interviewed...several former workshop members expressed disgust at how they'd let themselves be destructively seduced. Some of the seductions were literal....
>
> Everywhere, the human potential movement left casualties, but at Esalen these losses were more dramatic—a rash of suicides.[15]

It is only reasonable to expect that Antichrist will use psychiatry for subjugation and suppression even more efficiently than the Soviets have done. In the Soviet Union and other Communist countries today, allegedly no one is harassed, imprisoned, or killed for believing in God or practicing Judaism or wanting to immigrate to Israel. There is supposedly complete freedom to do any of those things. However, only the insane, by very definition, would believe in God or want to leave a Communist paradise; therefore those who do must be deranged, and giving them "treatment" is a kindness.

As in the Soviet Union today, persecution and death under

Antichrist will simply be humane treatments applied in loving concern for those who are out of touch with reality. Psychiatry will no doubt play an important role. Commenting upon Freud's ability to produce his own semantic, masquerade it as science, then use it to destroy his enemies, Szasz writes:

> Clearly, the idea that disagreement is a disease, and that he who defies authority is deranged and should be disposed of by the methods of social repression then in vogue, is very old indeed.[16]

Psychologists and psychiatrists have usurped God's authority over society by replacing the moral laws that He placed in human conscience with their new "scientific" standards. Thomas Szasz has pointed out that "the birth of psychiatry occurs...when the 'cure of souls' becomes the 'treatment of mental diseases.' "[17] If the psychiatrist calls homosexuality, lesbianism, incest, adultery, fornication, and mate-swapping perfectly normal options or alternate lifestyles, who is to disagree? Anyone clinging, in the face of such "expert" opinion, to the moral absolutes of conscience is branded as neurotic, prudish, fanatical, or worse, and in desperate need of therapy. The following favorite story from the Soviet Union applies equally to the absolute power of psychiatrists in the West to rule by labeling—and will be even more applicable under Antichrist.

> Two rabbits met on a trail. "Where are you going in such a hurry?" one asked.
> "Haven't you heard?" replied the other rabbit. "All camels are going to be sent to Siberia for seven years of hard labor."
> "But we're not camels," said the first rabbit, trying to shrug off a wave of fear.
> "Of course not," came the quick reply. "But when *they've* accused you of being a camel, who do you think will dare to believe you're a rabbit?"

As Freud and his followers viewed and still view those who believe in God as mentally ill and deluded, so anyone opposing Antichrist will be considered insane. Psychiatrists will no doubt be very busy supporting and working for the new world government, for psychiatry will be a valuable tool in maintaining the Antichrist's New Age Paradise. Szasz describes the "stock-in-trade of the psychopathologist" thus: "The deviant is branded as 'demented' and deprived first of his language, then of his life....Thus, when Freud developed his own lexicon of loathing, called it psychoanalysis, and used it to smite his enemies, he did nothing new...."[18] There will be no escaping prescribed "therapy" under Antichrist. The extent to which the preparatory rationale is becoming accepted is ominous; for example, this statement in the *American Journal of Psychiatry*: "There is widespread prejudice among mental health professionals that treatment must be voluntary....To serve, we risk the abuse of our powers; to avoid that risk is not to serve at all."[19] Of course, forced "treatment" will be for the "good" of the patient, and that is what matters. Viktor E. Frankl explains:

> In my department at the Vienna Polyclinic, we use drugs, and use electro-convulsive treatment. I have signed authorization for lobotomies without having cause to regret it. In a few cases, I have even carried out transorbital lobotomy.
> However, I promise you that the human dignity of our patients is not violated in this way....
> What matters is not a technique or therapeutic approach as such, be it drug treatment or shock treatment, but the spirit in which it is being carried out.[20]

There is no way to anticipate the genius of the "treatments" and amazing "therapies" that will be used during the Great Tribulation to "cure" those who deviate from Antichrist's program. Death would be preferred. The evil that will be flaunted and that society will engage in as officially approved methods of "group therapy" to promote the spirit of the New Age could be mind-boggling. Consider the following "therapies" that are already accepted:

> Sandi Enders, an attractive brunette of 26 who intends to become an occupational therapist, is earning her way through San Jose State University working as a sexual therapist.
> She charges $50 for a two-and-a-half hour session—including lovemaking—in her sensuously decorated apartment with its incense burner and heated water bed.[21]

Now you can release pent-up pain, anger, and fear through Dr. Casriel's own technique of "scream therapy"....[22]

The psychologist treated the patient with "Rage Reduction Therapy," a therapy method which involves physical stimulation of the rib cage area.
As a result of this therapy, the patient was physically and mentally abused for 11 hours, resulting in severe bruising of the upper half of the body. Also, there was a complete kidney failure for seven days.[23]

A new technique is gaining ground in addiction therapy: skydiving...."Not all that radical," says pediatrician Henry Bruyn, the program's medical advisor...."Technically, we are an encounter group, with a Gestalt basis."[24]

Everywhere the Staggering Evidence

The process of seduction and acceptance of the Lie is not only blatant in psychology, but almost everywhere in today's society; not only in Eastern cults and the religious science cults, but in medicine, sociology, the physical sciences, and even in evangelical Christianity. The process follows the pattern of Satan's own seduction, and the results are predictable: the belief that Self is all-important, that it has infinite potential, that it can create its own reality by *thinking* (positive, possibility, visualization, etc.), and thus, whether boldly stated or implied, that man in fact is God. Self even becomes the object of worship.

If we are to do anything to stop this process that will usher in the reign of Antichrist, we must first of all recognize the spirit of Antichrist in our own day. Then we must stand boldly against it. Mistakenly describing the Antichrist to one another as some bizarre monster, we have failed to see the connection between him and what is happening in today's world. To depict him as some obviously evil ogre who blatantly dispenses mass murder is to set everyone up for complete deception when this reasonable, loving man comes forth to lead the human race to ever-higher heights of achievement, love, and brotherhood. Yes, he is a beast, but not on the surface. It will all seem so beautiful.

The thousands of New Age groups and institutions will be only too eager to cooperate with this wonderful humanitarian who stands for the fulfillment of their dreams. The American Civil Liberties Union (ACLU) will use its rhetoric to support Antichrist's suppression and oppression, and will do it in the name of liberty and justice for all (as it operates today). For example, groups of Christians who are every bit as competent in science as evolutionists and who simply ask for an honest presentation of creation in public schools as an alternative to evolution are ridiculed and repressed in the name of science and academic freedom. Supported by the ACLU, evolutionists demand the exclusive right to push their viewpoint, which is no more scientific and no less religious than creationism. However, they have their own definitions of science and religion, which are forced upon everyone in the name of freedom...freedom from even listening to an alternate viewpoint.

H.G. Wells predicted that "The Plan" must operate "in the name and for the sake of science and creative activity."[25] Denying the existence of God and claiming, as does Carl Sagan (voted Humanist Man of the Year in 1981), that the Cosmos is all there ever was or ever will be, the physicist began to wonder whether there would be any noise when a tree fell in the forest if there were no one there to hear it. Realizing that the observer cannot divorce himself completely from what he observes, scientists concluded that something of the observer is in everything he sees. This brought an even more radical question to mind: would there be anything at all in the entire universe to see if there were no one to see it? The answer that many scientists are accepting agrees with Hinduism and the latest theory that the Cosmos is not a mechanism but a Mind.

In a new book, physicist Roger Jones has said: "I reject the myth of reality as external to the human mind, and I acknowledge consciousness as the source of the cosmos. It is mind that we see reflected in matter."[26] In a paper delivered at the 1981 Nobel Conference, philosopher of science Karl Popper declared, "Our minds are largely makers of our place in nature." Theologian Wolfhart Pannenberg expounded on the common spiritual origin of mind and nature.[27] Hundreds of such examples could be given. In his new book *The Cosmic Eye: A Traveller's Guide to Inner Space*, Peter Lemesurier betrays in his own thinking the effects of this seduction of modern science and philosophy that deifies Self and, in the Western counterpart of Hinduism's identification of atman (individual soul) and Brahman (Universal Soul), equates mind with Mind:

> Far from the psyche being merely our tool for learning about life, the whole of life as we experience it is merely the psyche's tool for learning about itself....
>
> Whatever the mind can fully conceive will eventually come to birth....In whatever form, it is Mind that dismembers itself into Individual "souls" that are its scattered arms and legs...then attempts to recover its primal unity via techniques such as meditation.[28]

The preparation of the world for the Antichrist and the classic seduction process are pretty much summed up in one man whom we have already mentioned, Willis W. Harman. A professor of engineering-economic systems at Stanford University, senior social scientist at Stanford Research Institute International, president of Edgar Mitchell's Institute of Noetic Sciences, and one of the early organizers and an executive board member of the Association for Humanistic Psychology, Dr. Harman is a leading New Age theorist and extremely influential in spreading his philosophy, which he proclaims very boldly and equates with what he calls "the 'perennial wisdom,' the esoteric core of the world's religious traditions"—i.e., paganism and more specifically Hinduism. The following excerpts from his keynote address to the August 1979 annual meeting of the Institute for Transpersonal Psychology give as clear an outline of the Lie and the coming world religion as one could find anywhere:

> I heard a Canadian psychiatrist make a statement that has impressed me ever since. There is only one mental illness, he said, a wrong perception of self.
>
> ...there is ample evidence that auto-suggestion can be one of the most powerful tools for self-transformation. It is the central technique in many executive development seminars

[and]...a key element in a wide range of personal-change approaches, from "psychocybernetics" to "psychosynthesis" to *A Course in Miracles*....

Each of us has access to a...mind whose capabilities are apparently unlimited. The limits we do experience [are]...imposed by our beliefs....If [this]...mind...has access to all the knowledge available to consciousness and more, then...why not turn to it with *all* decisions...?

One of the better ways of strengthening the belief [in a "higher" mind is]...with auto-suggestion in the form of repeated self-reminding of one's intention to refer all choices to the creative/intuitive mind....

The findings of psychic research...indicate that effects of mind are not limited by distance or physical time...mind exists in co-extensive unity with the world it observes....

There seems no reason to doubt that my creative/intuitive mind might "have in mind" a "plan"....This idea of a "plan" coming from beyond consciousness seems implausible....Yet there is impressive testimony...in a vast literature on mysticism and religious experience....

A couple of generations ago most educated people were quite certain that materialistic science had clearly won the "warfare between science and religion," and that such improbable ideas as "mind over matter" were banished once and for all.

It now appears that...mind can remotely exert influence in the physical world.[29]

The Seduction of Christianity

The appearance of Antichrist is the climactic episode in the cosmic struggle between God and Satan for the souls of mankind. This is a spiritual battle ("For our struggle is not against flesh and blood, but against the rulers...the spiritual forces of wickedness in the heavenly places.")[30] that intimately involves each member of the human race individually. Those who refuse the love of the truth will be given by God "a deluding influence" to believe the Lie.[31] God is not seducing them. Satan has done that, and they have been his willing victims. This deluding influence from God simply helps them not to lose faith in their chosen Messiah, Antichrist, when judgment becomes very heavy during the tribulation.

The most convincing evidence that the awesome climax is

near is the seduction of Christianity by the Lie dressed in Biblical language. This is something new. The very Lie that we have explained in detail, which is at the heart of the New Age Movement, is also seducing Catholic, Protestant, liberal, and evangelical alike on a scale never before known. This is strong evidence indeed that the Antichrist could appear very soon—which means that the rapture may be imminent.

Typical of much that is happening within "Christian psychology," which has a stranglehold on the church, is the following from H. Newton Malony, a professor in the graduate school of psychology at one of the leading evangelical seminaries in the United States: "In Transactional Analysis terms, I stay as close to my Free Child as possible. I am confident, as was Berne, that there is within the child part of me an area of primitive intuition (often termed the Little Professor) which can be trusted. I implicitly count on this part of my own psyche to guide me...."[32] The connection to the "higher mind" that Willis Harman turns to for guidance in "*all* decisions" is clear.

The Catholic Church has reinstated to its good graces once-banned Pierre Teilhard de Chardin. His writings argue for "the coming of a deeply moral super-humanity ennobled by the universal spirit of the cosmic Christ" as human consciousness evolves through the "noosphere" to a future fourth layer of spirit enveloping earth, the "theosphere," where "the converging-but-distinctly individual human spirits transcend space and matter and mystically join god-omega at the omega point."[33] Teilhard's syncretism of Darwinism, Hinduism, and Christianity profoundly influenced the New Age Movement. In fact, the 185 New Age leaders surveyed by Marilyn Ferguson in preparation for writing *The Aquarian Conspiracy* rated Chardin at the top of the list of persons most influential in their lives![34]

The message of Rodney R. Romney's book *Journey to Inner Space: Finding God-in-Us* is summarized on the back cover like this: "MISSION: To find God. METHOD: By finding one's self." Senior minister of Seattle's First Baptist Church, Romney claims that Jesus expects His followers "to realize the Christ within their own consciousness."[35] Romney declares that Jesus was not God,[36] but "simply a man who knew the laws of God";[37] that "he claimed nothing for himself that he did not claim for his disciples"[38] (how could Christ's statement, "I am the way, and the truth, and the life; no one comes to the Father but through Me"[39] apply to anyone else but Christ?); that Jesus "resisted all attempts to worship or deify him"[40] (there are eight instances recorded in the Gospel of Matthew alone in which various persons fell down before Jesus and worshiped Him, and not once did He ever "resist"). Although Romney admits that Jesus clearly said, "I am the way," he insists that Jesus "meant that he was the 'Way-Shower' and not the way."[41] There are many ways, according to Romney. Some of those he names with approval are: tapping into a "powerful, invisible force" through reaching "higher realms of spiritual consciousness"[42]; Buddhist meditation (Zen);[43] Yoga;[44] Transcendental Meditation ("I believe that it could give fuller and deeper meaning to any religion if pursued conscientiously");[45] Sufism;[46] all of these, he says, are equally good paths to God—take your pick. Romney is only one of many people in the church to whom the following remarks by C.S. Lewis, addressed to a group of ministers in 1945, are appropriate:

I insist that...bounding lines must exist, beyond which your doctrine will cease either to be Anglican or to be Christian; and I suggest also that the lines come a great deal sooner than many modern priests think...and if you wish to go beyond them you must change your profession.

This is your duty not specially as Christians or as priests but as honest men....Men who have passed beyond these boundary lines...protest that they have come by their unorthodox opinions honestly [and]...come to feel like martyrs.

We never doubted that the unorthodox opinions were honestly held: what we complain of is your continuing your ministry after you have come to hold them.

...a man who makes his living as a paid agent of the Conservative Party may honestly change his views and honestly become a Communist. What we deny is that he can honestly continue to be a Conservative agent and to receive money from one party while he supports the policy of another.

We are to defend Christianity itself—the faith preached by

the Apostles, attested by the Martyrs,...we are defending Christianity; not "my religion."

The great difficulty is to get modern audiences to realize that you are preaching Christianity solely and simply because you happen to think it *true*...[not] because you like it or think it good for society....

Our business is to present that which is timeless (Truth, Christ) in the particular language of our own age. The bad preacher does exactly the opposite: he takes the ideas of our own age and tricks them out in the traditional language of Christianity.[47]

Diagnosis and Treatment

Christians have generally been and should continue to be in the forefront of relief work and charitable efforts, doing all we can to make this world a better place: safer, more moral, healthier, happier, more prosperous. We should be thrifty, hard-working, diligent, generous, and opposed to war, exploitation, and dishonesty—not just thinkers, but doers. At the same time, however, we must make it clear that these efforts are not the final answer. They are emergency first aid—but without radical surgery, the patient will die. We must boldly and lovingly proclaim that the real problem is that the human race at its very heart is morally sick unto death. Jeremiah said, "The heart is deceitful above all things, and desperately wicked."[48] Adding to this diagnosis, Jesus declared: "For out of the heart come evil thoughts, murders, adulteries, fornications, thefts, false witness, slanders. These are the things which defile the man."[49] Unpleasant and negative though it may be, this is certainly more realistic than denying the existence of evil, and is a much better explanation of war, rape, jealousy, and hatred than the Divine within, or the inherent goodness of man, or the specious claim that we are simply out of touch with our Higher Self.

The gospel declares that the only remedy is to give ourselves to Jesus Christ, believing that He died for our sins and rose again, and to invite Him to come into and cleanse our hearts. We must receive Him as Savior and Lord. "Too simplistic!" complains the psychologist; "Narrow-minded dogmatism!" cries the liberal. Yet both would be stunned if, after being examined by a doctor for a serious problem and asking for the results, the doctor replied: "I'm not so narrow-minded and dogmatic as to come up with a *definite* diagnosis. I would not want to push 'my truth' on you. What would you like? Open-heart surgery has been popular lately, or I could transplant a kidney. I believe that every person is entitled to the operation of his choice." No one denies that this is absurd. Yet when it comes to diagnosing society and establishing a basis for eternal destiny through a right relationship with God, suddenly everyone gets "broad-minded" and insists that God should have no principles of His own, but that He should go along with whatever we choose, as long as we are "sincere" about it. Other people, unwilling to come to the cross, turn Jesus Christ into a heavenly Psychiatrist, with whom they can endlessly discuss their problems without accepting what He so plainly said: "If anyone wishes to come after Me, let him deny himself, and take up his cross, and follow Me."[50]

Unless there is a definite diagnosis of the evil plaguing humanity and a genuine cure, there is no hope, no matter how much positive thinking we engage in. Paul said, "For I am not ashamed of the gospel [that Christ died for our sins, was buried and rose the third day from the dead],[51] for it is the power of God for salvation to everyone who believes."[52] Christians must stand firmly on this simple truth and declare it boldly and earnestly to the world. If out of fear of offending someone who believes differently we encourage the idea that a humanistic faith in ourselves and the brave pulling on bootstraps will eventually produce a utopian New Age, we are contributing to the deception of those we mislead. As retired seminary Professor Marchant King has said:

> If the atoning death of Christ is not central and absolutely essential to one's faith, that person has not entered into Christianity; he has no valid claim to being a follower of Biblical revelation.[53]

Some Practical Suggestions

The church in Germany in the 1930's largely went along with Hitler, deceived by his rhetoric about "positive Christianity." We must not allow ourselves and those around us to be seduced in the same way with the same Lie. The World Council of Churches, headed by Philip Potter, pursues a pro-Communist, anti-Western policy that is contrary to the beliefs of the majority of the members of the churches it represents. Yet church leaders in the West compromise and allow this. Like the United Nations, the WCC financially supports Marxist revolutionaries around the world, and gives not one dime to those suffering persecution for their faith in Communist countries. "Marxist governments in general—and the Soviet Union in particular—get kid-glove treatment by the WCC."[54] In the meanwhile, the Soviet KGB at the time it was headed by Yuri Andropov was apparently involved in an assassination attempt on Pope John Paul II.[55] What does it take for us to wake up?

We must courageously expose the deception that is preparing this world for the Antichrist. We must bring aid behind the Iron Curtain; we must comfort and help those who are suffering as prisoners of conscience in Soviet and other Communist prisons; we must help their families who are left destitute, Christians and Jews who are being persecuted for their faith. **Mission: Possible,** to whom this book is dedicated, and other worthy organizations are working diligently at this task. They need our assistance. They can provide names and addresses of prisoners and persecuted families to whom we should write letters of comfort. We must let Communist governments know that we are watching and are not deceived. We must also protest against and expose the same denial of religious freedom and forcing of atheism upon our own children in public schools here in the United States.

Have we failed to recognize the truly terrifying significance of the compromises we are making? The stakes are awesome; yet we too often play with real life as though it were a game of Monopoly—so distant and unreal is the holocaust that this world is even now embracing. Are we like Chamberlain returning from Munich, thoroughly outwitted and defeated by Hitler, imagining that his latest compromising surrender was a victory and declaring, "Peace in our time"? Step by step, a little here, a little there—unaware of or unconcerned about what our children are being taught in public schools, and the lies and glorification of evil they are absorbing through television in our own homes or from popular singing groups that flaunt their rebellion and perversion—we have begun to play the world's game with its rules on its terms...not knowing that, for a tenuous detente with the enemy, we have bartered the very souls of those depending upon us.

The solemn words of Churchill to the House of Commons after Chamberlain signed the Munich Pact were never more relevant than today regarding the condition of the church in relation to the forces of darkness, with which we are supposed to be locked in deadly combat, but too often act as though we have negotiated a treaty of peaceful coexistence:

> [The people] should know that we have sustained a defeat without war....They should know that we have passed an awful milestone in our history...and that the terrible words have for the time being been pronounced against the Western democracies: "Thou art weighed in the balance and found wanting."
>
> And do not suppose this is the end; this is only the first sip, the first foretaste of a bitter cup which will be proffered to us year after year unless, by a supreme recovery of moral health and martial vigor, we arise again and take our stand for freedom as in olden times.

We must be certain that the Christ we proclaim is clearly distinguishable from the New Age false Christs around us; we must be certain that we do not add to the confusion and thereby contribute to the preparation of the world for the Antichrist. Evangelicals would not give up the gospel, but too often they take the offense of the cross out of it and turn "born-again" into a cheap slogan. In order to make it palatable to unbelievers and to avoid offending sinners, some Christian leaders proclaim the gospel as a means to health, success, prosperity, and happiness instead of what it really is: the sovereign Creator's offer of mercy and grace to rebels who deserve nothing but eternal judgment, and must repent or perish. A gospel of self-esteem, self-worth, and self-acceptance may cause the unrepentant to feel good about themselves, but if we do not persuade people that the gospel must be accepted because it is *true*, and must be believed and embraced on God's terms, we are deluding both them and ourselves. We must not fail to warn those who reject Jesus Christ as Lord and Savior that they are consigning themselves to eternal disillusionment through the Lie they have believed—the Lie that dooms forever.

A Positive Note

Although it may seem unlikely to succeed, we are to attempt to persuade the entire human race to renounce the Lie and embrace the truth. Yes, the prophecies pronouncing judgment on this earth are unequivocal. But so was the judgment that God told Jonah to denounce against Nineveh: "Yet forty days and Nineveh will be overthrown!"[56] Nothing could be more clearly stated than that—yet Nineveh was not destroyed in forty days or even forty years. Why? God has promised, "If that nation against which I have spoken turns from its evil, I will relent concerning the calamity I planned to bring on it."[57] Nineveh repented and was spared. We must work, persuade, pray to God, and plead with unbelievers everywhere to repent and ask God to spare this world its holocaust. On the other hand, if so many people refuse to repent that the holocaust comes as prophesied, at least we have rescued millions who, because of their repentance and faith in Jesus Christ, will not be part of it. That is something well worth expending our lives for.

Yes, Jesus left His disciples with a positive note. He promises to return. The fulfillment of that promise is going to take those people who have believed in and are looking for Him out of this world before the holocaust. Yet no matter what circumstances we face, he has given us His peace and joy. Before going to the cross, Jesus said, "Peace I leave with you; My peace I give to you."[58] Forgetting that Jesus added to that comforting statement, "Not as the world gives do I give to you," many Christians have imagined that this peace is to be experienced through a sort of Christian Couéism, repeating frequently, "Every day and in every way I'm becoming happier, healthier, more successful, and more prosperous, and I'm feeling better and better about myself." They have confused New Age peace with the peace that Jesus paid for at Calvary—a peace that can only be experienced as He lives in the hearts of those who have received Him as Savior and Lord.

After the Antichrist's kingdom has ended in doom, Jesus will reign over this earth at last. Which of these kingdoms we will be in depends upon the choice we make now—for God's truth or for the Lie. It is amazing that after his years of satire and polemic against Christianity, that old atheist Bertrand Russell wrote the following in *The Impact of Science on Society*:

> The root of the matter is a very simple and old-fashioned thing, a thing so simple that I am almost ashamed to mention it, for fear of the derisive smile with which wise cynics will greet my words.
>
> The thing I mean, please forgive me for mentioning it, is love, Christian love or compassion.
>
> If you feel this, you have a motive for existence, a guide in action, a reason for courage, an imperative necessity for intellectual honesty.

CHAPTER NOTES

Chapter 1: A Contrary Scenario

1. *Los Angeles Times,* Aug. 16, 1982.
2. Ibid., Sep. 4, 1982.
3. Ibid., Aug. 18, 1982.
4. Ibid.
5. Robert Muller, *New Genesis* (New York, 1982), from front flap of jacket.
6. Ibid., back flap.
7. Ibid., p. xv.
8. Ibid., dedication page.
9. Muller, op. cit., p. 136.
10. Herman Kahn, "Coming: An Age of Prosperity," in *Reader's Digest,* Feb. 1983, pp. 124-127.
11. Matthew 24:37,38.
12. Revelation 3:17.
13. Proverbs 1:32.
14. 2 Thessalonians 2:7-12.

Chapter 2: Why the Optimism?

1. Melissa Everett, "Growing Up in the Nuclear Age," in *Whole Life Times,* Sep./Oct. 1982.
2. *The Initiator,* Vol. 1, No. 2.
3. World Health Organization (WHO) statistics cited in *World Goodwill Newsletter,* July/Aug./Sep. 1981.

4. Kimberly French, "Finding a Drop to Drink," in *Whole Life Times*, July/Aug. 1982.
5. Mark Satin, *New Age Politics: Healing Self and Society* (New York, 1978), p. 152.
6. World Health Organization (WHO) statistics cited in *World Goodwill Newsletter*, op. cit.
7. *Los Angeles Times*, Nov. 17, 1981.
8. Ibid., Oct. 16, 1981.
9. Ibid., Nov. 21, 1981.
10. Muller, op. cit., p. 4.
11. "Howard Ruff's Apocalypse Now," in *Newsweek*, May 18, 1981, p. 100.
12. Ibid., Oct. 16, 1981.
13. Ibid., Nov. 21, 1981.
14. Ibid.
15. Ibid., Sep. 11, 1982.
16. Ibid., Sep. 13, 1982.
17. *World Goodwill Newsletter*, Oct./Nov./Dec. 1982.
18. *Manchester Guardian*, as quoted in *World Goodwill Newsletter*, Oct./Nov./Dec. 1981.
19. *Los Angeles Times*, Sep. 30, 1982.
20. Ibid., Sep. 20, 1982.
21. Ibid., Oct. 16, 1982.
22. Ibid., Oct. 13, 1982.

Chapter 3: A Colossal Trap?

1. *Los Angeles Times*, Oct. 6, 1982.
2. *The Initiator*, op. cit.
3. Planetary Initiative for the World We Choose, *Organizing Manual*, Project Description/Attachment III-a.
4. Ibid.
5. *Los Angeles Times*, July 22, 1982.
6. Ibid.
7. Ibid.
8. Ibid.
9. Ibid.
10. H.G. Wells, *The Open Conspiracy, Blue Prints for a World Revolution* (New York, 1928), p. 196.

Chapter 4: What About World War Three?

1. *Los Angeles Times*, Aug. 24, 1982.

2. Ibid., Aug. 26, 1982.
3. Ibid.
4. Melissa Everett, "Will Civil Defense Work?" in *Whole Life Times,* Apr./May 1982, p. 43.
5. *Review of the News,* Oct. 14, 1981, p. 47 (as quoted in *Daily News Digest,* Nov. 4, 1981, p. 4).
6. *The Spotlight,* Sep. 13, 1982.
7. *Los Angeles Times,* July 16, 1982.
8. Ibid.
9. *Intercessors for America Newsletter,* Aug. 1, 1982.
10. Ibid.
11. *Los Angeles Times,* Oct. 15, 1982.
12. Ibid.

Chapter 5: The Coming World Government

1. H.G. Wells, op. cit., pp. 59-60.
2. Ibid.
3. Ibid., Preface and p. 24.
4. Norman and Jeanne MacKenzie, *The Fabians* (New York, 1977), pp. 323-24.
5. 2 Thessalonians 2:3.
6. Wells, op. cit., p. 200.
7. Lovat Dickson, *H.G. Wells: His Turbulent Life and Times* (New York, 1969).
8. Wells, op. cit., p. 33.
9. Ibid., pp. 18-19.
10. Mark Satin, op. cit.
11. Fritjof Capra, from a speech at Santa Barbara, CA, the Mind and Supermind Series, Santa Barbara Community College, May 3, 1982.
12. Satin, op. cit., p. 10.
13. Capra, op. cit.
14. *The Initiator,* op cit.
15. Wells, op. cit., Preface.
16. H.G. Wells, *Anticipation of the Reaction of Mechanical and Scientific Progress Upon Human Life,* as quoted in *The Beacon,* May/June 1977.
17. For documentation of a UFO-related conspiracy, see Jacques Vallee, *Messengers of Deception* (Berkeley, 1979).
18. *The Beacon,* Sep./Oct. 1975, pp. 145-48.
19. Revelation 13:16,17,
20. Revelation 13:15; 14:9,10.
21. Revelation 13:16.
22. 2 Thessalonians 2:7.
23. 2 Thessalonians 2:3.
24. Matthew 24:24.

25. William L. Shirer, *The Rise and Fall of the Third Reich* (New York, 1959), pp. 324-32; see also William Sheridan Allen, *The Nazi Seizure of Power* (New York, 1973), pp. 81, 109, 150, 199, 222-23.

Chapter 6: The New Age Movement

1. Wells, op. cit., p. 167.
2. Satin, op. cit., pp. 11, 148, 149.
3. Virginia Kay Miller, "Is Nuclear War in Our Future?" in *Whole Life Times,* July/Aug. 1982, pp. 37-38.
4. Lessica Lipnack and Jeffrey Stamps, *Networking: The First Report and Directory,* as quoted in *Whole Life Times,* July/Aug. 1982., p. 49.
5. Ibid.
6. Ibid.
7. Ibid., pp. 213-28.
8. Marilyn Ferguson, *The Aquarian Conspiracy: Personal and Social Transformation in the 1980s* (Los Angeles, 1980), p. 23.
9. International Cooperative Council, *Directory For A New World* (Los Angeles, 1979), p. 299.
10. Ibid.
11. Ferguson, op. cit., pp. 23-25.
12. Paul Robinson, "The Coming of Unenlightenment," in *Psychology Today,* Feb. 1980, pp. 108-14.
13. Ibid., p. 113.
14. Capra, op. cit.
15. *Los Angeles Times,* Mar. 16, 1982.
16. Ibid.
17. Ibid.
18. Ibid.
19. Ibid.
20. *SCP Newsletter,* Aug./Sep. 1982, p. 5.
21. 2 Thessalonians 2:1-12.
22. 2 Thessalonians 2:3.

Chapter 7: Truth or Lie?

1. *Los Angeles Times,* July 12, 1981.
2. Ibid.

3. Ibid.
4. Ibid.
5. *Brain/Mind Bulletin,* Oct. 4, 1982, p. 2.
6. *Los Angeles Times,* July 12, 1981.
7. Lewis, *The Abolition of Man* (New York, 1947), pp. 16-17.
8. Beverly Galyean, *Language From Within* (Long Beach, CA, 1976), p. 1.
9. Ibid.
10. C.S. Lewis, op. cit., p. 85.
11. Galyean, op. cit., p. 91.
12. *New Age,* May 1979, pp. 42-60.
13. See Raphael Gasson, *The Challenging Counterfeit* (Plainfield, NJ, 1966).
14. Elmer and Alyce Green, *Beyond Biofeedback* (New York, 1979), p. 317.
15. Dori Smith, "Education for the Future: Eliciting the Spark from Within," in *Whole Life Times,* Sep./Oct. 1982.
16. Ibid.
17. Ibid.
18. *Whole Life Times,* Apr./May 1982, Los Angeles Directory, p. 1.
19. *Moody Monthly,* May 1982, p. 20.
20. *Whole Life Times,* Apr./May 1982, loc. cit.
21. International Cooperative Council, op. cit., p. 12.
22. *SCP Journal,* Winter 1981-82, pp. 29, 31.
23. *The New Age Source,* June 1982, p. 15.
24. 2 Thessalonians 2:4.

Chapter 8: The Myth That Wouldn't Die

1. Brad Steiger, *Gods of Aquarius* (New York, 1976), p. 7.
2. Matthew 24:3, 29-31; Luke 21:25-28; Acts 2:16-21.
3. Russell Targ and Harold Puthoff, *Mind Reach* (New York, 1977), p. 111-19.
4. Luke 21:9-11.
5. Matthew 24:4,5,24 KJV.
6. Psalm 22:7,8,16,18; 41:9; 69:4,12; 109:24,25; Isaiah 53:3-12; Zechariah 11:7-13; 12:10.
7. John Keel, *UFOs: Operation Trojan Horse* (New York, 1970), p. 215.
8. Ruth Montgomery, *A Gift of Prophecy: The Phenomenal Jeane Dixon* (New York, 1965), p. 172.
9. Ibid.
10. Ibid.
11. Jack Gratus, *The False Messiahs* (London, 1975), p. 9.

12. C.S. Lewis, edited by Walter Hooper, *God in the Dock* (Grand Rapids, 1970).
13. John Cournos, *A Book of Prophecy* (New York, 1942), p. 22.
14. 1 John 4:1-3.
15. Isaiah 14:14 KJV.

Chapter 9: Violence, Mysticism, and Secularism

1. Isaiah 53:3-8; Zechariah 13:7.
2. Isaiah 9:6; 53:10-12; 66:15,16; Zechariah 12:10; 13:1; 14:1-21.
3. Psalm 110:1.
4. Matthew 22:41-46; Mark 12:35-37; Luke 20:41-44.
5. Isaiah 7:14; 9:6; Micah 5:2; Zechariah 12:10; Psalm 2:7.
6. Isaiah 53:4-8.
7. Isaiah 9:6 KJV.
8. Isaiah 53:7.
9. Micah 5:2.
10. John 7:52.
11. Matthew 12:46; 13:55; Mark 6:3; John 7:1-5.
12. Josh McDowell, *Evidence That Demands a Verdict* (San Bernardino, CA, 1972), p. 150.
13. Matthew 13:55 KJV.
14. Mark 6:3 KJV.
15. Matthew 13:55; Mark 6:3.
16. Luke 4:16,17.
17. Matthew 13:54; Mark 6:2.
18. Isaiah 7:14; 9:6; Micah 5:2; John 1:1; 8:58; Philippians 2:6.
19. Matthew 14:15-21; 15:32-38.
20. Matthew 17:27.
21. Luke 5:4-7; John 21:5-11.
22. Luke 24:42,43.
23. Matthew 26:17-29; Luke 22:7-20; Exodus 12:1-10,14.
24. John 1:14,18; 3:16, 18; 1 John 4:9.
25. Steve Scott, *Jesus and the Gurus* (Sacramento, CA: Christian Research Alliance, 1981).
26. Zechariah 9:9.
27. John 8:24,58,59.
28. John 10:30-33.
29. John 18:28-32.
30. Isaiah 53:4-8.

31. Lyle E. Bourne, Jr., and Bruce R. Eckstrand, *Psychology: Its Principles and Meanings* (New York, 1976), p. 23.
32. Paul C. Vitz, *Psychology As Religion: The Cult of Self-Worship* (Grand Rapids, 1977), p. 67.
33. E. Fuller Torrey, *The Death of Psychiatry* (New York, 1975), p. 14.
34. Vitz, op. cit.
35. Robert Jastrow, "The Case for UFOs," in *Science Digest,* Nov./Dec. 1980, pp. 83-85.
36. Ibid.
37. Martin L. Gross, *The Psychological Society* (New York, 1978), p. 3.
38. Ibid., p. 4.
39. *SCP Journal,* Vol. 1, No. 2, Aug. 1977, p. 22.
40. Muller, op. cit., pp. 120-21.
41. Donald Keys, *Earth At Omega: Passage to Planetization* (Boston, 1982), dedication page.

Chapter 10: Preparation for Delusion

1. Andrija Puharich, *Uri: A Journal of the Mystery of Uri Geller* (New York, 1974), Frontispiece.
2. Ibid., pp. 167-70.
3. Ibid., p. 112.
4. Jacques Vallee, *Messengers of Deception* (Berkeley, 1979), pp. 204-05.
5. Joel Greenberg, "Close Encounters, All In The Mind?" in *Science News,* Feb. 17, 1979, pp. 106-07; John DeHerrera, "Does Hypnosis Create Contactees?" in *Second Look,* May/June 1980, pp. 16-17.
6. Martin and Deidre Bobgan, *Hypnosis and the Christian* (tentative title, to be released summer 1983 by Bethany Publishers, Minneapolis, MN), Chapter 2.
7. Greenberg, op. cit.
8. Greenberg and DeHerrera, op. cit.
9. Greenberg, op. cit.
10. Ibid.
11. Bobgan, op. cit., Chapter 3.
12. Ibid, Chapter 6.
13. Ibid.
14. *Los Angeles Times,* Feb. 3, 1975, front page; Nov. 25, 1981, Part V, page 1.
15. Ibid., Mar. 12, 1982.
16. Ibid.
17. Bobgan, op. cit., Chapter 2.
18. Ibid.

19. Ibid.
20. Ibid.
21. Ibid.
22. *Science News,* Jan. 16, 1982, p. 42.
23. *New Century Encyclopedia of Names* (New York, 1954), p. 1104.
24. *Encyclopaedia Britannica* (Chicago, 1979), Vol. III, p. 187.
25. David Wallechinsky and Irving Wallace, *The Peoples Almanac* (New York, 1975), p. 525.
26. Thomas Szasz, *The Myth of Psychotherapy* (New York, 1978), p. 49.
27. Ibid.
28. W. Brugh Joy, M.D., *Joy's Way* (Los Angeles, 1979), pp. 8-9.
29. *Encyclopaedia Britannica,* op. cit.
30. Wallechinsky and Wallace, op. cit.
31. Szasz, op. cit., p. 50.
32. Bobgan, op. cit., Chapter 1.
33. Carl Rogers, *Counseling and Psychotherapy* (Boston, 1942), p. 244, as quoted in *SCP Journal,* Winter 1981-82, p. 13.
34. MacKenzie, op. cit., p. 145.
35. Ibid., pp. 45-54.
36. Arthur H. Nethercot, *The First Five Lives of Annie Besant* (London, 1960), pp. 321-23.
37. McCandlish Phillips, *The Spirit World* (Wheaton, 1970), pp. 21-24.
38. Ibid.
39. Ibid.
40. Ibid.

Chapter 11: Hitler, The Almost-Antichrist

1. Revelation 13:8.
2. Gerald Suster, *Hitler: The Occult Messiah* (New York, 1981), pp. 100, 107.
3. Jean-Michel Angebert, *The Occult and the Third Reich* (New York, 1974), p. 201.
4. Suster, op. cit., p. 109.
5. Angebert, op. cit., p. 20.
6. William Shirer, *Berlin Diary,* as quoted by Gerald Suster, op. cit., pp. 140-41.
7. A.J.P. Taylor, *Thus Spake Hitler in Europe: Grandeur and Decline,* as quoted by Suster, op. cit., p. 119.
8. Trevor Ravenscroft, *The Spear of Destiny* (New York, 1973), p. 187.
9. Angebert, op. cit., p. 233.
10. Ibid.
11. Suster, op. cit., p. 119.

12. Ibid., p. 141.
13. Ibid., p. 118.
14. Shirer, *Rise and Fall*, p. 64.
15. From a tape of the news conference.
16. Ravenscroft, op. cit., p. 274.
17. Suster, op. cit., p. 118.
18. Ravenscroft, op. cit., pp. 224, 229.
19. Ibid., p. 229.
20. Louis Pauwels and Jacques Bergier, *The Morning of the Magicians* (New York, 1960), p. 219.
21. Suster, op. cit., p. 109.
22. Ibid., pp. 97, 141.
23. Pauwels and Bergier, op. cit., as cited by Suster, p. 138.
24. Suster, op. cit., p. 120.
25. Herman Rauschning, *Hitler Told Me So,* quoted by Angebert, op. cit., p. 234.
26. Pauwels and Bergier, op. cit., p. 219.
27. Suster, op. cit., p. 131.
28. Ibid., p. 115.
29. Brennan, *Occult Reich;* Pauwels and Bergier, op. cit., cited in Suster, op. cit., p. 99.
30. Suster, op. cit., p. 85.
31. Ibid., p. 77.
32. Marc Hillel and Clarissa Henry, *Of Pure Blood* (New York, 1976), from the cover.
33. Suster, op. cit., p. 180.
34. Ibid., p. 181.
35. Ibid., p. 191.
36. Ibid., p. 183.
37. Ibid., p. 192.
38. Ibid., p. 181.
39. Angebert, op. cit., Introduction.

Chapter 12: The Aryan Connection

1. 2 Corinthians 4:4.
2. Rene' Gue'non, *Le Theosophisme, histoire d'une pseudo-religion* (Paris, 1921), as quoted by Pauwels and Bergier, op. cit., p. 221.
3. Nels F. Ferre', Foreword in Surjit Singh, *Christology and Personality* (The Westminster Press, 1961), as quoted by Brooks Alexander, *Occult Philosophy &*

Mystical Experience, published by Spiritual Counterfeits Project, P.O. Box 2418, Berkeley, CA 94702.

4. *Far East Economic Review,* article by Kedar Man Singh, quoted in *Update,* Sep. 1981 (published by The Dialog Center, Aarhus, Denmark), under "News Items."

5. See *TM in Court: The Complete Text of the Federal Court's Opinion* in the case of Malnak vs. Maharishi Mahesh Yogi, published by SCP, P.O. Box 2418, Berkeley, CA 94702.

6. Johannes Aagaard, "Hinduism's World Mission," in *Update,* Sep. 1982.

7. Ibid.

8. Ibid.

9. Ibid.

10. Ibid.

11. Ibid.

12. Shirer, *Rise and Fall,* p. 330.

13. *Moody Monthly,* July/Aug. 1979; *The Milwaukee Journal,* June 3, 1978.

14. Aagaard, op. cit., "Hindu Scholars, Germany and the Third Reich."

15. Ibid.

16. Ibid.

17. Ibid.

18. Suster, op. cit., p. 182.

19. Ibid., p. 183.

20. Ibid., p. 185.

21. Benjamin Creme, "The Gospel Story and the Path of Initiation," in *Share International,* June 1982, p. 14.

22. Suster, op. cit., p. 141.

Chapter 13: Marxism—Pattern of the Future

1. L.I. Brezhnev, *The Great October Revolution and Mankind's Progress.* Report at a jubilee meeting of the Central Committee of the CPSU, the Supreme Soviet of the USSR, and the Supreme Soviet of the RSFSR to mark the sixtieth anniversary of the Great October Socialist Revolution (Moscow: Notosti Press Agency Publishing House, 1977), pp. 5, 32.

2. Aleksandr Solzhenitsyn, "Wake Up! Wake Up!" in *Reader's Digest,* Dec. 1975, pp. 69-74.

3. Ibid.
4. Ibid.
5. Brezhnev, op. cit., pp. 5, 6.
6. *The Journal,* Nov. 1982 (Summit Ministries, P.O. Box 207, Manitou Springs, CO 80829), p. 2.
7. *Socialist International Information,* Nov. 1970, as quoted in Rose L. Martin, *The Selling of America* (Santa Monica, CA, 1973), p. 17.
8. *The Journal,* op. cit., p. 5.
9. Karl Marx and Friedrich Engels, *Historisch-kritisch Gesamtausgabe, Werke, Schriften, Briefe* (Complete historical critical edition: Works, Writings, Letters) on behalf of the Marx-Engels Institute, Moscow, published by David Rjazanov (Frankfurt-am-Main, 1927), I, i(2), pp. 55-57.
10. Ibid., "Invocation of One in Despair," I, i(2), pp. 30-31.
11. *Los Angeles Times,* Feb. 21, 1979.
12. Vladimir Ilyich Lenin, in a personal letter to the Russian author Gorki in 1913.
13. Francis A. Schaeffer, "A Perspective for Christians on Military Preparedness," in *Intercessors for America Newsletter,* Nov. 1, 1982 (P.O. Box 1289, Elyria, OH, 44036).
14. *Los Angeles Times,* Feb. 10, 1978, Part I, p. 7.
15. *Harvard University Gazette,* June 8, 1979. Address delivered by Aleksandr Solzhenitsyn, recipient of honorary Doctor of Letters degree.
16. *Los Angeles Times,* July 19, 1982, Part II, p. 5.
17. *The Spotlight,* op. cit.
18. Cited in June 28, 1982, letter from Congressman Ron Paul.
19. Ibid.
20. *Harvard University Gazette,* June 8, 1979, loc. cit.
21. *Reader's Digest,* op. cit.
22. *Peking Review* (Red China), Jan. 23, 1976, p. 41.
23. W. Robert Lee, *The United Nations Conspiracy* (Los Angeles, 1982), p. 23.
24. Ibid., pp. 205-09.
25. *Congressional Record,* Oct. 26, 1971, p. S16764.
26. *The Journal,* op. cit., p. 3.
27. I.P. Tsamerian and S.L. Ronin, *Equality of Rights Between Races and Nationalities in the USSR* (UNESCO, 1962), pp. 11-13, 37.
28. Martin and Deidre Bobgan, *The Psychological Way/The Spiritual Way* (Minneapolis, 1979), p. 55.
29. Thomas Szasz, op. cit., p. 184.

30. Sigmund Freud, *The Future of an Illusion,* translated and edited by James Strachey (New York, 1961), p. 43.
31. E. Fuller Torrey, op. cit., p. 107.
32. John Barron, *KGB: The Secret Works of Soviet Agents* (New York, 1974), pp. 155-57.
33. G.B. Chisholm, "The Reestablishment of Peacetime Society: The Responsibility of Psychiatry," in *Psychiatry* 9:3-11, 1946.

Chapter 14: Capitalism—Over the Cliff

1. *Famous American Quotes* (Lynchburg, VA: Old-time Gospel Hour).
2. Ibid.
3. *Harvard Gazette,* op. cit.
4. Ibid.
5. *Famous American Quotes,* op. cit.
6. Leo Buscaglia, *Love* (New York, 1972), p. 16.
7. Leo Buscaglia, *Personhood: The Art of Being Fully Human* (New York, 1978), p. 116.
8. 1 John 4:7,8.
9. Buscaglia, *Love,* p. 107.
10. Buscaglia, *Personhood,* p. 88.
11. Buscaglia, *Love,* pp. 124-25.
12. Ibid., p. 157.
13. Buscaglia, *Personhood,* p. 128.
14. John 13:34.
15. Buscaglia, *Personhood,* p. 105.
16. Joy, op. cit., p. 7.
17. Buscaglia, *Personhood,* p. 102.
18. Buscaglia, *Love,* p. 195.
19. Ibid., p. 49.
20. Ibid., p. 40.
21. Martin L. Gross, op. cit., p. 3.
22. Ferguson, op. cit., pp. 241-42.
23. Ibid., pp. 99-101.
24. Buscaglia, *Love,* pp. 133, 139, 161, 195.
25. Gross, op. cit., pp. 4-5.
26. Carl G. Jung, *Two Essays on Analytical Psychology.*
27. Abraham Maslow, *Main Currents in Modern Thought.*
28. Ferguson, op. cit., pp. 99-101.
29. *Self Acceptance: Real Encounter,* front page; *Questions and Answers About Life-*

spring, p. 3; *The Family News,* Vol. 1, No. 2, July 1978, p. 14.

30. Green, op. cit., pp. 56, 342-43.
31. *Los Angeles Times,* Sep. 4, 1981, Business p. 1.
32. Ibid.
33. Ibid.
34. "Total Success catalog featuring the Love Tapes, For going beyond positive thinking and hypnosis...to develop your potential" (Effective Learning Systems, Inc.), pp. 17-19.
35. Ibid., p. 18.
36. Ibid.
37. *Congressional Record,* Proceedings and Debates of the 94th Congress, First Session, Vol. 121, No. 15, Feb. 5, 1975, S1466.
38. *SCP Journal,* July 1977.
39. Simon & Schuster promotional material for *The Turning Point.*
40. Ibid.
41. John Bliedman, "Scientists in Search of the Soul," in *Science Digest,* July 1982, p. 105.
42. Buscaglia, *Personhood,* p. 17.

Chapter 15: Disappearance and Collapse

1. 1 Corinthians 15:50-52.
2. 1 Thessalonians 4:13-18.
3. Revelation 19:14.
4. *A Secular Humanist Declaration,* Endorsed by 58 leaders of thought, including Isaac Asimov, Sir A.J. Ayer, Sir Francis Crick, et al (USA, 1980), p. 24.
5. *World Goodwill,* published by the Lucis Trust.
6. 2 Thessalonians 2:11.
7. 2 Thessalonians 2:12.
8. M.E. Haselhurst, "The Plan and its Implementation," in *The Beacon,* Sep./Oct. 1975, p. 147.
9. Ibid., p. 146.
10. *Humanist Declaration,* op. cit.
11. *1979 Directory For A New World* (Unity in Diversity, Los Angeles), pp. 12-15.
12. Carl Rogers, "Are Human Abilities Expanding? A Psychotherapist's View," in *Science Digest,* Dec. 1979, p. 36.
13. Matthew 24:36.
14. Matthew 24:42.
15. Matthew 24:37-41.
16. Revelation 3:17.

17. Mark 13:35,36.
18. Matthew 24:44.
19. Planetary Initiative for the World We Choose, *Organizing Manual* (New York, 1982), p. 11.

Chapter 16: When Antichrist Takes Control

1. Sir John Hackett, *World War III, The Untold Story* (New York, 1982).
2. Ibid.
3. Mary Bailey, "Externalizing the Mysteries—Part I," in *The Beacon*, Nov./Dec. 1975, p. 171.
4. Alice Bostok, "1975—The Magical Year," in *The Beacon*, Nov./Dec. 1976, p. 370.
5. 2 Thessalonians 2:11.
6. David Spangler, *Reflections on the Christ* (Findhorn, Scotland, 1978), pp. 40-44.
7. Manly P. Hall, *The Secret Teachings of All Ages* (Los Angeles, 1969), p. XXI.
8. Robert Macoy 33°, *General History of Freemasonry*.
9. Hall, op. cit.
10. *Ojai Valley News*, Aug. 8, 1979, p. G-4.
11. Creme, loc. cit., p. 14.
12. Muller, op. cit., p. 145.
13. Ibid., dedication page.
14. *Los Angeles Times*, Sep. 3, 1978.
15. Ibid.
16. 2 Thessalonians 2:10,12.
17. *1982 Catalogue* (Heartwood: California College of Natural Healing Arts).
18. John 10:27.
19. Levi H. Dowling, *The Aquarian Gospel of Jesus the Christ: The Philosophic and Practical Basis of the Religion of the Aquarian Age of the World* (Santa Monica, CA, 1907), p. 48.
20. Alice Bailey, *The Rays and The Initiations* (Lucis Trust), p. 79.
21. *1979 Directory for a New World* (Los Angeles), p. 300.
22. Ibid.
23. *SCP Newsletter*, Oct./Nov. 1982.
24. Ibid.
25. *World Goodwill Newsletter*, July/Aug./Sep. 1982.
26. Jeremiah 17:9.
27. Matthew 15:19.

Chapter 17: Russia and the Coming Holocaust

1. *Los Angeles Times,* Sep. 18, 1982.
2. *Intercessors for America Newsletter,* Oct. 1, 1982.
3. Thomas Scott, Rector of Aston Sandford, *The Holy Bible, With Explanatory Notes, Practical Observations, and Copious Marginal References* (London, 1828), comments on Ezekiel 38.
4. Ezekiel 38:2-6.
5. Genesis 10:1-3.
6. *Los Angeles Times,* Aug. 8, 1982, p. I-8.
7. Personal interview for the film "Russia and the Coming Holocaust."
8. 2 Samuel 7:12-16; Psalm 132:11; Jeremiah 23:5; In the New Testament see also: Matthew 1:1; 22:42; John 7:42; Acts 2:25-32; 13:23; Romans 1:2; etc.
9. Psalm 22:16; 69:8; 118:22; Isaiah 53:3; Zechariah 12:10.
10. Jeremiah 16:14,15; 23:3-8; 30:3-11; Ezekiel 37:21-28; 38; 39; Joel 3:1,2; Amos 9:14,15; Obadiah 20,21; Zechariah 12:8-10; 14:2-5.
11. Psalm 118:26; Daniel 9:26; Haggai 2:7-9; Zechariah 11:13; Malachi 3:1.
12. Memorandum re KGB Show Trials from Lynn Singer, President Union of Councils for Soviet Jews, to Supporters and Volunteers, Fall of 1982.
13. Personal letter from Avital Scharansky, enclosed with the above.
14. Zechariah 12:2-9; 14:2-5; Joel 3:1,2.
15. Marv Rosenthal, "I Will Make Jerusalem a Cup of Trembling!" in *Israel My Glory,* Oct./Nov. 1982, p. 2.
16. Zechariah 12:2,3 KJV.
17. Isaiah 13:6-13; Joel 1:15; 2:1; Ezekiel 30:3; Zephaniah 1:7; 1 Thessalonians 5:2; 2 Peter 3:10-12; etc.
18. Isaiah 34:1,2,8; 61:2; 2 Thessalonians 1:7-10; etc.
19. Maharishi Mahesh Yogi, *On The Bhagavad-Gita,* p. 101. Cited and commented upon in "Who Is This Man and What Does He Want?" Available from SCP, P.O. Box 2418, Berkeley, CA, 94702.
20. *Ojai Valley News,* Aug. 8, 1979, p. G-14.
21. Revelation 11:3.
22. Revelation 11:5,6.
23. Daniel 9:27.
24. *Denver Post,* Mar. 21, 1982.
25. Revelation 11:7.
26. Revelation 11:10.
27. Revelation 13:17.
28. Revelation 13:2.
29. Revelation 12:9,12.
30. Revelation 13:3.
31. Revelation 13:7.
32. Revelation 13:5.
33. Revelation 13:15; 6:11; 7:9,14.
34. Matthew 24:15-20.

35. *Los Angeles Times,* Aug. 2, 1982; Sep. 12, 1982, pp. 1-18.
36. *Los Angeles Times,* June 5, 1981; July 3, 1981; Feb. 11, 1982.
37. *U.S. News and World Report,* June 7, 1982, p. 48.
38. *Brain/Mind Bulletin,* July 12, 1982, p. 3.
39. Ibid.
40. Revelation 9:6.
41. Revelation 13:4.
42. Charles Fillmore, "Fear Not," a tract printed and distributed by Unity School of Christianity, Unity Village, MO.
43. Ibid.
44. Matthew 24:22.
45. Matthew 24:27.
46. Revelation 1:7.
47. Zechariah 12:10.
48. John 10:30.
49. Isaiah 53:2-5.
50. *Intercessors for America Newsletter,* Nov. 1, 1982.

Chapter 18: Escape from Delusion

1. Proverbs 17:22.
2. Matthew 19:26.
3. Philippians 4:13.
4. Matthew 9:22.
5. Matthew 21:21.
6. Kenneth E. Hagin, "Having Faith in Your Faith," in *The Word of Faith,* Sep. 1980, p. 3.
7. Mark 11:22.
8. 2 Thessalonians 2:9,10.
9. Revelation 18:13; cf. ch. 18.
10. Vitz, op. cit.
11. *Los Angeles Times,* July 20, 1982, Part 1, p. 17.
12. *Science Digest,* op. cit., Dec. 1979.
13. Carl Frederick, *est: Playing the Game the New Way* (New York, 1974), p. 171.
14. *Brain/Mind Bulletin,* Oct. 4, 1982.
15. Jeffrey Klein, "Esalen Slides Off the Cliff," in *Mother Jones,* Dec. 1979, pp. 26-33.
16. Szasz, op. cit., p. 161.
17. Ibid., p. 69,
18. Ibid., p. 160.

19. Richard R. Parlour, "The Myth of Voluntary Therapy" (letter to the editor), in *American Journal of Psychiatry,* 131, May 1974, p. 161.
20. Viktor E. Frankl, " 'Nothing but—': On Reductionism and Nihilism," in *Encounter,* Nov. 1969, p. 56.
21. "All About the New Sex Therapy," in *Newsweek,* Nov. 27, 1972, p. 71.
22. Advertisement for *A Scream Away From Happiness,* by Daniel Casriel, M.D., in *New York Times Book Review,* Oct. 8, 1972, p. 14.
23. *Abraham v. Zaslow,* California Superior Court, Santa Clara County, Docket No. 245862 (1972), *Citation,* 26, Mar. 15, 1973, pp. 169-70.
24. "Ex-Addict Sky Jumpers: 'Sky-high' on Mutual Trust," *Medical World News,* Sep. 1, 1972, p. 7.
25. H.G. Wells, *Open Conspiracy,* p. 26.
26. Roger Jones, *Physics as Metaphor* (University of Minnesota Press, 1982).
27. Richard Elvee, editor, *Mind in Nature* (1982).
28. Peter Lemesurier, *The Cosmic Eye: A Traveller's Guide to Inner Space* (Moray, Scotland, 1982).
29. Willis W. Harman, "Rationale for Good Choosing," in *Journal of Humanistic Psychology,* Vol. 21, No. 1, Winter 1981.
30. Ephesians 6:12.
31. 2 Thessalonians 2:9-12.
32. H. Newton Malony, "Psychotherapy: Where the Rubber Hits the Road," a paper in response to Gary R. Collins, Finch Symposium, Jan. 1978.
33. *Los Angeles Times,* Oct. 11, 1981, I-B, p. 1.
34. Ibid.
35. Rodney R. Romney, *Journey to Inner Space: Finding God-in-Us* (Nashville, 1980), p. 29,
36. Ibid., p. 30.
37. Ibid., p. 28.
38. Ibid.
39. John 14:6.
40. Romney, op. cit., p. 30.
41. Ibid.
42. Ibid., p. 73.
43. Ibid., p. 82.
44. Ibid., p. 83.
45. Ibid., p. 84.
46. Ibid., p. 85.
47. Lewis, *God in the Dock,* pp. 89-93.
48. Jeremiah 17:9 KJV.
49. Matthew 15:19,20.
50. Mark 8:34.
51. 1 Corinthians 15:1-8.
52. Romans 1:16.
53. Marchant A. King, "Digging Deeper: Let's Study Hebrews 9," in *Moody Monthly,* July/Aug. 1982, pp. 55-58.

54. Joseph A. Hariss, "Which Master Is the World Council of Churches Serving...Karl Marx or Jesus Christ?" in *Reader's Digest,* Aug. 1982.
55. *Los Angeles Times,* Jan. 18, 1983, p. 1.
56. Jonah 3:4.
57. Jeremiah 18:8.
58. John 14:27.

Russia and the Coming Holocaust

Nuclear war! Is it inevitable?

Russia on the move! Do these moves coincide with Ezekiel 38 or 39, pushing us all toward global starvation, ecological collapse...and Armageddon?

From film smuggled past the Iron Curtain, learn the truth about the church and fate of Christians in the USSR. See Soviet prisons.

Inside the American Embassy in Moscow, the "Siberian Seven" speak their view. So does Georgi Vins and a leading soviet editor and radio-TV commentator who turned from Marx to Christ!

RUSSIA AND THE COMING HOLOCAUST reflects the power and purpose of the Soviet Union in its push for world domination.

16 mm Full Color, 35 Minutes
Also Videotape Available

For information contact:
NEW LIBERTY FILMS
1805 W. Magnolia
Burbank, California 91506
(213) 842-6167
or
MISSION: POSSIBLE
P.O. Box 2014
Denton, Texas 76201
(817) 382-1508